W9-BES-119

Surviving the Design of a 200 MHz RISC Microprocessor

Lessons Learned

Surviving the Design of a 200 MHz RISC Microprocessor

Lessons Learned

Veljko Milutinović

IEEE Computer Society Press
Los Alamitos, California

Washington • Brussels • Tokyo

Library of Congress Cataloging-in-Publication Data

Milutinović, Veljko
    Surviving the design of a 200 MHz RISC microprocessor: lessons learned / Veljko Milutinović
        p.   cm.
    Includes bibliographical references (p.).
    ISBN 0-8186-7343-5
    1. RISC microprocessors.   I. Title
QA76.5.M531426   1997
621.39 ' 16—dc20

                                                                95-52094
                                                                CIP

IEEE Computer Society Press
10662 Los Vaqueros Circle
P.O. Box 3014
Los Alamitos, CA 90720-1264

IEEE Computer Society Press Order Number BP07343
Library of Congress Number 95-52094
ISBN 0-8186-7343-5

Additional copies may be ordered from:

IEEE Computer Society Press	IEEE Service Center	IEEE Computer Society	IEEE Computer Society
Customer Service Center	445 Hoes Lane	13, Avenue de l'Aquilon	Ooshima Building
10662 Los Vaqueros Circle	P.O. Box 1331	B-1200 Brussels	2-19-1 Minami-Aoyama
P.O. Box 3014	Piscataway, NJ 08855-1331	BELGIUM	Minato-ku, Tokyo 107
Los Alamitos, CA 90720-1264	Tel: +1-908-981-1393	Tel: +32-2-770-2198	JAPAN
Tel: +1-714-821-8380	Fax: +1-908-981-9667	Fax: +32-2-770-8505	Tel: +81-3-3408-3118
Fax: +1-714-821-4641	mis.custserv@computer.org	euro.ofc@computer.org	Fax: +81-3-3408-3553
Email: cs.books@computer.org			tokyo.ofc@computer.org
http://www.computer.org/cspress			

Assistant Publisher: Matt Loeb
Technical Editor: Pradip Srimani
Acquisitions Editor: Bill Sanders
Acquisitions Assistant: Cheryl Smith
Advertising/Promotions: Tom Fink
Production Editor: Lisa O'Conner
Cover Design: Alex Torres
Cover Image: Milić Stanković

Printed in the United States of America

The Institute of Electrical and Electronics Engineers, Inc

Table of Contents

Foreword

The process of designing a computer is a long and involved one. After completion, few designers look forward to documenting the details. As a minimum, the designer describes the final version of the design so that users (at least) can effectively master it. Sometimes, an energetic design group may publish a paper on one of the more novel features found in the design. More rarely, designers provide a more comprehensive design description and the tradeoffs that were involved in the final implementation. Such papers are very valuable lessons for the next generation of designers because they represent case studies in computer design. The more articulated the discussion of the tradeoffs, the more valuable the paper or book. Thus, in the computer architecture literature, works that have described machines such as the IBM 360/91, the Denelcor HEP, the VAX processor family, and the RISC-I have provided extraordinary insight and have been very valuable to the field. Indeed, such works have been important not only because of the innovations that were contained in those particular designs, but because of the discussion of the tradeoffs and the context in which the designs were done.

In this book, Professor Milutinović takes the case study process one step further. He does not simply discuss the tradeoffs that created the resultant design, but describes the context of the design process. The original design competition to be judged by a government sponsor, press releases on the project, the CAD tools that were selected and used, the standard gate library, as well as the technology context—all set the stage for the final design tradeoffs. As in many designs, some elements are fixed at the beginning. In this case, the instruction set had already been fixed as the SU-MIPS-Core instruction set. The target technology was gallium arsenide, an exotic technology even today, and significantly more exotic in the timeframe of the mid-to-late 1980s in which Professor Milutinović described this design work.

Of special interest is the architecture case study in Chapter 6. Professor Milutinović elaborates the constraints and step by step analysis used in arriving at a final design. Equally important are the final two retrospective chapters (7 and 8). Chapter 7 is a retrospective on technology and architecture, including an insightful and critical analysis of the gallium arsenide compound with CMOS. Chapter 8 reviews the influence of specific applications on architectural tradeoffs and points to a methodology for performance enhancement.

This book is not about the state of the art of design tools or architecture issues; rather, it is about the context of design and the experiences learned from dealing with design constraints and tradeoffs made under these constraints. This book is for those who are interested in understanding the design process and comparing their own experiences to those of one of the best known contributors to the computer systems design art.

Michael Flynn
Stanford University

Preface

This book describes the design of a 32-bit RISC, developed through the first DARPA effort to create a 200 MHz processor on a VLSI chip. The presentation contains only the data previously published in the open literature (mostly in the IEEE journals) or covered in a Purdue University graduate course on microprocessor design (taught by the author). The project was very much ahead of its time, and the scientific community was informed about its major achievements through research papers and invited presentations (see the list of references and the short biographical sketch of the author at the end of the book). However, it is only just now that the need has appeared to publish this book, with all generated experiences and lessons learned (several years after the project was successfully completed), because of the recent appearance of the first commercially available microprocessors clocked at or above 200 MHz (IBM, DEC,SUN, MIPS, Intel, Motorola, NEC, Fujitsu, and so forth).

The main purpose of this book is to take the reader through all phases of the project under consideration and to cover all theoretical and technical details necessary for the creation of the final architecture and the final design. Special emphasis is put on the research and development methodology utilized in the project.

The methodology of this project includes the following elements: creation of candidate architectures, their comparative testing on the functional level, selection and final refinement of the best candidate architecture, its transformation from the architecture level to the design level, logical and timing testing of the design, and its preparation for fabrication, including the basic prefabrication design for efficient postfabrication testing.

Special emphasis is devoted to the software tools used in the project (discussing only the aspects relatively independent of the technological changes) and to RISC architectures that have served as the baselines for the project (discussing only the aspects which had a strong impact on this effort and the later efforts to design commercial RISC machines to be clocked at or above 200 MHz).

While writing the book, the main intention of the author was to create a text which, after a detailed reading, enables readers to design a RISC machine on their own once they find themselves in an environment which offers all the prerequisites for such a project. This goal seems to have been accomplished fairly successfully. After years of teaching the course related to this book (first at Purdue University and then at several other universities around the world), former students have called from time to time telling the author how useful this knowledge was once they faced the design of a new VLSI processor in companies like Intel, Motorola, IBM, NCR, AT&T, ITT, Boeing, Encore, Hyundai, or Samsung. This was proof that the effort was not only worthwhile, but was also a source of great satisfaction for all the hard and dedicated work over the years.

This book's main purpose is to serve as a textbook; it has been drawn from various versions of the author's undergraduate courses which are dedicated to microprocessor design for VLSI. The first version of this book was created several years ago and was tested in a number of university courses (Purdue, UCLA, Sydney, Tokyo, Frankfurt, Darmstadt, Dortmund, Pisa, Budapest, Warszaw, Belgrade, Podgorica, and so forth), commercial tutorials (L'Aquila, Genoa, Dubrovnik, Zagreb, Los Angeles, Miami, and so forth), in-house tutorials (NASA, Aerospace Corporation, Honeywell, Fairchild, Encore, Intel, RCA, TOT, IBM, NCR, CERN, GMD, and so forth) and preconference tutorials (ISCA, HICSS, WESCON, MIDCON, IRE, EUROMICRO, ETAN, ETRAN, and so forth).

This version of the book includes all the comments and suggestions from many generations of students. The course is now being taught at the undergraduate level of the University of Belgrade, and most of the comments and suggestions have come from the Belgrade students. Without their active interest, it would have been impossible to create the latest iterations of refinement.

The author especially thanks **David Fura,** now at Boeing, for his contributions during the early phases of the development of this book. Also, to Charles Gimarc, now at Symbios Logic, Alex Silbey, now at SGI, and Erik Feldman, now at Intel.

The author also thanks his friends from the former RCA, **Walter Helbig,** Bill Heaggarty, Jeff Pridmore, and Wayne Moyers. This effort would not have been possible without their enthusiastic help. The author learned a lot from these extraordinary and experienced individuals through daily engineering interactions. Some of the lessons learned, after they have withstood the test of time (in the jointly published research papers), have been incorporated and elaborated in this book.

The structure of this book is as follows. The first chapter contains an introduction into the architecture and design of RISC microprocessors for VLSI. The first chapter also contains the definitions of the main terms and conditions of the DARPA project which serves as the basis for this book.

The second chapter discusses the research and design methodology of interest (both for the general field of computer architecture and design and for the particular project of a new RISC design described here).

The third chapter introduces the general field of hardware description languages (HDLs), with a special emphasis on the language which was used in the project under consideration (ISP').

The fourth chapter gives a general introduction to the VLSI design techniques and concentrates on one specific design technique (standard cell VLSI) which was used in the design of the 32-bit machine considered here.

The fifth chapter talks about the prefabrication design phases and the postfabrication testing phases in general and discusses the case of the CADDAS package used in the RCA effort.

The sixth chapter presents the RISC architecture in general and talks about the SU-MIPS and the UCB-RISC architectures, one of which served as the baseline for this research; the other helped through its overall impact on the field. The focus was on the architectural issues which survived the two architectures and whose impact spreads to the latest RISC machines at the technological edge.

The seventh chapter considers the interaction between the RISC style microprocessor architecture and the VLSI implementation technology. This part includes some general notions and concentrates on the emerging GaAs technology.

The eighth chapter considers the interaction between the RISC style microprocessor architecture and its applications in the fields of multimedia and neural computing in general and focuses on the problems which have their roots in the issues presented earlier in the book.

The ninth chapter represents a summary of lessons learned and experiences generated throughout this project. This chapter also gives some thoughts about the future development trends.

The tenth chapter gives a survey of the open literature in the field (both the literature of general interest and the literature of special interest for the subject treated in this book).

The original text was developed in Serbian and typeset by the author; the translation to English and typsetting by the publisher may have changed the precise meaning of some statements.

Veljko Milutinović

emilutiv@etf.bg.ac.yu

Acknowledgments

Very warm thanks are due to Dr. Borivoj Lazić, Dr. Dejan Živković, Dr. Jovan Djordjević, and Dr. Aleksandra Pavasović, all from the University of Belgrade, for their valuable comments during the review of the manuscript. Thanks are also due to Mr. Vladan Dugarić, for drawing all the figures in this book, as well as for the effort he put into designing the layout of the book. Last, but not least, thanks also go to numerous students, on all five continents, for their welcome comments during the preparation of the manuscript, and for their help in finding small inaccuracies. Of all the half dozen unknown referees of this book, the author is especially thankful to the one who was kind enough to make deep and thoughtful in-line comments on almost all pages of the manuscript. Finally, thanks to you, dear reader, for choosing to read this book. It has been made entirely out of recyclable ideas—please let the author know if you decide to reuse some of them.

1

An Introduction to RISC Processor Architecture for VLSI

This chapter consists of two parts. The first part contains the definition of this book's goal and explains many issues which are key to understanding the rest of the book. The second part contains the basic information about the entire project and its rationales.

1.1 The Goal of This Book

The goal of this book is to teach the reader how to design a RISC[1] microprocessor on a VLSI[2] chip, using the approaches and tools from a DARPA sponsored effort to design a 200 MHz RISC chip for the Star Wars program (see the enclosed paper by Helbig and Milutinović).

Commercial microprocessors can be conditionally classified into two large groups: RISCs and CISCs[3]. There are two reasons why it was decided that this book, with the above defined goal, is based on a RISC architecture. First, RISC processors (on average) have better performance. Second, RISC processors (on average) are less complex, and consequently more appropriate for educational purposes.

Commercial RISC machines are implemented either on a VLSI chip or on a printed circuit board (using components of lower level of integration). On-chip implementations are superior in price, speed, dissipation, and physical size. In addition, the design process is more convenient, because it is based more on software tools and less on hardware tools.

After studying this book, the reader will be able (on his/her own) to design a RISC processor on a chip (on condition that all other prerequisites are satisfied, and the environment is right for this type of effort).

This book stresses the holistic approach to RISC design for VLSI. That includes the activities related to the creation and evaluation of the most suitable processor architectures, which use the same research and development methodology as the original DARPA sponsored project.

The presentation in this book is based on two different efforts to realize a 32-bit microprocessor on a VLSI chip: one for silicon technology and one for GaAs technology. The author was involved in both projects, and his intention now is to pass on to the reader both the generated technical knowledge and the information about the many lessons learned throughout the entire effort. As already indicated, both projects were a part of the Star Wars program; together, they are also known as *MIPS for Star Wars*, or *On-Board Computer for Star Wars*.

---

[1]RISC = Reduced Instruction Set Computer
[2]VLSI = Very Large Scale Integration
[3]CISC = Complex Instruction Set Computer

1.2   The "On-Board Computer for Star Wars" Project

The basic goal of the "On-Board Computer for Star Wars" program was to realize a 200 MHz RISC microprocessor on a single chip, using the newly emerging GaAs technology (the average speed was expected to be around 100 MIPS, or about 100 times the speed of VAX-11/780). At the same time, a 40 MHz silicon version also had to be implemented. Figures 1-1 and 1-2 show the following: advertising material for the 32-bit and the eight-bit versions of the GaAs RISC/MIPS processor of RCA, and excerpts from commercial magazines which discuss the entire DARPA program in general, particularly focusing on the approach taken at Purdue University for RCA.

Initially, there were about a dozen different teams competing for funds on the GaAs project. DARPA selected only three teams:

a)   McDonnell Douglas (doing both the technology and the architecture).

b)   A team consisting of Texas Instruments (technology) and Control Data Corporation (architecture).

c)   RCA Corporation, which decided to do the work in cooperation with a spin-off company of Tektronix called TriQuint Corporation (technology) and Purdue University (architecture).

This book is based on the approach taken at Purdue University, which was described in numerous papers (for example, [1]–[4]). The primary paper, written by Helbig and Milutinović, represents the apex of the entire effort and is reprinted later in this book.

The DARPA plan (according to the publicly released information) was that the initial prototype be completed by the end of the 1980s so that the serial production could go through the 1990s. As already indicated, this book covers the theoretical aspects of the problems related to the creation of the prototype. Practical aspects of the problems related to the serial production and related issues are outside the scope of this book.

MICROPROCESSORS

DARPA EYES 100-MIPS GaAs CHIP FOR STAR WARS

PALO ALTO

For its Star Wars program, the Department of Defense intends to push well beyond the current limits of technology. And along with lasers and particle beams, one piece of hard-ware it has in mind is a microprocessor chip having as much computing power as 100 of Digital Equipment Corp.'s VAX-11/780 superminicomputers.

One candidate for the role of basic computing engine for the program, officially called the Strategic Defense Initiative [*ElectronicsWeek*, May 13, 1985, p. 28], is a gallium arsenide version of the Mips reduced-instruction-set computer (RISC) developed at Stanford University. Three teams are now working on the processor. And this month, the Defense Advanced Projects Research Agency closed the request-for-proposal (RFP) process for a 1.25-μm silicon version of the chip.

Last October, Darpa awarded three contracts for a 32-bit GaAs microprocessor and a floating-point coprocessor. One went to McDonnell Douglas Corp., another to a team formed by Texas Instruments Inc. and Control Data Corp., and the third to a team from RCA Corp. and Tektronix Inc. The three are now working on processes to get useful yields. After a year, the program will be reduced to one or two teams. Darpa's target is to have a 10,000-gate GaAs chip by the beginning of 1988.

If it is as fast as Darpa expects, the chip will be the basic engine for the Advanced Onboard Signal Processor, one of the baseline machines for the SDI. "We went after RISC because we needed something small enough to put on GaAs," says Sheldon Karp, principal scientist for strategic technology at Darpa. The agency had been working with the Motorola Inc. 68000 microprocessor, but Motorola wouldn't even consider trying to put the complex 68000 onto GaAs, Karp says.

A natural. The Mips chip, which was originally funded by Darpa, was a natural for GaAs. "We have only 10,000 gates to work with," Karp notes. "And the Mips people had taken every

possible step to reduce hardware requirements. There are no hardware interlocks, and only 32 instructions."

Even 10,000 gates is big for GaAs; the first phase of the work is intended to make sure that the RISC architecture can be squeezed into that size at respectable yields, Karp says.

Mips was designed by a group under John Hennessey at Stanford. Hennessey, who has worked as a consultant with Darpa on the SDI project, recently took the chip into the private sector by forming Mips Computer Systems of Mountain View, Calif. [*ElectronicsWeek*, April 29, 1985, p. 36]. Computer-aided-design software came from the Mayo Clinic in Rochester, Minn.

The GaAs chip will be clocked at 200 MHz, the silicon at 40 MHz

The silicon Mips chip will come from a two-year effort using the 1.25-μm design rules developed for the Very High Speed Integrated Circuit program. (The Darpa chip was not made part of VHSIC in order to open the RFP to contractors outside that program.)

Both the silicon and GaAs microprocessors will be full 32-bit engines sharing 90% of a common instruction core. Pascal and Air Force 1750A compilers will be targeted for the core instruction set, so that all software will be interchangeable.

The GaAs requirement specifies a clock frequency of 200 MHz and a computation rate of 100 million instructions per second. The silicon chip will be clocked at 40 MHz.

Eventually, the silicon chip must be made radiation-hard; the GaAs chip will be intrinsically rad-hard. Darpa will not release figures on the size of its RISC effort. The silicon version is being funded through the Air Force's Air Development Center in Rome, NY.

–Clifford Barney

ElectronicsWeek/May 20, 1985

Figure 1-1. A brochure about the RCA's 32-bit and eight-bit versions of the GaAs RISC/MIPS processor, realized as a part of the MIPS for Star Wars project. The baseline architecture for both projects was the Stanford University MIPS[4] architecture—an early and famous RISC style architecture developed by Professor John Hennessy and his associates. This architecture was also developed through a DARPA sponsored project. The Stanford University MIPS architecture (SU-MIPS) is described in detail later in this book.

[4]Microprocessor without Interlocked Pipeline Stages

RCA
GaAs

A Heritage
of Excellence

**32-bit MICROPROCESSOR
TEST CHIP**

Process
- E/D GaAs MESFET
- 1-μm gate

PLA
- Instruction decode unit
- Fully automated folded PLA
- 2.5-ns decode time

32-bit ALU
- Standard cell layout (MP2D)
- 3.5-ns add time

Register file
- Custom layout
- Sixteen 32-bit words
- 4.5-ns read access time
- 4.5-ns write time

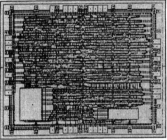

8-bit CPU

- RISC architecture
- Architecture and design complete
- >100 MIPS throughput
- ≥200 MIPS clock rate operation

SYSTEM SPECIFICATION (BEHAVIOR)
SYSTEM DECOMPOSITION (STRUCTURE)
SUBSYSTEM SPEC (BEHAVIOR)
SUBSYSTEM DECOMPOSITION (STRUCTURE)
MODULE SPEC (BEHAVIOR)
MODULE DECOMPOSITION (STRUCTURE)
DIRECTLY IMPLEMENTABLE PRIMITIVE (BEHAVIOR)

DESIGN DECOMPOSITION

Hierarchical System Decomposition

Research in this team began in January of 1982, and it is carried out by the CISD High-Speed Fiber Optic Group, ATL, and RCA Laboratories at Princeton. The first result of this multimillion-dollar program was a 100-Mbit ECL fiber optics network; research soon produced a 200-Mbit system that was successfully evaluated by the Johnson Space Flight Center of NASA in 1986, and it has since led to 500-Mbit GaAs testbed. A 1-Gbit GaAs fiber optics network is now entering development.

"GaAs technology demands the best from academia and industry. RCA stands at the cutting edge of research and application in this field."
Professor Veljko Milutinovic, Purdue University Authority on GaAs Computer Design

ACHIEVEMENTS

RCA's increasing knowledge of GaAs gigabit logic developments has yielded valuable expertise: We are one of the first in the field to have announced an 8-bit CPU in development. Our efforts have resulted in unclassified examples on the previous page.

*For information contact:
Wayne Moyers,
Manager of Advanced Programs,
Advanced Technology Laboratories,
Moorestown Corporate Center, Moorestown, NJ 08057
(609) 866-6427*

Figure 1-1. *(Continued)* A brochure about the RCA's 32-bit and eight-bit versions of the GaAs RISC/MIPS processor, realized as a part of the MIPS for Star Wars project.

A McGRAW-HILL PUBLICATION   THREE DOLLARS

Electronics
THE WORLDWIDE TECHNOLOGY WEEKLY   OCTOBER 7, 1985

HAS THE AGE OF VLSI ARRIVED FOR GaAs?

RYE BROOK, NY

So far, gallium arsenide integrated circuits have touched off excitement mostly among people involved in solid-state device development. But at this week's International Conference on Computer Design (ICCD) in Rye Brook, the excitement should ripple through computer designers as well: a total of seven papers and one panel are devoted to GaAs very large-scale-integration technology.

The excitement has built to the point where Purdue University researcher Veljko Milutinovic proclaims that the age of VLSI has arrived for GaAs. Actually, the circuit densities that most researchers in GaAs are now getting for logic circuits and memories are just approaching LSI. But they are becoming technically and economically feasible for computer designs.

"There have been several significant advances [in digital GaAs chips] worldwide in the past year," says Joe Mogab, director of materials and wafer processing at Microwave Semiconductor Corp., the Siemens AG subsidiary in Somerset, NJ. He notes, for example, that Nippon Telegraph & Telephone Corp. has demonstrated a 16-K static random-access memory containing over 100,000 FETs.

Milutinovic will describe an 8-bit GaAs microprocessor that was developed jointly by Purdue and RCA Corp. The team also has a 32-bit chip in the works.

An unorthodox approach taken at Purdue University (West Lafayette, Ind.) may solve the problem.

Electronic Design • September 5, 1985

RISCing a GaAs Processor

Within the last two years, there has been significant progress in two types of GaAs digital chips: static RAMs and gate arrays. RAMs have increased in density from 4 kbits to 16 kbits this year alone, and gate arrays have increased from 1000 gates to 2000 gates. Because of the high-speed characteristic of these parts, and GaAs parts in general, professor Veljko Milutinovic and graduate student David Fura at Purdue University (West Lafayette, IN) believe that multiple-chip GaAs processor configurations are less desirable than configurations containing only one chip. "This is because the large amount of interchip communication typical for multichip configurations greatly diminishes the inherent GaAs gate-switching speed advantage."

A PennWell Publication   OCTOBER 15, 1985

COMPUTER DESIGN

Figure 1-2. Fragments from various technical and commercial magazines in 1985 discussing the MIPS for Star Wars project in general, and specifically addressing the Purdue University approach to the RCA project.

NEWSFRONT

32-bit GaAs μP hits
200 MIPS at RCA

Electronic Design • May 29, 1986

BY CAROLE PATTON

Moorestown, N.J.—A 32-bit gallium arsenide microprocessor owes its 200 MIPS speed to a reduced instruction set strategy. RISC, says the chip's developer, RCA Corp.'s Advanced Technology Laboratories, is crucial to realizing this highly mobile compound's potential for an ultrafast microprocessor—considered next to impossible in the past due to its relatively low on-chip transistor counts compared to silicon.

Where there seems to be enough space, silicon designers often seek higher speeds by moving computing functions into the hardware. But to build a GaAs CPU that could hit the desired 200 MIPS, RCA turned to Purdue University (West Lafayette, Ind.) for a specialized software compiler and a strategy that aggressively transplants hardware functions into software. But Purdue's Veljko Milutinovic admits, "GaAs chips will probably never match the transistor-count potential of silicon."

Guest Editor's Introduction

GaAs
Microprocessor
Technology

Veljko Milutinovic,
Purdue University

GaAs マイクロプロセサ向き アーキテクチャを探る

Veljko M. Milutinovic
David A. Fura
米パーデュー大学

Walter A. Helbig
米 RCA 社

GaAs LSI マイクロプロセサ向きアーキテクチャについての基本橄を報告している。Si と比較したとき，GaAs LSI は集積度が低く，チップ内の速度に対する外部メモリへのアクセス速度の比が大きいといった特徴がある。こらを考慮すると RISC（reduced instruction set computer）アーキテクチャ採用するのが妥当と思われる。命令数を抑え，実行制御回路を簡単にする一方，大容量のレジスタ・ファイルを採用する。パイプライン構造も，Si マイクロプロセサとは異なり，命令フェッチを遅らせないための工夫がより重要となる。　　（本誌）

Figure 1-2. *(Continued)* Fragments from various technical and commercial magazines in 1986 discussing the MIPS for Star Wars project in general, and specifically addressing the Purdue University approach to the RCA project.

2

An Introduction to RISC Design Methodology for VLSI

This chapter is divided into two parts. The first part globally defines and explains the typical phases of RISC design for VLSI. The second part precisely defines the basic design stages of a specific project, which (apart from some minor differences) is closely related to the project which is the subject of this book.

2.1 Basic Stages of a RISC Processor Design for VLSI

The most important question which arises during the design of a RISC processor for VLSI is not "how," but "what" to design. In other words, VLSI design is now a classic engineering discipline, and it can be mastered with relative ease. The difficult part, requiring much creative work, is the design of the internal architecture of the processor to be implemented on a VLSI chip, that is, its microarchitecture. That is why this book focuses on the problems that arise during the design of a processor's architecture, and on the tools and techniques for the comparison of different architectures. The details of the VLSI design are considered to be less important: the contemporary approach to the VLSI system design presupposes this order of priorities.

The first task that has to be completed while designing a new processor on a VLSI chip is the generation of several candidate architectures of approximately the same VLSI area, or of approximately the same transistor count.

The second task is comparing all of the candidate architectures, in order to measure the execution speed of the compiled code. This is originally written in some high-level programming language which, naturally, represents the application for which the new processor is targeted.

The third task is selecting one candidate architecture and its realization at the level of logic elements compatible with the software tools chosen for the later VLSI design.

The fourth task implies the usage of software tools for VLSI design. The basic steps that have to be taken are: schematic entry, logic and timing testing, and placement and routing of the logic elements and their interconnects.

7

The fifth task is generating all the required masks for the chip fabrication; this narrows down to a careful utilization of the appropriate software tools.

The sixth task is the fabrication itself; it is followed by the postfabrication testing.

An approach for solving the aforementioned problems is described in the following section, using the MIPS for Star Wars project as an example. For the reader's convenience, the absolute and relative durations of the relevant time internals have been excluded since they have no significance in this book; the assumed duration of a single phase is taken to be one year.

2.2 Typical Development Phases for a RISC Microprocessor

The question which arises here is how to organize the work, so that the six tasks discussed earlier can be efficiently completed. Here is how it was done, with some modifications, during the project which serves as the basis for this book.

2.2.1 Request for Proposals

The request for proposals was issued on January 1 of the year X. Among other issues, it specified:

   a)   Architecture type (SU-MIPS, Stanford University MIPS);

   b)   Maximum allowed transistor count on the VLSI chip (30,000);

   c)   Assembler with all associated details (CORE-MIPS), but without any requirements concerning the machine language (the one-to-one correspondence between the assembly and machine level instructions was not required, that is, it was allowed to implement a single assembly level instruction as several machine level instructions); and

   d)   A set of assembly language benchmark programs, representing the final application.

2.2.2 Choice of Contestants

The three contestants were chosen by January 1 of the year $X + 1$, based on the proposals submitted by October 1 of the year X. The proposal had to specify the modifications of the SU-MIPS architecture that would speed up the new design to the maximum extent. The SU-MIPS architecture was developed for the silicon NMOS technology which, compared to the chosen technology, (GaAs E/D-MESFET) was slower by a factor of 20. The main question, therefore, was the way in which to modify the baseline architecture, in order to achieve the speed ratio of the two architectures (new versus baseline) that was close to the speed ratio of the two technologies (GaAs E/D MESFET versus Silicon NMOS). It was clear from the very beginning that the choice of an extremely fast technology would require some radical architectural modifications; if that fact were not realized, then the speed ratio of the two architectures would not even come close to the speed ratio of the two technologies. This is perhaps the place to reiterate that the basic question of VLSI system design is not "how," but "what" to design.

2.2.3 Creating the Most Suitable Architecture

Each contestant team had completed, secretly and independently of each other, the following tasks during the next one-year-period:

a) Formed several candidate architectures, each one with the estimated transistor count of less than 30,000.

b) Wrote a simulator of each candidate architecture capable of executing the specified benchmarks (after being translated from assembly language to machine language) and capable of measuring the benchmark execution times. All contestant teams were required to write their simulators in ISP'—a high-level HDL (*Hardware Description Language*) which is available through the ENDOT package. This package is intended for functional simulation of processors and digital systems. The architecture description was formed in ISP', and the simulation was carried out using the ENDOT package, which executed the benchmarks, and collected all relevant data for the statistical analysis and the measurement of the speed of the architecture being analyzed. There are other HDLs, and VHDL is one of them (VHDL is short for Vhsic HDL, or *Very High Speed Integrated Circuit Hardware Description Language*). Each HDL is usually just a part of some software package for simulational analysis with which a designer can construct various simulation experiments. In general, the architecture simulators can be made using general purpose programming languages such as C or PASCAL. However, using HDLs results in much less effort being expended on the project, and the number of engineer hours can even be decreased by an order of magnitude.

c) Ranked all candidate architectures according to the timing of the supplied benchmark programs.

d) Considered in detail the reasons of particular architectures scoring extremely high or extremely low. The best candidate architecture was refined by using elements of other highly ranked architectures so that it became even better. Finally, the definitive architecture was frozen, ready to go into the "battle" with other contestants' submissions.

e) Made a detailed design, first on the RTL level (*Register Transfer Level*), then using the logic elements compatible with the VLSI design software that would be used later in the project. This stage was necessary to confirm that the resulting architecture could really be squeezed into the 30,000 transistor limit.

2.2.4 Comparison of the Contestants' Architectures

By January 1 of the year $X + 2$, the research sponsor ranked the architectures of the three contestants, using the above mentioned predefined benchmark programs, and the ISP' simulators that the three teams realized internally. Two teams were selected to be further funded by the sponsor. The third team was left the choice of quitting the contest, or continuing on the company's own funding. The contestants who decided to go on were allowed access to the complete details of the other contestants' projects.

2.2.5   Final Architecture

The teams that remained in the contest did the following by January 1 of the year $X + 3$:

a)   They used their last chance to change the architecture. The quality of the design after the changes had been incorporated was verified using the ENDOT package. Then the architecture was effectively frozen, that is, it was decided to not change it, even if a major improvement resulted from a new idea.

b)   They developed the architecture into an RTL model, and froze it.

c)   They chose a family of logic elements. (The projects described here used the 1.25 μm CMOS silicon and the 1 μm E/D-MESFET GaAs technologies. This book will discuss the two technologies in more detail later.) The final logic diagram was formed, using exclusively the standard logic elements belonging to the chosen logic element family, including the standard elements for connection to the pads of the chip that was being designed.

d)   They centered further effort on the software packages for VLSI design. These packages, and the related design methodology, will be discussed in much detail later in this book. Only the basic facts, in the context of the project being discussed, will be mentioned in the text that follows.

1.   The logic diagram has to be transformed into the form which precisely defines the topology of the diagram, and formatted for the existing VLSI design software packages. In this case, it is the netlist, where each logic element is described with one line of the text file; that line specifies the way this element is connected to other elements. The netlist can be formed directly or indirectly. In the former case, any text editor can be used. In the latter case, graphics oriented packages are used to enter the diagram, and it (the diagram) is translated automatically, and without errors, into a netlist, or some other convenient form. The netlist can also be formed using high-level hardware description tools, or using state transition tables for the state machine definition. This phase of the design is usually called *logic entry* or *schematic capture*.

2.   After forming the netlist (the logic diagram, represented in a specific way), it must be verified by using software for logic and timing testing. If this software shows that "everything is OK," the designer can proceed to the following steps. Note that the absolute confidence in the design cannot be established in the case of complex schematic diagrams. Consequently, this phase of the design is very critical. It is usually called *logic and timing testing*.

3.   After being tested, the netlist is fed to the software for placement and routing. The complexity of this phase depends on the technology that will be used to fabricate chips. In the case of design based on the logic symbols, as in this project, there are three different approaches to chip fabrication. One possibility is to make all N mask levels[1] before the design begins. Then, after the design is over, some of the existing interconnects are activated, while the rest remain inactive (the complete set of interconnects is prefabricated). This approach to VLSI design is generally called *Programmable Logic VLSI* (or PL VLSI). The designer has a minimal influence on the placement and routing (or sometimes none whatsoever). Another possibility is to prefabricate all the necessary mask levels,

---

[1]The value of N depends on the underlying technology: it is an integer, usually between 7 and 14 [5].

except those defining the interconnects, meaning that the first $N-1$ or $N-2$ mask levels are prefabricated. In this case, the designer defines only the remaining one or two mask levels. This approach is called *Gate Array VLSI* (or GA VLSI). The designer has some degree of influence on the placement and routing. The third possibility is that no mask levels are prefabricated. In this case, the designer creates all N levels of the mask after the design process is over. This approach is called *Standard Cell VLSI* (SC VLSI). Now the designer has plenty of influence on the placement and routing process, and that process can get very complicated. These approaches will be discussed later in this book. This phase is usually called *placement and routing*. The process generates a number of output files, two of which are important to this discussion. These are the *fabrication file*, which represents the basis for chip fabrication, and the *graphics file*, which is actually a photomicrograph of the chip, and can be used for visual analysis of the layout of the logic elements on the chip.

4. The final part of the design process is the realization of the remaining mask levels (except when using the PL VLSI), and the chip fabrication itself.

In the project described here, the three teams completed all the stages of the design, and thus developed their first prototypes which, although working at the highest possible speeds, were still slower than required.

2.2.6 Fabrication and Software Environment

Each team fabricated the lower-than-nominal-speed prototype by January 1 of the year $X + 4$, and the full-speed preseries examples became available by January 1 of the year $X + 5$.

Efforts for completing the software environment paralleled the activities that led to chip realization. This included the translators, from the relatively complex assembly languages of the CISCs like the Motorola 680x0 ($x = 0, 1, 2, 3, 4$, and so forth) and the 1750A, to the relatively simple RISC-type assembly language, the CORE-MIPS. It also included the compilers for high-level languages C and Ada.

3

An Introduction to Hardware Description Languages

This chapter is divided into two parts. The first part discusses hardware description languages in general. The second part discusses the ISP' hardware description language, and specifically focuses on the ENDOT package for hardware analysis.

3.1 Introduction

Nowadays, one cannot imagine the development of new computer architectures without using high-level hardware description languages (HDLs). Hardware can be described on a low level, that is, using logic gates (GTL, *Gate Transfer Level*), on a medium level (RTL, *Register Transfer Level*), or on a high level (FBL, *Functional Behavior Level*).

This chapter concentrates on the HDLs that can be used to describe hardware on the functional level, which is particularly useful when a designer attempts to develop and analyze a new architecture. A simulator of the architecture can be easily generated from this description, thus allowing the assembly language programs to be executed on the simulator. If the designer has to choose from several candidate architectures, and if the measure of quality of the architecture is the execution speed for a given benchmark program (or a set of benchmark programs), then all he (or she) has to do is to execute the benchmark(s) on the simulator of every candidate architecture, and write down the execution times. The best architecture is chosen according to the criterion of minimum execution time (for the same hardware complexity).

There are lots of useful hardware description languages; however, there are very few that stand out, especially when it comes to functional level simulation. Two of them are VHDL and ISP'. The former one has been accepted as the IEEE standard (IEEE 1076). The latter one has been accepted by DARPA as the mandatory language for the project this book is based on, as well as a number of other projects in the field.

Compared to ISP', the basic advantages of VHDL are:

a) The language VHDL is generally more capable. This advantage is important in very complex projects; however, for the majority of problems, it is insignificant, thus making the ISP' good enough most of the time.

b) The FBL description in VHDL can easily be translated to a GTL description, that is, to the level of the chosen logic gate family which is oriented toward the technology that will be used during the fabrication process; this is not true in the case of the ISP' language. This advantage is important if the implementation that follows assumes the chip realization in VLSI, but it is of no significance if the implementation is based on standard off-the-shelf processor components, such as the popular micro-processors and peripherals on a VLSI chip.

c) Since VHDL became a standard, many models of popular processors and support chips exist, thus enabling the designer to use these rather than develop his (her) own models. This is important if the architecture being developed is based on standard components, but it is of no significance if an entirely new architecture is being developed.

The basic advantages of the ISP' language over the VHDL are:

a) The ISP' language is simpler, so it is easier to learn and use.

b) ISP' is faster, thus shortening execution times of the simulations.

c) ISP' exists within the ENDOT package which contains efficient tools for gathering the statistical information pertaining to the test program execution.

Fortunately, the ENDOT package contains a very useful utility which enables the user to combine the advantages of both ISP' and VHDL languages. This utility is the ISP' to VHDL translator. It allows the initial research (gathering of the statistical information, and so on) to be done in ISP' while the rest of the activities on the project can be done in VHDL, utilizing to the fullest its more sophisticated features.

Another useful feature of the ENDOT package is the existence of an ISP' to C translator. This feature enables a hardware description to be treated by some C-to-silicon compilers. After a series of steps a VLSI mask can be obtained and used in the fabrication process [6].

The details of the ISP' language and the ENDOT package can be found in [7] and [8]. Some useful ENDOT application notes are referred to in [9]–[12]. As for the details of the VHDL language and the MODEL TECHNOLOGY package, which contains a VHDL com-piler and debugger, it is best to consult [13]–[15]. The rest of this book will center only on the issues of the ISP' language and the ENDOT package.

3.2   ENDOT and ISP'

Basically, in order to design the simulator for a processor using the ENDOT package and the ISP' language, one has to create the following files:

a) **.isp:** The file with an arbitrary name and the extension **.isp** contains the processor description, as well as the description of the program and data memory. If so desired, two files can be created—one for the processor, and one for the program and data memory. In the latter case, the two **.isp** files must have different names. Generally, one can have more **.isp** files [for processor(s), memory(ies), peripheral(s), and so on].

b) **.t:** The file having the **.t** extension describes the structure of the simulated system. If a single **.isp** file contains the descriptions of the processor and the memory, the **.t** file is rather trivial in appearance, and will contain only the mandatory part which defines the clock period duration, the names of the files which contain the translated description of the system, and the assembled test program that will be executed (an example follows). If, on the contrary, there are two (or more) **.isp** files containing separate descriptions of the processor and the memory, then the **.t** file must contain a detailed description of the external connections between the two **.isp** files. The term *external connections* refers to the pins of the processor and memory chips, and these descriptions are given in the two mentioned **.isp** files. In the case of a multiprocessor system with several processor chips, several memory modules, and other components, the **.t** file can become quite complex because it contains the description of all the connections between the **.isp** files in the system. To manage this complexity a separate topology language has been developed, but it transcends the scope of this book.

c) **.m:** The file having the **.m** extension contains the information needed to translate the assembly language instructions into the machine language. It includes a detailed correspondence between the assembly and the machine instructions, as well as other elements which will be discussed later.

d) **.i:** The file with the **.i** extension contains the information necessary for both loading the description of the system into the memory and for connecting the different parts of the system description.

e) **.b:** Apart from the aforementioned files, the designer has to create a file with the program that is going to be executed. This file can have any name and any extension, but the extension **.b,** either with or without additional specifiers such as **.b1, .b2,** and so on, is most commonly used. It is assumed that the test program is written in the assembly language of the processor that is being simulated.

The ENDOT package contains three groups of software tools described below: hardware tools, software tools, and postprocessing and utility tools. Using these tools, one first creates the executable simulation file (applying the tools on the five files mentioned earlier in this passage), and then analyzes the results by comparing them to the expectations that were prepared earlier.

The hardware tools are:

a) the ISP' language,
b) the ISP' compiler—*ic,*
c) the topology language,
d) the topology language compiler—*ec* (ecologist),
e) the simulator—*n2,* and
f) the simulation command language.

The software tools are:

a) metaassembler—*micro,*
b) metaloader, that comes in two parts: the interpreter—*inter,* and the allocator—*cater,* and
c) a collection of minor programs.

The postprocessing and utility tools are:

a) statement counter—*coverage,*
b) general purpose postprocessor—*gpp,*
c) ISP' to VHDL translator—*icv,* and
d) a collection of minor programs.

As stated earlier, the ENDOT package greatly simplifies the road that one has to travel in an attempt to transform an idea of a new architecture into an analysis of the simulation results, even if the architecture is a very complex one. This will be shown through a simple example, which is preceded by some short explanations.

3.2.1   Definition of the ISP' Program Declaration Section

The ISP' program has two basic segments: the declaration section and the behavior section.

The declaration section contains the definitions of the language constructs used in the behavior section. There are six different subsections that can appear in the declaration section of an ISP' program.

a) **macro:** This subsection is used to define easy to remember names for the objects in the program. It is highly recommended that this subsection type be used frequently in professional ISP' programming.

b) **port:** This subsection defines the names of objects that will be used for communications with the outside world. They are typically related to the pins of the processor, memory, or some other module (chip), whose description is given within some **.isp** file.

c) **state:** This subsection is used to define the names of sequential objects (with memory capability), but without the possibility of defining their initial values. These objects are typically the flip-flops and the registers of the processor. One should be aware that the state of most flip-flops and registers is undefined immediately after the powerup.

d) **memory:** This subsection is also used to define the names of sequential objects (with memory capability), but with the possibility of defining their initial values. It is most frequently used to define the memory for programs and data. One should be aware that the contents of the ROM memory is fully defined immediately after the powerup.

e) **format:** This subsection is used to specify the names for fields within the objects that have memory. Typically, it is used to define the fields of the instruction format.

f) **queue:** This subsection is used to specify the objects used for synchronization with the external logic.

3.2.2   Definition of the ISP' Program Behavior Section

The behavior section contains one or more processes. Each process has a separate declaration part, followed by the process body, and is made up of the ISP' statements.

Contrary to the traditional high-level languages which execute statements in sequence, the ISP' statements inside a block execute in parallel. For example, the sequence

$$a = b;$$
$$b = a;$$

leaves both a and b with the same value in a traditional high-level language program. The ISP' language would, on the other hand, interpret this sequence of statements as an attempt to swap the values of the variables a and b. This is a consequence of the inherent parallel execution in ISP'.

If, for some reason, there is a need for the sequential execution of two statements, the statement **next**, or some complex statement that contains it, should be inserted between them. One of these complex statements is **delay**. It contains two primitives: the first primitive introduces the sequentiality into the execution stream and is referred to as *next*, and the second primitive is a statement that updates the clock period counter and is referred to as *counter-update*.

The ISP' language supports four different process types.

a) **main:** This process type executes as an endless loop. This means that the process is reexecuted once it has completed, continuing to loop until the end of the simulation. This is precisely the manner in which processor hardware behaves, fetching instructions from the moment it is powered to the moment the power is cut off, or to the moment when some special instruction or event is encountered, such as HALT, HOLD, WAIT, and so on.

b) **when:** This process type executes once for each occurrence of the specified event.

c) **procedure:** This process type is the same as a subprogram or a procedure in a traditional high-level language. It is used to build a **main** or **when** process in a structured, top-down manner.

d) **function:** This process type is the same as a function in a traditional high-level language.

3.2.3 Examples of ISP' Program Declaration and Behavior Sections

Figures 3-1 and 3-2 show simple examples of clock generator and counter in the ISP' language. After reading this book, readers are encouraged to browse through the original documentation that is shipped with the ENDOT package.

Figure 3-1 shows the **wave.isp** file, describing the clock generator in terms of the ISP' language. Its declaration section contains the definition of the output pin, which carries the clock signal. The behavior section makes sure that the duration of the logic level "zero," as well as the duration of the logic level "one," are exactly 50 time units. The actual duration of the time unit will be specified in the **.t** file.

Figure 3-2 shows the **cntr.isp** file which describes the clocked counter in the ISP' language. Its declaration section contains the following definitions:

a) the definition of the input pin (CK), through which the clock signal is fed into the module;

```
port
    CK 'output;
main  CYCLE :=
    (
        CK = 0;
        delay(50);
        CK = 1;
        delay(50);
    )
```

Figure 3-1. File **wave.isp** with the description of a clock generator in the ISP' language.

```
port
    CK  'input,
    Q<4> 'output;
state
    COUNT<4>;
when  EDGE(CK:lead)  :=
    (
        Q = COUNT + 1;
        COUNT = COUNT + 1;
    )
```

Figure 3-2. File **cntr.isp** with the description of a clocked counter in the ISP' language.

b)   the definition of the four output pins (Q), which lead the four-bit result out; and

c)   the definition of the internal register which holds the current clock period count (COUNT).

The behavior section makes sure that the number one is added to the previous count on every leading (positive) edge of the clock signal, and writes this value into the internal register COUNT and the output pins Q. Keyword LEAD is a part of the ISP' language, and it denotes the leading edge of the signal.

The files **wave.isp** and **cntr.isp** contain the source code written in the ISP' language; now is the time to generate the files **wave.sim** and **cntr.sim**, which contain the object code. The ISP' compiler *ic* does that job.

3.2.4   Creating a .t File

The next step is to create the **.t** file using the topology language. This step is important because we have to define the connections between the descriptions in the **.sim** files. The sections that a program in topology language contains are listed below:

a)   **signal:**   This section contains the signal declarations, that is, it specifies the connections between the objects contained in the **.sim** files. A general form of the signal declaration, using the original ENDOT package terminology, looks like this:

signal_name[*<width>*][, *signal_declarations*]

This means that we first specify the signal name, then the signal width (number of bits), and the two are followed by optional declarations which will not be discussed here.

b)   **processor:**   This section contains the declaration of one processor, that is, of one element of the system, whose description is contained in one **.sim** file. The **.t** file can contain many **processor** sections, one for each **.sim** file. A general form of the processor declaration looks like this:

processor_name = "filename.sim";
   [**time delay** = *integer*;]
   [**connections** *signal_connections*;]
   [**port** = *signal_name*[, *signal_connections*];]
   [**initial** *memory_name* = l.out]

In short, we have to define the processor name (mandatory) and then we (optionally) define:

1) Specific time delays;
2) Signal connections; and
3) Initial memory contents.

An example is given later in the book.

c) **macro:** This section contains the easily remembered names for various topology objects.

d) **composite:** This section contains a set of topology language declarations. A general form of this section is:

> **begin**
> > *declaration* [*declaration*]
>
> **end**

Therefore, the declarations are contained inside a **begin-end** block. Readers should consult the original ENDOT documentation for further insight.

e) **include:** This section is used to include a file containing the declarations written in the topology language. For details, refer to the original ENDOT documentation.

3.2.5 Example of a .t File

Figure 3-3 shows the file **clcnt.t**, which defines the topology of the system composed of the **wave.sim** and **cntr.sim** files, and the associated hardware components.

The **signal** section defines the connections between the files **wave.sim** and **cntr.sim**, while the two separate **processor** sections define the details of the incorporation of the files **wave.sim** and **cntr.sim** into the system.

The following step is the creation of two object files containing the description of the system. To this end, we use the ecologist (*ec*). The input files are:

a) The .t file;

```
signal
    CLOCK,
    BUS<4>;
processor CLK = "wave.sim";
    time delay = 10;
    connections
        CK = CLOCK;
processor CNT = "cntr.sim";
    connections
        CK = CLOCK,
        Q = BUS;
```

Figure 3-3. File **clcnt.t** with a topology language description of the connection between the clock generator and the clock counter, described first in the **wave.isp** and then in the **cntr.isp** files.

b)   All the **.sim** files; and

c)   The **l.out** file, if the system contains a predefined program. The output file has the extension **.e00**, and it contains the object code that represents the entire system.

In the case of the example analyzed here, the input files are:

clcnt.t
wave.sim
cntr.sim

The output file is:

clcnt.e00

3.2.6   Simulation

For simulation we use the program *n2*. The required input files are **.e00**, all the **.sim** files, and the optional file **l.out**. If we want to record the simulation results for later processing, the usual extension given to the output file is **.txt**.

In our example, the input files for the *n2* are:

wave.sim
cntr.sim
clcnt.e00

The output file, if we want to create it, is:

clcnt.txt

During the simulation, we use the simulation command language. We will briefly mention only some of its commands (a detailed list is available in the ENDOT documentation).

a)   **run:**   This command starts or continues the simulation.

b)   **quit:**   This command ends the simulation and exits the simulator.

c)   **time:**   This command prints the current simulation time on the terminal (the number of clock periods that have elapsed since the beginning of the simulation).

d)   **examine** *structure(s):*   This command gives the user a means of gaining insight into the contents of different structures. For example, we can see the contents of a register after the simulation was interrupted.

e)   **help** *keyword:*   This command enables the user to get on-line help on the specified keyword.

f)   **deposit** *value structure:*   This command enables the user to change the contents of specified structures. For example, we can set the contents of a register to a specific value after the simulation is interrupted.

g)   **monitor** *structure(s):*   This command enables the user to gain insight into the contents of various structures while simultaneously setting the break points. The details are given in the ENDOT manuals.

The example presented in Figure 3-4 contains only the hardware elements and hardware tools that have been described so far. In general, more complex systems include both software and hardware components. We will discuss the existing software tools next.

3.2.7 The .m File

If the test program was written in the assembly language of the processor that is to be simulated, it has to be translated into the machine language for that same processor. This process can be done using a program called *metamicro*. The input files for this program are: the **.m** (containing the description of the correspondence between the assembly and machine instructions), and the **.b** (containing the test program). The output file is **.n** (containing the object code of the program). The **.m** file, apart from the description of the correspondence between the assembly and the machine instructions, also contains the specification of the file with the test program, in the **begin-end** section, with the following general form:

```
begin
    include program.b$
end
```

3.2.8 The .i File

There is one more file that has to be prepared. It has the extension **.i**, and it contains the information for the linker/loader, and describes the method of resolving addresses during the linking and loading process. This file is first interpreted using the program *inter*. The input file is **.i**, and the output file is **.a**, which contains the executable object code before the linking and loading process. The linking and loading are done using the program *cater*. The input files for the *cater* are **.n** and **.a**, and the output file is **l.out**, containing the object code of the program ready to be executed.

After the execution of the test program is over, one can analyze the results of the simulation using the aforementioned postprocessing and utility tools. The reader is advised to try them out, and to learn more about them by using the **help** and the documentation that comes together with the ENDOT package.

Figure 3-4 shows a possible sequence of operations that have to be carried out during a successful ENDOT session, as in the case of our clocked counter example. The details of Figure 3-4 should be quite clear by now. One more thing to remember is that the programs included in the ENDOT package have various command line options. The option **-h** (hardware) in the command line of the program *ec* specifies that we intend to simulate only the hardware. The alternatives are: **-s**, if we simulate only the software, and **-b** if we simulate both hardware and software. The option **-s** in the command line of *n2* specifies that the output is saved in a (script) file with the specified name (**clcnt.txt**).

```
begin
    ❶    vi wave.isp
    ❷    vi cntr.isp
    ❸    ic wave.isp
    ❹    ic cntr.isp
    ❺    vi clcnt.t
    ❻    ec -h clcnt.t
    ❼    n2 -s clcnt.txt clcnt.e00
end
```

Figure 3-4. Assuming that the environment is the UNIX operating system, this sequence of operations have to be executed in order to perform an ENDOT simulation.

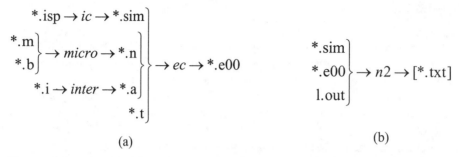

(a)   (b)

Figure 3-5. A typical sequence of ENDOT system program calls for the case of (a) making and (b) running the model of a stored program machine.

It is strongly recommended that the reader tries out this example using a computer. A sample simulation run using ENDOT package is given in Figure 3-6. Afterwards, it would be wise to try out the complete processor simulation of an educational RISC machine, for example, the one described in [9]. Simulation will no longer be discussed in this book. Here, we only show a typical sequence of ENDOT system program calls for the case of making and running the model of a stored program machine (see Figure 3-5).

```
simulation: clcnt (snapshot = 00)
date created: Fri Mar 24 20:51:29 1995
simulation time = 0
> monitor write stop CNT:Q    Breakpoint: triggered on write into structure Q.
tag 1
> examine CNT:Q               This enables one to see the contents of a structure.
CNT:Q = 0 X (port data)
> run                         This runs the simulation,
500                           until the first breakpoint is reached.
      1:    write CNT:Q = 1   The result of a write triggers the break.
>
> examine CNT:Q
CNT:Q = 1 (port data)         As expected, the number one is written into Q
> run                         after 500 time units.
1500
      1:    write CNT:Q = 2   After another 1000 time units,
> examine CNT:Q               the number two is written into Q.
CNT:Q = 2 (port data)
> run
2500
      1:    write CNT:Q = 3
> run
3500
      1:    write CNT:Q = 4
> time
3500
> quit                        After the simulation is over,
                              we return to the UNIX system.
```

Figure 3-6. A sample simulation run using ENDOT package.

In addition to the above mentioned simulator, there are many more simulators in existence at the User Library of ENDOT, including several popular 16-, 32-, and 64-bit microprocessors. A detailed investigation into their structure can enhance the reader's understanding of the process of creating a professional simulator for a commercial microprocessor.

The ISP' language and the ENDOT package have been used not only in the RISC/MIPS projects of DARPA (for GaAs and silicon versions of the processor), but also in the development of a number of more or less known processors. These tools have been used in the development of the Motorola 68000 and other members of its family [16], various Gould (now Encore) superminicomputers [17], and in the design of the famous SPUR processor at the University of California at Berkeley, which is one of the descendants of the original RISC I and RISC II processors.

3.2.9 Example of MIPS for Star Wars Benchmark Programs

We now return to the MIPS for Star Wars project, which represents the basis of this book. Let us assume that we have completed the ENDOT simulators for several different new architectures, and that we can determine which one is the best by executing certain test programs (before we make an attempt to realize it using appropriate VLSI design tools).

To this end, the MIPS for Star Wars project used the programs listed in Figure 3-7. Of all the realized candidate architectures, only one was chosen for the VLSI implementation. That architecture was selected according to the criterion of the shortest execution times for the benchmarks from Figure 3-7. However, the usage of test programs is not the only possibility. That is why we will now discuss the general methodology of computer system performance evaluation. (Reference [18] gives a more detailed approach to this problem.)

3.2.10 General Methodology of Computer System Performance Evaluation

The computer system workload is the set of all inputs (programs, data, commands, and so on) the system receives from its environment. It is not possible to evaluate the computer system

1.	ackp.p
2.	bubblesortp.p
3.	fftp.p
4.	fibp.p
5.	intmmp.p
6.	permp.p
7.	puzzlep.p
8.	eightqueenp.p
9.	quickp.p
10.	realmmp.p
11.	sievep.p
12.	towersp.p
13.	treep.p

Figure 3-7. List of benchmark programs, written in Pascal (.p), used during the MIPS for the Star Wars project to compare different solutions to the problem. These were submitted by different teams competing in the project.

performance using the true workload. Even though the computer system might carry out its intended functions while the measurement takes place, the workload is sampled only for a limited period of time. The true workload is a function of the inputs received by the system during its entire lifetime.

A workload used in performance evaluation has to comply with certain requirements. The most important requirement is the representability (that is, the ability to represent the workload of the target application). It is very difficult to achieve representability, especially during the design of the processor intended for a wide spectrum of applications. The workload has to be specified in advance and used to compare the architectures that have been generated during the research. More often than not, it is the customer's, rather than the contractor's, responsibility of supplying the workload. In the case of the Star Wars project, the customer supplied, in advance, all of the competing teams with the test programs (see Figure 3-7), and has received some unfavorable criticism due to the nonrepresentability of the test programs (that is, they did not reflect the end user target application very well). The construction of a representative workload is a separate problem which will not be discussed here. The reader is advised to consult an appropriate reference, such as [18].

The workload used in performance evaluation has to comply with other requirements as well:

a) The workload has to be easy to construct;

b) Execution cost of the workload must be minimal;

c) Measurement has to be reproducible;

d) Memory complexity of the workload has to be small;

e) The machine has to be independent of the workload (allowing the possibility of evaluating other systems' performance as well, for the purpose of comparison).

The relative importance of these requirements depends on the actual experiment (the important aspects of one experiment can be insignificant in another experiment).

3.2.11 Natural and Synthetic Workloads

There are two basic classes of workloads. These are the *natural workload*, and the *synthetic workload*.

The *natural workload* is made up of a sample of the production workload (for example, the sample of the actual activity of the system executing its intended application). It is used for certain measurements of the system performance in parallel with the workload generation. All remaining cases represent the *synthetic workloads*.

The nonexecutable workloads are defined using the statistical distributions of the relevant parameters, and are used in analytical analyses (based on mathematical models). These workloads are usually defined using various functions of the statistical distribution, such as probabilities, mean values, variances, distribution densities, and so on, or parameters such as the instructions from a specified instruction set, memory access times, procedure nesting depth, and so on. This group also contains the so called *instruction mixes*, or the probability tables for the instructions from an assembly-level instruction set, and *statement mixes*, or the probability tables for typical high-level language statements and constructs.

Instruction mixes can be specific (when generated for a specific application), or standard (which is suitable for comparison of different general purpose systems). Some of the well known instruction mixes are the Flynn mix for assembler instructions and the Knuth mix for high-level language statements and constructs [18].

The executable workloads are defined as one or more programs, and they are usually used in simulation analyses (using a software package for the simulation analysis, such as ENDOT). These workloads are usually specified in the form of synthetic jobs or benchmark programs.

3.2.11.1 Synthetic Jobs   *Synthetic jobs* are parametric programs with no semantic meaning. A *parametric program* is a program with certain probabilities defined in it (probabilities of high-level language constructs or machine language instructions, as well as some of the above mentioned parameters of the nonexecutable workloads). The value of each parameter can be specified prior to the program execution. A program with no semantic meaning is a program that does not do anything specific, but only executes loops to achieve the effects specified by the parameters. This explanation makes it clear that the synthetic job is actually an executable version of some nonexecutable workload.

There are numerous methods of constructing a synthetic job which represents an executable version of some nonexecutable workload. Two widely used methods are: the Buchholz which is based on the flowchart with variable parameters, and the Kernighan/Hamilton, which is similar but more complex (see [18]). There are various methods of synthetic job usage in the comparative performance evaluation. The most widely used and quoted method is the Archibald/Baer [19].

3.2.11.2 Benchmark Programs   *Benchmark programs* are nonparametric programs with semantic meaning. They do something useful, for example the integer or real matrix multiplication (a typical numerical benchmark program), or searching and sorting (typical nonnumerical benchmark programs). The test programs can be: extracted benchmarks, created benchmarks, and standard benchmarks.

If the test program represents the inner loop which is the most characteristic of the target application, then it is referred to as the *kernel program*. Kernel programs usually contain no input/output code. However, since the original enthusiasm for the RISC processor design has become saturated, and due to the fact that the RISC design methodology (as described in this book) has shifted its emphasis toward the input/output arena, in the broadest sense (including the memory subsystem) the input/output code will be included more and more often in the kernel programs.

3.2.12 Summary

If we assume that by this time, we have completed (with the aide of a number of representative benchmark programs) the comparative evaluation of all candidate architectures and that we have decided upon the best candidate architecture, then the task that awaits us is the VLSI chip design. The following step, therefore, is specifically related to the VLSI design, and is the subject of the following chapter.

4

An Introduction to VLSI

This chapter is divided in two parts. The first part discusses the basics of the VLSI chip design. The second part discusses several VLSI chip design methodologies.

4.1. The Basics of VLSI Chip Design

The term *VLSI*, in its broadest sense, denotes the implementation of a digital or analog system in very large scale integration, as well as all associated activities during the process of design and implementation of the system. In particular, the term VLSI means that the transistor count of the chip is larger than 10,000 (different sources quote different figures). The following example summarizes the transistor counts for various integration scales (the most frequently encountered figures are given here):

SSI: more than 10 transistors per chip
MSI: more than 100 transistors per chip
LSI: more than 1,000 transistors per chip
VLSI: more than 10,000 transistors per chip

As previously stated, the actual figures should not be taken unconditionally. Some sources quote the same figures, but refer to the gate count instead of the transistor count. The number of transistors per gate ($N_{t/g}$) depends on the integrated circuit design technique and on the fan-in (N_u). For instance:

NMOS (Si): $N_{t/g} = 1 + N_u$

CMOS (Si): $N_{t/g} = 2 N_u$

ECL (Si): $N_{t/g} = 3 + N_u$ (conditionally)

In the case of GaAs technology used in the project described in this book, the following formula holds true:

E/D-MESFET (GaAs): $N_{t/g} = 1 + N_u$

Therefore, when we speak of the chip complexity, we have to stress the fact that our figures refer to one of the two counts (transistor count or gate count). The term *device* is often confusing because some sources use it to denote the transistor, and others to denote the gate.

4.1.1   A Classification of VLSI Design Methodologies

The VLSI design methodologies can be classified as:

a)   Design based on geometric symbols—*full-custom (FC) VLSI;*

b)   Design based on logic symbols; and

c)   Design based on behavioral symbols—*silicon compilation* or *silicon translation (ST).*

Design based on logic symbols can be divided further into three subclasses:

b_1)   Standard cell (SC) VLSI;

b_2)   Gate array (GA) VLSI; and

b_3)   Programmable logic (PL) VLSI (see Table 4-1).

In Table 4-1, the figures in parentheses denote the number of VLSI mask layers necessary for the prefabrication process, or before the design of the chip is begun (the value before the comma), and the number of VLSI mask layers necessary for the final fabrication process, or after the chip design is complete (the value after the comma). The total number of VLSI mask layers is governed by the chosen fabrication technology and the chip realization technique.

4.1.2   More on VLSI Classification

The FC VLSI and the SC VLSI technologies require no prefabrication. The VLSI mask layers are created after the design process is completed. In the case of the FC VLSI, all necessary VLSI mask layers are created directly from the circuit design based on the geometric symbols. In the case of the SC VLSI, one extra step is required, namely the translation of the design based on the logic symbols into the design based on the geometric symbols. Among the most renowned US manufacturers of VLSI chips based on the SC and FC technologies are VLSI Technology (Silicon) and TriQuint (GaAs).

The GA VLSI technology requires that all VLSI mask layers be prefabricated (except one or two which define the interconnects, and these layers are specified by the designer, after the design process is complete). Among the most renowned US manufacturers of the GA VLSI chips are Honeywell (Silicon) and Vitesse (GaAs).

The PL VLSI technology has all mask layers prefabricated, and there is no final fabrication. Only the interconnects have to be activated after the design is completed. The interconnects are prefabricated along with the rest of the chip. They are activated by writing the

Table 4-1.   Summary of VLSI Design Methodology Classifications

VLSI
  Design based on geometric symbols
    FC VLSI $(0, N)$
  Design based on logic symbols
    SC VLSI $(0, N)$
    GA VLSI $(N-1, 1$ or $N-2, 2)$
    PL VLSI $(N, 0)$
  Design based on behavioral symbols
    ST VLSI $(0, N$ or $N-K, K$ or $N, 0)$; $K = 1, 2$

appropriate contents into the on-chip ROM or RAM memory. Among the most renowned US manufacturers of the PL VLSI chips are Actel, Altera, AT&T, Cypress, Lattice, and Xilinx.

With SC VLSI no mask layers are prefabricated, leaving the designer with complete freedom in placement and routing. With GA VLSI there are $N-1$ or $N-2$ mask layers prefabricated, significantly reducing the placement and routing freedom. With PL VLSI all mask layers are prefabricated, allowing for only minimal placement and routing flexibility.

The ST VLSI technology is based on FC VLSI, SC VLSI, GA VLSI, or PL VLSI in the chip fabrication domain; it is based on general purpose HLLs (like C) or special purpose HLLs (like HDLs) in the chip design domain.

4.1.3 VLSI Design Activities

All these methods have the following common basic design activities:

a) Logic entry or schematic capture;

b) Logic and timing testing; and

c) Placement and routing.

These activities have a specific form in the case of FC VLSI and ST VLSI (these two methods will not be further elaborated here).

For the three design methodologies based on logic symbols, the schematic entry and logic/timing testing are identical. The most striking differences, however, occur in the placement and routing arena. These differences are due to the differing levels of placement and routing flexibility of chip elements in different technologies, which, in turn, is governed by the number of prefabricated mask layers. An explanation follows.

4.1.4 Basic Elements of VLSI Chip Design

In practical terms, the basic elements of SC VLSI chips, standard cells, have equal heights and different widths, the latter dimension being a function of the standard cell complexity. Standard cells are aligned in channels to ease the burden of the placement and routing software. Interconnects are grouped in the interconnect channels. A typical layout is given in Figure 4-1. The height of a standard cell channel is equal for all channels because the height of each standard cell is the same. The height of an interconnect channel depends on the number of interconnects, and it differs from channel to channel on the same chip. In plain English, this means that the standard cell channels *are not* equidistant.

In GA VLSI, the basic elements, the gates, have all the same dimensions (all gates share the same complexity). The gates are placed in the gate channels during the prefabrication process. The interconnects are realized through prefabricated interconnect channels. The interconnects are made for two purposes: to form RTL elements, and to connect them in order to make the designed VLSI system. A typical layout is shown in Figure 4-2. In this case, not only the gate channels, but also the interconnect channels are fixed in size. In other words—gate channels *are* equidistant.

In PL VLSI, the basic elements, the macrocell blocks (logic elements of a significant complexity), are prefabricated and interconnected. A typical layout is given in Figure 4-3. The intersections of channels contain the interconnect networks, which are controlled by the contents of RAM or ROM memory.

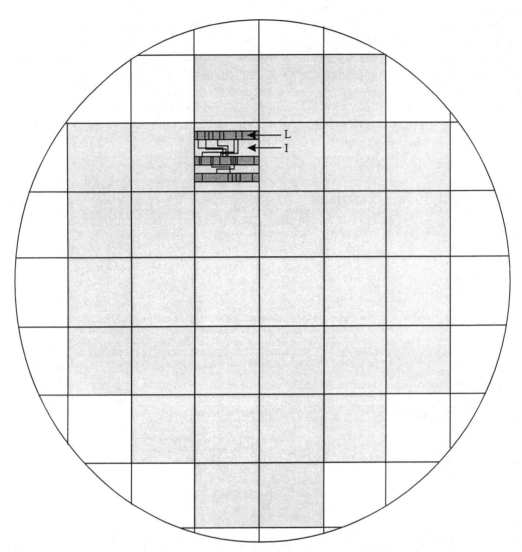

Figure 4-1. Sketch of the semiconductor wafer containing a large number of chips designed using the SC (Standard Cell) VLSI methodology. Symbol L refers to logic channels, and symbol I refers to interconnect channels. The channels containing standard cells have the same width and are not equidistant. The channels containing connections have a varying width—their widths are governed by the number and the structure of connections that have to be made. They take up a relatively small portion of the chip area (around 33 percent in this sketch). The total chip area is as big as the implemented logic requires (the chip utilization is always close to 100 percent).

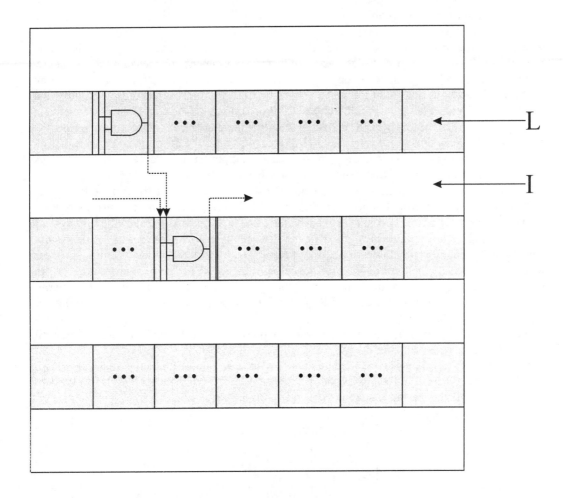

Figure 4-2. Sketch of the chip designed using the GA (Gate Array) VLSI methodology. The channels that contain the gates are of the same width and are equidistant. Symbol L refers to logic channels, and symbol I refers to interconnect channels. The channels that contain the connections are also of the same width—their widths are predetermined during the prefabrication process. They take up more chip area (around 50 percent in the sketch). The total chip area is always bigger than the area required by the logic, because the prefabricated chips of standard dimensions are used (the chip utilization is virtually always below 100 percent—the designers are usually very happy if they reach 90 percent).

4.1.5 Design and Fabrication Costs

The differences between these three design methodologies influence the design cost and the fabrication cost. The design cost is made up from two components: creative work that went into the design, and the design cost in specific. The cost of the creative work depends on the scientific and technical complexity of the problem that is being solved through the VLSI chip realization. The design cost depends on the number of engineer hours that went into the design process. No matter what technology was chosen (SC, GA, or PL VLSI), the cost of schematic entry and logic testing is about equal. This is because the complexity of that process depends on the diagram complexity and not on the chip design methodology. However, the placement and routing cost is at its peak in SC VLSI and at its bottom in PL VLSI. This is because SC VLSI offers great flexibility and takes a lot of engineer hours to be fully utilized. This, in turn, raises the cost of the placement and routing process. On the other hand, the hours spent in the placement and routing increase the probability that the chip will have a smaller VLSI area, thus reducing the production run cost.

Chip fabrication cost is made up from two basic components: the cost of making masks and the production run cost, after mask layers have been made.

In SC VLSI, the complete cost of making N mask layers falls on the individual buyers because no masks are made before the design and the different buyers cannot share any kind of cost. However, this initial cost is offset when the production starts because the unit cost of SC VLSI chips is lower since they probably have the smallest VLSI area for the same system complexity. This is attributable to the extremely flexible placement and routing process which maximizes the number of logic elements per area unit. The interconnect channels can be narrow (only the area absolutely needed by the interconnects will be occupied). In general, chip cost is proportional to the chip VLSI area raised to the power of x, where x is typically between two and three.

In GA VLSI, the cost of making the first $N-1$ or $N-2$ mask layers is shared between all buyers because it is the same for everybody. The total cost of making masks is less since the cost is shared, the large scale production reduces cost per unit, and only one or two mask layers are specific. On the other hand, the production cost of GA VLSI chips is greater because the system of a given complexity requires larger VLSI area than in the case of SC VLSI. This is because of

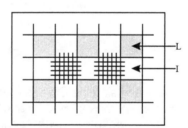

Figure 4-3. Sketch of the chip designed using the PL (Programmable Logic) VLSI methodology. Symbol L refers to logic channels, and symbol I refers to interconnect channels. The areas containing the macrocells (shaded) take up only a fraction of the chip area (around 25 percent in the sketch). The channels containing the connections take up the rest of the area (around 75 percent in the sketch), and their intersections contain the interconnection networks that are controlled using either RAM (XILINX) or ROM (ALTERA) memory elements. The sketch shows one of the many possible internal architectures that are frequently implemented. The total chip area is always quite bigger than the area required by the logic, because prefabricated chips of standard dimensions are used (the chip utilization is virtually always below 100 percent—the designers are usually very happy if they reach 80 percent).

the significantly restricted placement and routing flexibility, which leads to less efficient logic element packing. The interconnect channels are equidistant and are frequently wider than necessary for the specific design. Also, the chip has standard dimensions, and if the first smaller standard chip would not accommodate the design, a part of the used chip always remains unused.

In PL VLSI, the cost of all N mask layers is shared between the buyers, since all mask layers are the same for everybody. Thus, the mask making cost is minimal. However, since these chips offer the smallest logic element packing density because of their internal structure, the production cost of these chips is the highest. This is due to the minimal flexibility in the placement and routing, and to the large VLSI area devoted solely to the interconnection purposes. Also, since the chips are standard, parts remain unused every time.

When all these cost determining factors are considered, the following can be said. If large scale production will follow, it is best to use the FC VLSI design methodology. In the case of smaller scale, but still relatively large series productions, it is best to use the SC VLSI design methodology. In the case of a relatively small series, the best solution is the GA VLSI design methodology. For small series and individual chips, it is best to design for the PL VLSI, or the ST VLSI. Although the boundaries are somewhat blurred, because they also depend on nontechnical parameters, one can still frequently stumble upon some numbers as shown in the following example (these are to be regarded only as guidelines; N_{sp} refers to the number of chips in the serial production):

FC: $\qquad 10000 < N_{sp}$

SC: $\qquad 1000 < N_{sp} < 10000$

GA: $\qquad 100 < N_{sp} < 1000$

PL: $\qquad 10 < N_{sp} < 100$

ST: $\qquad 1 < N_{sp} < 10$

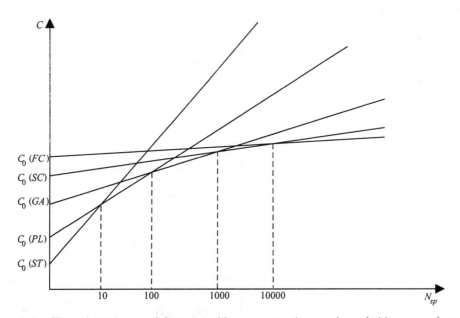

Figure 4-4. The dependency of the cost with respect to the number of chips manufactured. The C-axis represents the total cost of the design and manufacturing processes for the series comprising of N_{sp} VLSI chips. The value C_0 that corresponds to $N_{sp} = 0$ represents the sum of two components. They are: the cost of the design and the cost of all the masks that have to be made after the design is complete.

The typical dependencies of total cost (C) on the number of chips in the series (N_{sp}) are given in Figure 4-4. It is obvious from the figure that the initial cost (at $N_{sp} = 0$) is the largest for FC VLSI, then drops off through SC and GA VLSI, and reaches its minimum for PL VLSI and ST VLSI.

4.2   The VLSI Design Methodologies

This section will clarify some basic facts about FC VLSI, SC VLSI, GA VLSI, and PL VLSI, respectively.

4.2.1   FC VLSI

As previously stated, the FC VLSI methodology is based on geometric symbols. In this methodology the details have to be taken into account while strictly respecting the technology requirements. Each device technology and each circuit design technique is characterized with a certain number of VLSI mask layers. Different mask layers correspond to different technology processes used in the fabrication. Each VLSI mask layer contains a set of nonoverlapping polygons. The dimensions and positions of these polygons define the coordinates of areas on which certain technology processes will take place.

Geometrically speaking, in accordance with the technology requirements, polygons from different mask layers overlap partially. In the case of structured design procedures for the FC VLSI methodology, a minimal geometry, or minimal resolution lambda (λ) is defined. In these conditions, minimal (and sometimes maximal) overlaps are defined in terms of integer multiples of lambda (λ rules).

4.2.1.2   FC VLSI Silicon Technology   Figure 4-5 shows the steps in implementing a CMOS transistor in silicon technology as well as the geometric structure of each VLSI mask layer [5]. Figure 4-6 gives the lambda rules for the CMOS structure from Figure 4-5. Detailed explanations can be found in [5].

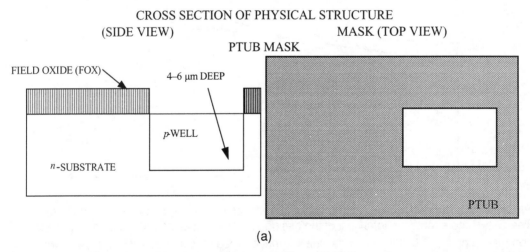

(a)

Figure 4-5.   The steps of implementation of a silicon CMOS transistor and the geometric structure of the corresponding VLSI masks: (a) mask number one.

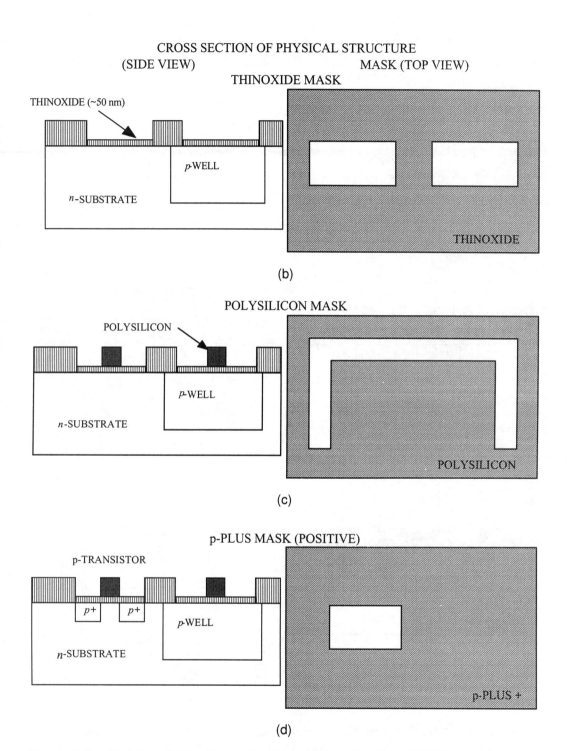

Figure 4-5. *(Continued)* The steps of implementation of a silicon CMOS transistor and the geometric structure of the corresponding VLSI masks: (b) mask number two, (c) mask number three, and (d) mask number four.

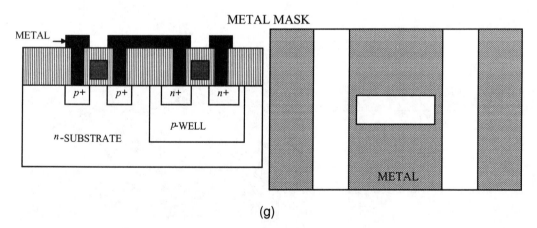

CROSS SECTION OF PHYSICAL STRUCTURE
(SIDE VIEW)   MASK (TOP VIEW)
p-PLUS MASK (NEGATIVE)

n-TRANSISTOR

$p+$ $p+$ $n+$ $n+$

n-SUBSTRATE p-WELL

p-PLUS -

(e)

CONTACT MASK

CONTACT CUTS

$p+$ $p+$ $n+$ $n+$

n-SUBSTRATE p-WELL

CONTACT

(f)

METAL MASK

METAL

$p+$ $p+$ $n+$ $n+$

p-WELL

n-SUBSTRATE

METAL

(g)

Figure 4-5. *(Continued)* The steps of implementation of a silicon CMOS transistor and the geometric structure of the corresponding VLSI masks: (e) mask number five, (f) mask number six, and (g) mask number seven.

Mask		Feature	Dimension
Thinox	A1.	Minimum thinox width	2λ
	A2.	Minimum thinox spacing (n^+ to n^+, p^+ to p^+)	2λ
	A3.	Minimum p-thinox to n-thinox spacing	8λ
p-well	B1.	Minimum p-well width	4λ
	B2.	Minimum p-well spacing (wells at same potential)	2λ
	B3.	Minimum p-well spacing (wells at different potential)	6λ
	B4.	Minimum distance to internal thinox	3λ
	B5.	Minimum distance to external thinox	5λ
Poly	C1.	Minimum poly width	2λ
	C2.	Minimum poly spacing	2λ
	C3.	Minimum poly to thinox spacing	λ
	C4.	Minimum poly gate extension	2λ
	C5.	Minimum thinox source/drain extension	2λ
p-plus	D1.	Minimum overlap of thinox	$1{,}5\text{–}2\lambda$
	D2.	Minimum p-plus spacing	2λ
	D3.	Minimum gate overlap or distance to gate edge	$1{,}5\text{–}2\lambda$
	D4.	Minimum spacing to unrelated thinox	$1{,}5\text{–}2\lambda$
Contact	E1.	Minimum contact area	$2\lambda\times2\lambda$
	E2.	Minimum contact to contact spacing	2λ
	E3.	Minimum overlap of thinox or poly over contact	λ
	E4.	Minimum spacing to gate poly	2λ
	E5.	n^+ source/drain contact	
	E6.	p^+ source/drain contact	
	E7.	V_{SS} contact	
	E8.	V_{DD} contact	See [5]
	E9.	Split contact V_{SS}	
	E10.	Split contact V_{DD}	
Metal	F1.	Minimum metal width	$2\text{–}3\lambda$
	F2.	Minimum metal spacing	3λ
	F3.	Minimum metal overlap of contact	λ

Figure 4-6. The lambda rules that have to be satisfied when forming the geometrical structures for various mask levels in the implementation of a silicon CMOS transistor.

For example, the first (silicon) 32-bit RISC processors realized at Berkeley and Stanford universities, were based on the $\lambda = 3$ μm technology. The silicon version of the RISC processor in the project MIPS for Star Wars was based on the $\lambda = 1.25$ μm, while all modern 64-bit RISC processors are based on submicron technologies ($\lambda < 1$ μm).

4.2.1.2 FC VLSI GaAs Technology GaAs technology has similar rules, as well. In the case of E/D-MESFET GaAs technology, used in the project which serves the base of this book, there were 11 mask layers, and λ rules were defined through the CALMA GDSII system. In particular, the technology for the GaAs version of the RISC processor for the MIPS for Star Wars project was based on the $\lambda = 1$ μm.

As previously mentioned (in the case of FC VLSI), a careful design leads to minimal VLSI area, and this has a corresponding positive effect on cost, speed, and dissipation. On the other hand, a lot of engineering time is required, mainly affecting cost in the small series.

Many factors determine what will be designed using the FC VLSI methodology. It is generally advisable to use it in the following cases:

a)   The design of standard logic elements which will be used as standard cells in the SC VLSI methodology. The complexity of standard cells can differ from case to case. If the most complex standard cells in the standard cell family are one-bit gates and one-bit flip-flops, then we refer to it as the *semicustom SC VLSI*. If the complexity of the standard cells reaches the levels of coder/decoder, multiplexer/demultiplexer, or adder/subtractor, then we have the *macrocell SC VLSI*. In the former case, the VLSI area of the chip is almost identical to the area of the FC VLSI chip. In the latter case, the number of engineer hours can be drastically reduced. The design of standard cells (using FC VLSI) is done either when a new standard cell family is being created (by the manufacturer of the software tools for the SC VLSI), or when an existing family is being expanded (by the user of the software tools for the SC VLSI).

b)   The design of VLSI chips with highly regular and repetitive structures, such as memories and systolic arrays.

c)   The design of chips without highly repetitive structures, but planned to be manufactured in enormous quantities. This includes popular general purpose microprocessors (Intel 486, Motorola 68040, and so on), on-chip microcontrollers (Intel, Motorola, and so on), or on-chip signal processors (Intel, Motorola, and so on).

d)   The design of chips without highly repetitive structures which will not be manufactured in enormous quantities, if they are relatively simple.

Most of the manufacturers of processor chips of either general or specific purposes do not satisfy the above mentioned conditions. They have to resort to a method other than the FC VLSI.

4.2.2   SC VLSI

As stated previously, the SC VLSI methodology is based on the logic symbols, which requires solid understanding of the architectural issues, rather than the microelectronics technology details.

Figure 4-7 depicts a CMOS standard cell family that was used in the design of the silicon version of the RISC processor for the MIPS for Star Wars project.

Figure 4-8 shows a typical standard cell in the E/D-MESFET standard cell family, used in the design of the GaAs version of the RISC processor for the MIPS for Star Wars project. Other cells in the GaAs family have approximately the same complexity as their silicon counterparts, except for the missing multi-input AND elements and the tristate logic elements (which, in turn, mandates the use of multiplexers).

The SC VLSI design methodology is suitable for a large (but not enormous) series of chips (see the graph in Figure 4-4). For example, a prototype of the first 32-bit GaAs RISC microprocessor (RCA) was designed using the SC VLSI methodology. The only exceptions were the register file and the combinational shifter, which were designed using the FC VLSI methodology. They were, in turn, treated as two large standard cells. Since FC and SC VLSI methodologies share many features, particularly the number of mask layers (N), they can be freely mixed. Most often, the highly repetitive structures such as register files and combinational shifters are typically designed using the FC VLSI methodology, while the rest of the chip (random logic) is typically designed using the SC VLSI methodology. Many of the specialized processors on the VLSI chip are designed in this way.

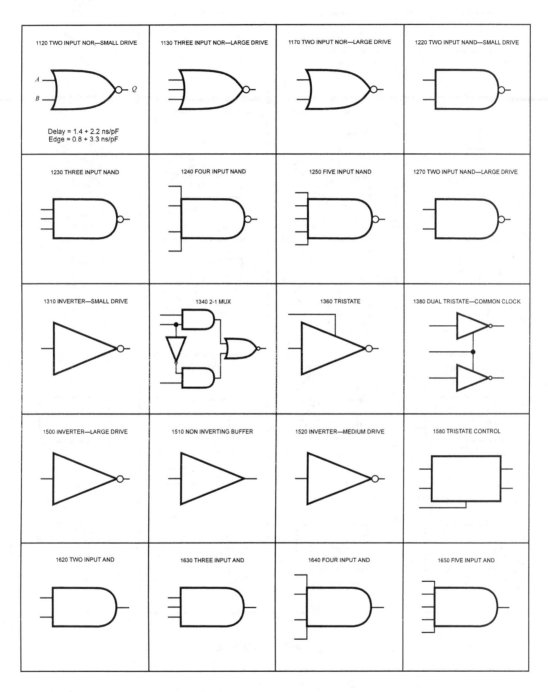

Figure 4-7. The CMOS standard cell family used in the design of the silicon version of the RISC/MIPS processor within the MIPS for Star Wars project.

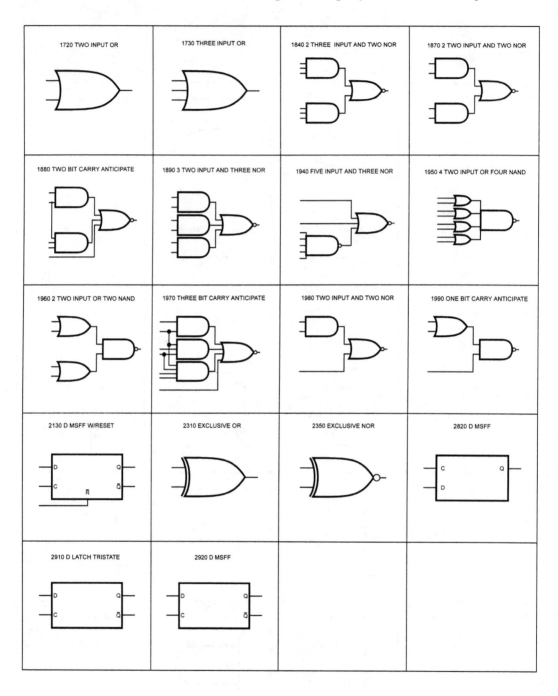

Figure 4-7.   *(Continued).*

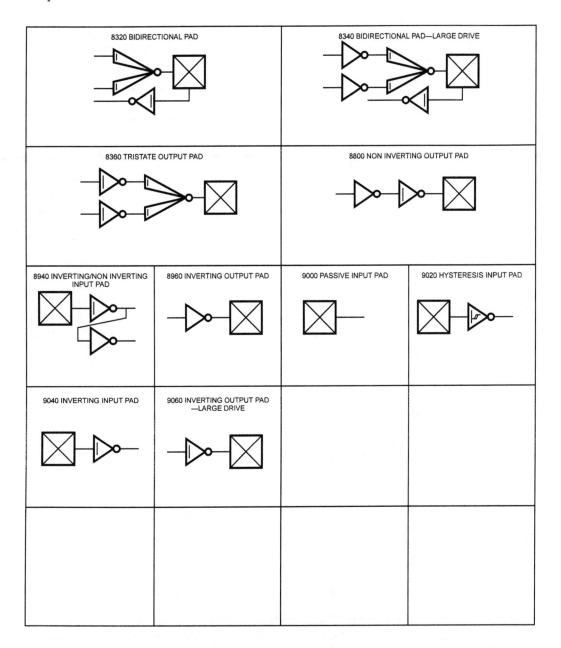

Figure 4-7. *(Continued).*

Two input NAND
6 devices   4010

Cell height: 68 μm
Cell width: 36 μm

Logic Symbol

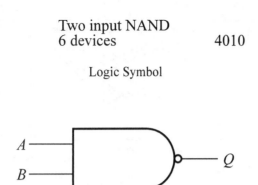

Truth Table

A	B	Q
0	0	1
0	1	1
1	0	1
1	1	0

Input A:

Rise delay:	117 ps +0,26 ps/fF
Fall delay:	95 ps +0,30 ps/fF
Rise time:	117 ps +0,57 ps/fF
Fall time:	217 ps +0,60 ps/fF

Input B:

Rise delay:	198 ps +0,26 ps/fF
Fall delay:	100 ps +0,34 ps/fF
Rise time:	242 ps +0,59 ps/fF
Fall time:	223 ps +0,61 ps/fF

$V_{DD} = 2$ V

Power:	610 mW

Pin Capacitance:

Pin Q:	1 fF
Pin A:	150 fF
Pin B:	150 fF

Figure 4-8. The GaAs E/D-MESFET standard cell family: a typical standard cell from the GaAs E/D-MESFET family of standard cells used in the design of the GaAs version of the RISC/MIPS processor for the MIPS for Star Wars project.

Standard Cell Overview

Cell Number	Cell Description	Transistor Count
4010	two-input NAND	6
4020	two-input AND, two-input NOR	10
4030	two-input AND, three-input NOR	14
4040	two-input AND, four-input NOR	18
4050	two-input AND, five-input NOR	22
4100	invertor	1
4110	two-input AND, two-input NOR	8
4120	two-input AND, three-input NOR	12
4130	two-input AND, four-input NOR	16
4140	two-input AND, five-input NOR	20
4200	two-input NOR	6
4210	two-input AND, three-input NOR	10
4220	two-input AND, four-input NOR	14
4230	two-input AND, five-input NOR	18
4300	three-input NOR	8
4310	two-input AND, four-input NOR	12
4320	two-input AND, five-input NOR	16
4330	four-input NOR	10
4410	two-input AND, five-input NOR	14
4500	five-input NOR	12
4700	latch	14
4710	latch with RESET	22
4720	latch with SET	20
4800	MSFF	22
4810	MSFF with asynchronous RESET	25
4820	MSFF with asynchronous SET	23
4830	MSFF with synchronous RESET	24
4840	MSFF with synchronous SET	22
8100	ECL→E/D input pad	7
8200	E/D→ECL output pad	6

Figure 4-8. *(Continued)* The GaAs E/D-MESFET standard cell family: a review of various standard cells from the GaAs E/D-MESFET family, as well as their complexities, expressed in transistor count.

4.2.3 GA VLSI

The GA VLSI methodology is also based on logic symbols; however, the placement and routing freedom is restricted. This methodology is gradually becoming obsolescent, and this book will not devote special attention to it. It was the basis from which the PL VLSI methodology has evolved. There are, however, a number of random logic chips which are parts of large systems and are manufactured in large series; these are often designed using the GA VLSI methodology.

4.2.4 PL VLSI

The PL VLSI methodology is also based on logic symbols, but has truly minimal placement and routing capabilities. A bright future awaits PL VLSI. Consequently, a large number of small-scale production VLSI systems have been realized using this methodology. The same applies for many prototypes (which will, eventually, be redesigned in SC VLSI, to be mass produced). The speed of PL VLSI prototype systems is typically lower than nominal (PL VLSI is inferior to SC VLSI with respect to the speed).

The internal structure of some popular PL VLSI chips from ALTERA (PLD VLSI) and one PL VLSI chip from XILINX (LCA VLSI) are given in Figures 4-9 [20] and 4-10 [21], respectively. Interested readers can find more details in the original literature from ALTERA and XILINX.

4.2.5 Summary of SC VLSI, GA VLSI, and PL VLSI

A summary of SC VLSI, GA VLSI, and PL VLSI is given in Figure 4-11. It is based on the following design parameters:

a)   Number of prefabricated mask levels;
b)   Number of designer specified mask levels;
c)   Designer freedom;
d)   Design cost;
e)   Chip area utilization;
f)   Chip size;
g)   Chip speed; and
h)   Fabrication cost per chip.

4.2.6 ST VLSI

The ST (Silicon Translation) VLSI methodology is currently emerging and still under development. As already indicated, it is also known as silicon compilation VLSI methodology. It implies that the input model is derived in some general-purpose high level language (C, C++) or some special-purpose high level language (ISP', VHDL). See Appendix C for one illustration of this methodology.

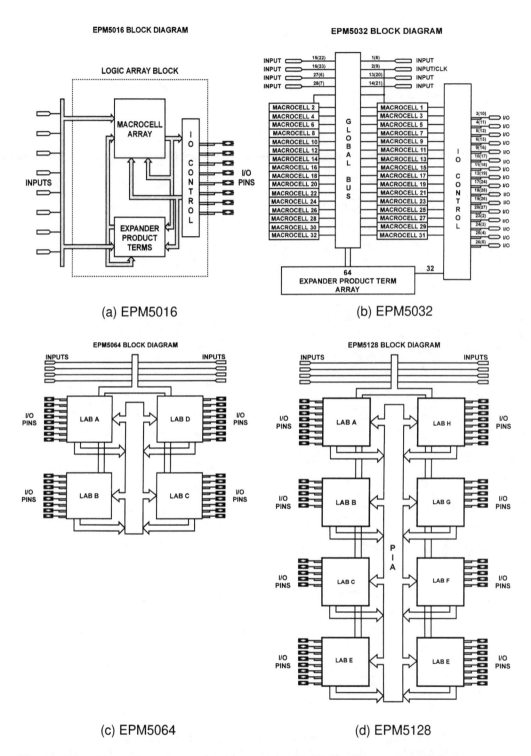

(a) EPM5016

(b) EPM5032

(c) EPM5064

(d) EPM5128

Figure 4-9. Internal structure of some popular PL VLSI chips manufactured by Altera [20]. Symbol PIA refers to Programmable Interconnect Array. See the original manufacturer's literature for the internal structure of the latest Altena products.

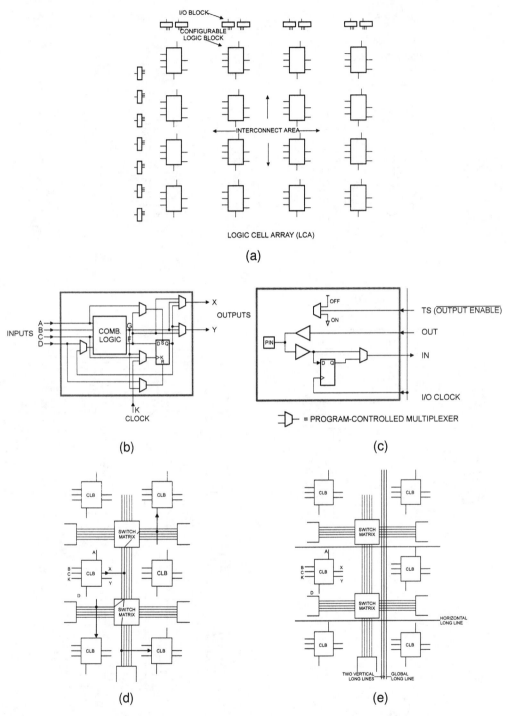

Figure 4-10. Internal structure of some popular PL VLSI chips manufactured by Xilinx [21]: (a) General structure of the reconfigurable cell array, (b) internal structure of the reconfigurable logic block, (c) internal structure of the input/output block, (d) general purpose interconnect, and (e) long line interconnect. See the original manufacturer's literature for the internal structure of the latest Xilinx products.

VLSI Methodology	Number of Prefabricated Mask Levels	Number of Designer Specified Mask Levels	Designer Freedom	Design Cost	Chip Area Utilization	Chip Size	Chip Speed	Fabrication Cost Per Chip
SC	0	n	high	high	$\approx 100\%$	small	high	low
GA	n – 1 to n – 2	1 to 2	medium	medium	$< 100\%$	medium	medium	medium
PL	n	0	low	low	$\ll 100\%$	large	low	high

Figure 4-11. A summary of SC VLSI, GA VLSI, and PL VLSI.

5

VLSI RISC Processor Design

This chapter is divided in two parts. The first part discusses the basic elements of prefabrication design (schematic entry, logic and timing testing, and placement and routing). The second part discusses the basic elements of postfabrication chip testing.

5.1 Prefabrication Design

As previously stated, VLSI system design process consists of three basic phases:

a) schematic entry,
b) logic and timing testing, and
c) placement and routing.

These three phases will be reviewed in this section only in the SC VLSI context. There are two reasons for this approach. One is the consistency with the baseline project described in this book (mainly the semicustom SC VLSI was used). The other is the high complexity of the SC VLSI design process which leads to the following conclusion: after mastering the SC VLSI design process intricacies, readers will easily comprehend the GA VLSI or the PL VLSI design processes as well. This is because the schematic entry and the logic and timing testing phases are almost identical for all three design approaches, while the placement and routing phase is the most complex with the SC VLSI.

In the MIPS for the Star Wars project, the chief design methodology was semicustom SC VLSI (with a few items designed using the FC VLSI). The software package CADDAS was used [22]. It includes: the schematic entry program VALID, the logic and timing test program LOGSIM [23], and the placement and routing program MP2D [24].

The schematic entry phase serves the purpose of forming the file (or database) with a detailed description of the circuit that is being realized on a chip. This file (or database) then serves as the base of the later logic and timing testing and placement and routing processes. It most often comes in the shape of a netlist. In the case of the CADDAS package, the netlist structure requires that each standard cell is described in one line of text. This line defines the connectivity for each pin of the standard cell it stands for. The explanation that follows is based on a simple example.

Figure 5-1 shows the block diagram of a digital modem modulator with FSK modulation which provides speeds of up to 1200 bit/s (which is in accordance with the CCITT standard). This circuit has three inputs: FQ (higher frequency clock signal), $S103$ (binary data signal), and $F105$ (CCITT command signal "request to send"). The circuit has two outputs: $FSKOUT$ (binary modulated data signal) and $S106$ (CCITT control signal "ready to send"). The correlation between the signals $S105$ and $S106$ is shown in Figure 5-2. Figure 5-3 shows one possible configuration of the circuit from Figure 5-1, using only standard cells from Figure 4-7. The netlist for the circuit in Figure 5-3 is shown in Figure 5-4. Understanding the details from Figures 5-1 through 5-3 is not mandatory for the comprehension of the netlist structure in Figure 5-4.

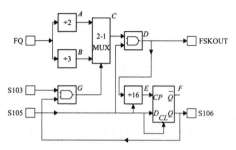

Figure 5-1. An example of practical work using the SC VLSI methodology: schematic diagram of a digital modulator for a modem with the FSK modulation, and the data transfer rate of 1200 bps, according to the CCITT standard. Input signals, FQ, S103, and S105, and output signals, FSKOUT and S106, are defined by the CCITT standard. The complete understanding of the functionality of the diagram is not a prerequisite for the comprehension of the following text.

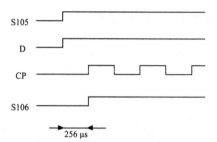

Figure 5-2. An example of practical work using the SC VLSI methodology: timing diagram illustrating the relation between the data signal (D), the clock signal (CP), and the control signals (S105 and S106).

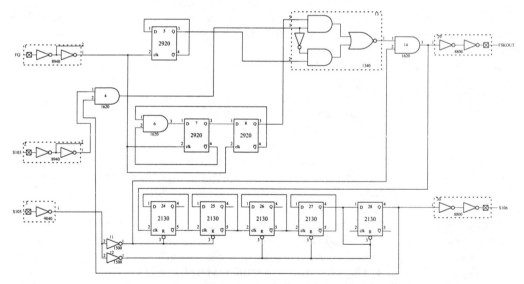

Figure 5-3. An example of practical work using the SC VLSI methodology: one possible configuration of the block diagram shown in Figure 5-1, using only the standard cells shown in Figure 4-7. Each standard cell has two numbers associated with it. The first number (2920, 8940, and so on) refers to the standard cell part number (as defined by the designer of the standard cell family), while the second number (1, 2, and so on) refers to the original number of the standard cell in the diagram (as defined by the designer of the diagram).

In CADDAS, the netlist file is usually called **connect.dat**. Lines beginning with an asterisk denote comments. Fields in individual lines start at columns 1, 9, 17, 25, 33, 41, 49, 57, 65, and 73. This is clarified by comments in the sixth and the seventh line of the **connect.dat** (see Figure 5-4). A detailed explanation of each column follows.

The first column contains the name of the standard cell. This name has been defined by the designer of the standard cell family. For instance, the name *S*8940 denotes a standard cell containing the input pad and the inverting/noninverting input buffer. The last column contains the ordinal number that the standard cell has been assigned by the designer of the circuit. Thus, number one stands for the first standard cell in the circuit.

Columns two through nine, at positions nine through 65 contain information about the connections of the standard cell pins with other standard cells. For example, the symbol 1P1 appears four times:

```
*
* A simple FSK modulator for voice-band data modems.
* Implemented with the RCA CMOS/SOS standard cell family.
* Author: Salim Lakhani.
*
* Column numbers:
*       09      17      25    33      41    49      57      65    73
* Pin numbers:
*       1       2       3     4       5     6       7       8

S8940   1P1     1P2     FQ                                          1
S8940   2P1     2P2     S103                                        2
S9040   3P1     S105                                                3
S1620   2P1     28P8    4P3                                         4
S2920   5P4     1P1     5P3   5P4                                   5
S1620   8P4     7P4     6P3                                         6
S2920   6P3     1P1     7P3   7P4                                   7
S2920   7P3     1P1     8P3   8P4                                   8
NEXT    11
S1500   11P1    3P1                                                 11
S1500   12P1    3P1                                                 12
S1340   13P1    5P3     4P3   DUMMY   8P3                           13
S1620   13P1    11P1    14P3                                        14
NEXT    24
S2130   24P5    14P3    11P1  DUMMY   24P5  DUMMY   DUMMY   24P8   24
S2130   25P5    24P5    11P1  DUMMY   25P5  DUMMY   DUMMY   25P8   25
S2130   26P5    25P5    12P1  DUMMY   26P5  DUMMY   DUMMY   26P8   26
S2130   27P5    26P5    12P1  DUMMY   27P5  DUMMY   DUMMY   27P8   27
S2130   12P1    27P8    12P1  DUMMY   28P5  DUMMY   DUMMY   28P8   28
S8800   14P3    FSKOUT                                             29
S8800   28P8    S106                                               30
```

Figure 5-4.   An example of practical work using the SC VLSI methodology: the file **connect.dat**. It contains the diagram from Figure 5.3, formatted according to the rules set forth in the CADDAS manual. One standard cell has one line assigned to it. The first column contains the part number of the standard cell. The last column contains the ordinal number of the standard cell in the diagram. Other columns (between the first and the last) define the connections between the standard cells (details are given in the text).

a)   With the first standard cell, in the position associated with pin #1;

b)   With the fifth standard cell, in the position associated with pin #2;

c)   With the seventh standard cell, in the position associated with pin #2; and

d)   With the eighth standard cell, in the position associated with pin #2.

The fact that the same symbol (1P1) appears in all four places denotes that the corresponding pins are connected. The designer could have used any other name instead of 1P1, but 1P1 conforms to the convention used to name the connections. The rule is simple: if a connection has one source and n destinations ($n = 1, 2, ...$), then its name is formed by concatenating the ordinal number of the source standard cell and the ordinal number of the source pin. In the symbol 1P1, the first 1 denotes the standard cell, and the second 1 denotes the pin number in that standard cell, which is the source of the signal 1P1. Therefore, the signal 28P5 originates from the fifth pin of the standard cell 28.

The entire netlist can be viewed as a matrix with m rows and n columns, where m is the number of the standard cells in the circuit, and n is the maximum standard cell pin count for the chosen standard cell family. In the example given in Figure 5-4 $m = 19$ and $n = 8$. It may seem confusing at first that $m = 19$, because the standard cell ordinal numbers run from 1 to 30. This is the consequence of skipping the numbers 9, 10, and 16 through 23, and using the NEXT directive. Its existence enables the designer to use parts of the circuit either in other projects or in the variations of the same project.

A mention of the variable DUMMY is in order. It denotes the physically nonexistent pins of the standard cells (such as pins 4, 6, and 7 of the standard cell 24), which were existent in the previous implementations of the same standard cell in another technology. This is due to compatibility reasons. Any other symbol could have been used instead of the symbol DUMMY. This symbol is defined in the **drop.dat** file, which will be explained later.

5.1.1   LOGSIM and Mandatory Files

After the netlist has been created, it is time to perform logic and timing testing. In the CADDAS package the program LOGSIM is used to perform this task. The basic input file for LOGSIM is **connect.dat**. With this file, several other secondary files have to be created. Some of them are mandatory, while the others are not; but they often significantly reduce the effort needed to test the design. The mandatory files are **lmode.dat**, **gen4.dat** (or **gen.dat**), and **print.dat**. These will be explained in the following paragraphs.

5.1.1.1   The lmode.dat File   Figure 5-5 shows the **lmode.dat** file. It is one of the mandatory files for the LOGSIM program. This example contains only two lines (the other lines are comments, and are not a part of the file). The first line (CTRL) defines various relevant options: if the bit position corresponding to the option contains one, it is selected; if the position holds zero, the option is not selected.

For example, in the case shown in Figure 5-5 the following options are selected: PRINT (column 15), CONNECTIVITY (column 30), OVERRIDE INITIAL CONDITION (column 35), and CONSISTENCY BYPASS (column 40). All options and their meanings are explained in the caption of Figure 5-5. The second line (SPEC) defines the maximum simulation run time, expressed through the number of time intervals. All relevant details are explained in [23].

1		10	15	20	25	30	35	40	45	50
CTRL			1			1	1	1		
SPEC	1000									

Figure 5-5. An example of practical work using the SC VLSI methodology: the file **lmode.dat**. The valid options in the control line (CTRL) are as follows. Column 10, COMPARE option: the optional file **compare.dat** has to exist. Column 15, PRINT option: the mandatory **print.dat** file specifies which signals will be printed out; otherwise, all the signal generator outputs and all of the standard cell outputs will be printed out. Column 20, SPIKE option: if this option is selected, and if a short irregular signal appears during the simulation, the appropriate warning message will be printed out. Column 30, CONNECTIVITY option: all the output loads for the standard cells and the signal generators will be printed out, which matters in the cases when the output loads affect the timing of the signals. Column 35, OVERRIDE INITIAL CONDITION option: the simulation will be performed even if the desired output state of the outputs cannot be effected during the initialization. Column 40, CONSISTENCY BYPASS option: the simulation will continue even if the inconsistency of the output values of the standard cells is detected. Column 50, COMPRESS option: normally, a new line is output whenever the input or the output of any standard cell changes; if this option is selected, a new line is output only when one of the signals from the **print.dat** file changes. The second control line (SPEC) is the place to specify the desired simulation time.

5.1.1.2 The gen4.dat File Figure 5-6 shows the **gen4.dat** file, which is also mandatory. This particular example contains three lines, one for each input pin (*FQ*, *S*103, and *S*105). The first line begins with the symbol GENF, to denote periodic input signal. The second and the third lines begin with the symbol GEN to denote aperiodic signals. The format of the **gen4.dat** file is free, meaning that only the relative position of the specifier is significant. The following facts hold true for the example shown in Figure 5-6:

a) The signal *FQ* is periodic, and starts with logic zero; the number of repetitions of the sequence is 250, and the periodic repetition starts at the beginning of the simulation. The number of time intervals between the logic level changes is four, and the sequence has the binary form of 10, wherein one and zero last four time intervals each.

b) The signal *S*103 is aperiodic; it starts with the logic zero, after 500 time intervals becomes one, then it stays that way to the end of the simulation run (if the simulation lasts longer than 500 time intervals, as specified in the **lmode.dat** file).

c) The signal *S*105 is also aperiodic; it starts with logic zero, after 50 time intervals becomes one, after the 500th interval becomes zero, after the 550th interval again becomes one, and stays that way until the end of the simulation (if it lasts longer than 550 time intervals).

All relevant details are explained in [23].

5.1.1.3 The print.dat File Figure 5-7 shows the **print.dat** file, also mandatory for the LOGSIM package. In this example, it contains 7 lines. The first line (POSPNT) defines the number of windows for monitoring the selected signals (one window), and the number of columns in the printout (25 columns). Some of the 25 columns will contain signal values, while the others will stay empty, to enhance the readability. The second line (SLOT) defines the start (0) and the end (1000 decimal) of the window through which the signals will be monitored,

GENF	FQ	0	250	0	4	10		
GEN	S103	0	500	1				
GEN	S105	0	50	1	500	0	550	1

Figure 5-6.   An example of practical work using the SC VLSI methodology: the contents of the **gen4.dat** file. For the periodic signals (GENF), one must assume the following: the first of the five specifiers refers to the logic level at the beginning of the simulation; the second specifier refers to the number of periods in the waveform that is being specified in the GENF line; the third specifier refers to the time index of the first logic level change, meaning that the periodic behavior starts at that time; the fourth specifier refers to the length of the interval during which the value specified in the fifth specifier lasts, expressed through the number of the simulation intervals; the fifth specifier defines the logical sequence that repeats itself. For example, GENF GORAN 0 2 100 50 10 specifies a periodic signal, named GORAN, with the initial value of 0: at time index 100, a positive transition occurs; at time index 150, a negative transition occurs; and at time index 200, another positive transition occurs, and that is the end of the first of the two periods. At time index 250, a negative transition occurs again, and lasts until the time index 300, when the second period ends, and stays that way until the end of the simulation (if the simulation still runs after the time index 300). The following rules apply to aperiodic signals (GEN): the first specifier defines the initial logic level, at time index 0 (that is, at the beginning of the simulation); the second specifier defines the time index of the first transition, and so on. The total number of the specifiers in the GEN line is $N + 1$, where N stands for the total number of signal changes. For example, GEN MILAN 0 50 100 specifies an aperiodic signal named MILAN, with the following characteristics: initial value is equal to 0, the first positive transition occurs at time index 50, the first negative transition occurs at time index 100, and the value of 1 remains through the rest of the simulation.

denoting the time intervals of the simulation. The following five lines define the contents of all columns in the printout. Of these 25 columns, eight are reserved for the signals, and the remaining 17 are the empty columns, for enhanced readability (SKIP). All relevant details are explained in [23].

5.1.2   LOGSIM and Optional Files

One optional file is the **capinit.dat** file (see Figure 5-8). In this example, the file contains six lines which define the initial states of the Q and $\overline{Q}$ outputs of the three flip-flops. An adequate specification of the initial states can reduce the necessary number of time intervals for obtaining useful simulation results. All relevant details are explained in [23].

Another optional file is the **title.dat** (see Figure 5-9). This file contains one line which will appear across the top of each page of the printout.

There is one more optional file, not shown here, which can be very useful. This is the **compare.dat** file, which contains the specification of the expected output signals. During the simulation the LOGSIM package automatically compares the obtained outputs with the expected ones, at each time interval. The parameters that need to be specified are: the signal name, the time interval, and the expected logic level. Optionally, when the discrepancy is discovered the simulation can either be terminated or continued with the appropriate warning in the simulation logfile. All relevant details are explained in [23].

	1		5	10	15	20	25
	POSPNT				1	25	
	SLOT				0000		1000

(a)

1		8	18	28	38	48	58	68
PNT	FQ		SKIP	SKIP	5P3	SKIP	SKIP	
PNT	8P3		SKIP	SKIP	13P1	SKIP	SKIP	
PNT	SKIP		S103	SKIP	SKIP	S105	SKIP	
PNT	SKIP		SKIP	S106	SKIP	SKIP	SKIP	
PNT	FSKOUT							

(b)

Figure 5-7. An example of practical work using the SC VLSI methodology: contents of the **print.dat** file. The reader should notice that the parts (a) and (b) refer to the fragments of the same file. The fields in the POSPNT line are as follows: columns 13–15 specify the number of windows through which the signals are being monitored; columns 18–20 specify the number of columns in the printout; column 25 specifies the type of printout, with zeros and ones (if nothing is specified), or with L and H (if the column 25 contains the symbol H). The fields in the SLOT line refer to the beginning and end of the window through which the simulation is being monitored (two fields for the specification of one window, 2*N* fields for the specification of *N* windows). The PNT lines specify either the signals to be monitored (if their names are given, these correspond to the columns in the printout) or empty columns (if the SKIP keyword is specified).

INIT	5P4	0	(* D-FF #5: loop definition *)
INIT	5P3	1	(* D-FF #5: $Q/\overline{Q}$ consistency definition *)
INIT	7P4	0	(* D-FF #7: loop definition *)
INIT	7P3	1	(* D-FF #7: $Q/\overline{Q}$ consistency definition *)
INIT	8P4	0	(* D-FF #8: loop definition *)
INIT	8P3	1	(* D-FF #8: $Q/\overline{Q}$ consistency definition *)

Figure 5-8. An example of practical work using the SC VLSI methodology: the contents of the **capinit.dat** file. The first INIT line specifies that the initial value of the 5P4 signal is zero, and so on. Beside the INIT lines, this file can contain the CAP and the CAPA lines as well. The CAP lines provide users with capability to completely ignore the capacitance computations which are performed by the translator. The CAPA lines provide users with the capability to specify the capacitances to be added, when the translator computes the capacitances in the system.

An FSK modulator for the voice-band data modem

Figure 5-9. An example of practical work using the SC VLSI methodology: contents of the **title.dat** file. This file contains one line with, at most, 40 characters. That line appears on every page of the printouts of the logic and timing simulations.

5.1.3 Simulation

After all the necessary files have been prepared, the simulation can proceed. Some practical notes on the LOGSIM package usage are found in Figure 5-10.

The simulation is an iterative process. After some time, the designer can conclude that the basic design should be altered. If that is precisely what has happened, then the altered design (see Figure 5-11), using standard cells shown in Figure 4-7, should be tested. Its realization in the chosen standard cell family is shown in Figure 5-12. The corresponding netlist is shown in Figure 5-13. After the **connect.dat** file has passed all tests, it can be used in the process of placement and routing.

5.1.4 MP2D Placement and Routing Files

As previously mentioned, the CADDAS package contains the placement and routing program MP2D. Its basic input file is **connect.dat**. Besides this file, there are some other mandatory and optional files that need to be created which are necessary for the placement and routing process. The only mandatory file beside **connect.dat** is **mmode.dat**. It specifies a number of parameters necessary for the placement and routing process.

5.1.4.1 The mmode.dat File   The **mmode.dat** file is shown in Figure 5-4; reference [24] explains the relevant details. In this example, the file contains one line with three items. Columns 9 to 12 specify the identification number of the chip that is being designed; in this case it is 7777. Columns 13 to 16 contain the information about the technology that will be used during the fabrication of the chip, number 7 in our case, which corresponds to the 3 μm SOS/CMOS technology. Columns 25 to 28 contain information about the DOMAIN PLACEMENT option: the number one in our case stands for *yes* (DOMAIN PLACEMENT is enabled). This means that the **dmode.dat** file will have to be created in order to specify the required parameters for the DOMAIN PLACEMENT. This option means that the placement and routing will be done in accord to the user's wishes.

5.1.4.2 The dmode.dat File   Figure 5-15 shows the **dmode.dat** file. All details about creation of this file can be found in [24]. In our case, the file is empty (40 blanks), denoting that the user has not specified any requests, and that MP2D will perform its usual automatic placement and routing. This approach is correct in the first iteration. Later on, the user will probably specify some requirements in this file.

5.1.4.3 The drop.dat File   Figure 5-16 depicts the **drop.dat** file; all details regarding this file can be found in [24]. This file contains the list of signals (one line per signal) to be ignored by MP2D. In our example, the first one on the list is the DUMMY signal; these refer to the unused (physically nonexistent) pins on the standard cells which are present for compatibility reasons. Instead of the name DUMMY, any other name could have been used as well. The rest of the **drop.dat** file refers to the signals that are not connected.

5.1.4.4 The title.dat File   Figure 5-17 shows the **title.dat** file, which was seen before in this text. It is identical to the **title.dat** file for the LOGSIM program, although it does not have to be that way.

Guidelines for LOGSIM-Based Testing of a Digital (Processor) Module in DARPA-Sponsored Projects

1) Assuming that the module is designed using only the cells of the chosen standard cell family, one has first to fully comprehend the logic of the module.

2) A set of input and output test vectors has to be carefully prepared (on paper, offline). Also, the delay information which specifies how much different outputs will lag behind different inputs (this is of special importance for the later creation of the compare.dat file). The methodology of "divide and conquer" works well here. It is suggested that the entire work (which defines exhaustive testing) be created as a set of small testing experiments. Each of the small experiments should be precisely defined and documented.

3) Create the *connect.dat* file. This should be simple to comprehend, but time consuming and error prone.

4) Create the *capinit.dat* file. Both loops and $Q/\overline{Q}$ consistencies have to be defined by this file. This should be easy.

5) Create the *print.dat* file. This one should be easy. It defines the total amount of signals that have to be tested, which ones that will be, and for how many clock periods the *print-out* will go.

6) Create the *lmode.dat* file. This one should also be easy. It specifies how many clock periods the *simulation* will go, if the printout will be normal or condensed, and other options.

7) Create the *gen4.dat* file. This one represents your wish list of input test vectors. Since wish lists are easy to make, this task will be easy (except that you have to carefully include all possible input cases). The related thinking was done during task number two. Create a separate *gen4.dat* file for each of your experiments.

8) Create the *compare.dat* file. This one represents the expected values of output test vectors. Since all related thinking was done during task number two, this work should be nothing more than a careful translation of concepts from task number two into the format of the *compare.dat* file. This format should coincide with the format given in the *print.dat* file (only for signals that should be compared). Please, remember the important role of both the logic and the gate delays (see the comment in task number two). Remember that the number of *compare.dat* files has to be the same as the number of *gen4.dat* files.

9) Double check all your work on paper before you start the simulation. This will save you a lot of frustration.

10) Run the simulator program once for each *gen4.dat/compare.dat* pair. Hopefully, each time the output file *lprt.lst* is run it will contain no error messages (these are related to differences between *compare.dat* and the LOGSIM-generated output test vectors).

11) If everything is correct, document all your work before the results fade away from your head.

12) If something is wrong, then you have the opportunity to learn that the real-life design is an iterative process. If something is wrong, that may mean one or more of the following:

   a) Bug(s) in the logic.
   b) Logic correct, but *connect.dat* file contains error(s).
   c) Logic correct, but other LOGSIM files contain error(s).
   d) Logic correct, but *compare.dat* file contains error(s).

   Don't panic! Just cool down and recheck the logic diagram, *connect.dat* file, *compare.dat* file, and other input files in a well structured manner.

13) Remember, the worst thing that can happen is that your documentation (task number 10) claims that everything is okay, but the fabricated chip happens not to work. Note that RCA guarantees that if LOGSIM reports no timing errors, the MP2D will create the mask which works, on the condition that the design contains no logic errors. The LOGSIM and MP2D are responsible for timing errors; the designer(s) is(are) responsible for logic errors!

Figure 5-10. A guide for the LOGSIM program, based on the author's experience (the original version was developed May 4, 1985).

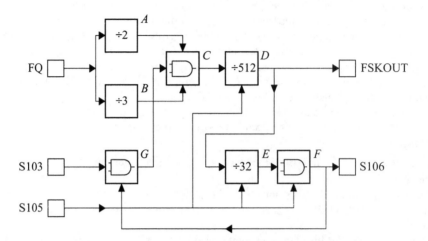

Figure 5-11. An example of practical work using the SC VLSI methodology. Block diagram of the final project, after all the changes pointed out by the LOGSIM program were entered.

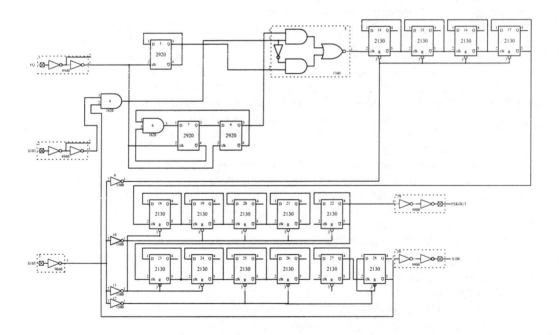

Figure 5-12. An example of practical work using the SC VLSI methodology. Detailed diagram of the final project from Figure 5-11, realized by exclusively using the standard cells from Figure 4-7.

```
*
* A simple FSK modulator for voice-band data modems.
* Implemented with the RCA's 3 µm single level metal CMOS/SOS standard cell family.
* Author: Aleksandar Purkovic.
*
* Column numbers:
*       09      17      25      33      41      49      57      65      73
* Pin numbers:
*       1       2       3       4       5       6       7       8
```

Cell	1	2	3	4	5	6	7	8	#
S8940	1P1	1P2	FQ						1
S8940	2P1	2P2	S103						2
S9040	3P1	S105							3
S1620	2P1	28P8	4P3						4
S2920	5P4	1P1	5P3	5P4					5
S1620	8P4	7P4	6P3						6
S2920	6P3	1P1	7P3	7P4					7
S2920	7P3	1P1	8P3	8P4					8
S1500	9P1	3P1							9
S1500	10P1	3P1							10
S1500	11P1	3P1							11
S1500	12P1	3P1							12
S1340	13P1	5P3	4P3	DUMMY	8P3				13
S2130	14P5	13P1	9P1	DUMMY	14P5	DUMMY	DUMMY	14P8	14
S2130	15P5	14P5	9P1	DUMMY	15P5	DUMMY	DUMMY	15P8	15
S2130	16P5	15P5	9P1	DUMMY	16P5	DUMMY	DUMMY	16P8	16
S2130	17P5	16P5	9P1	DUMMY	17P5	DUMMY	DUMMY	17P8	17
S2130	18P5	17P5	10P1	DUMMY	18P5	DUMMY	DUMMY	18P8	18
S2130	19P5	18P5	10P1	DUMMY	19P5	DUMMY	DUMMY	19P8	19
S2130	20P5	19P5	10P1	DUMMY	20P5	DUMMY	DUMMY	20P8	20
S2130	21P5	20P5	10P1	DUMMY	21P5	DUMMY	DUMMY	21P8	21
S2130	22P5	21P5	11P1	DUMMY	22P5	DUMMY	DUMMY	22P8	22
S2130	23P5	22P5	11P1	DUMMY	23P5	DUMMY	DUMMY	23P8	23
S2130	24P5	23P5	11P1	DUMMY	24P5	DUMMY	DUMMY	24P8	24
S2130	25P5	24P5	11P1	DUMMY	25P5	DUMMY	DUMMY	25P8	25
S2130	26P5	25P5	12P1	DUMMY	26P5	DUMMY	DUMMY	26P8	26
S2130	27P5	26P5	12P1	DUMMY	27P5	DUMMY	DUMMY	27P8	27
S2130	12P1	27P8	12P1	DUMMY	28P5	DUMMY	DUMMY	28P8	28
S8800	22P8	FSKOUT							29
S8800	28P8	S106							30

Figure 5-13. An example of practical work using the SC VLSI methodology: a netlist that corresponds to the detailed diagram shown in Figure 5-12.

Column number of the rightmost digit in the field	12	16	28
	7777	7	1

Figure 5-14. An example of practical work using the SC VLSI methodology: contents of the **mmode.dat** file. The field that spans columns 9–12 refers to the identification number of the chip that is being designed. The field that spans columns 13–16 refers to the technology that will be used during the fabrication. The field that occupies column 28 specifies whether the DOMAIN PLACEMENT option will ($\geq$1) or will not (0) be used. This option is explained in the text.

Figure 5-15. An example of practical work using the SC VLSI methodology: contents of the **dmode.dat** file. This file contains the user's wish list in the domain of placement and routing which the MP2D program must respect. In this case, the file is empty (40 blanks), meaning the user does not have any special requests about placement and routing, so the MP2D program will perform the entire placement and routing in the default manner.

```
DUMMY
1P2
2P2
14P8
15P8
16P8
17P8
18P8
19P8
20P8
21P8
23P8
24P8
25P8
26P8
28P8
FSKOUT
S106
```

Figure 5-16. An example of practical work using the SC VLSI methodology: contents of the **drop.dat** file. This file contains the list of signals to be ignored during the placement and routing process. The first signal is ignored, because it is physically nonexistent for historical reasons (DUMMY); the remaining signals are ignored because they physically exist, but are unused (*hanging* signals).

An FSK modulator for the voice-band data modem

Figure 5-17. An example of practical work using the SC VLSI methodology: contents of the **title.dat** file. This file can be used with the LOGSIM program as well as with the MP2D program. In this particular case, the designer has decided to have the same **title.dat** file for both programs (although he/she did not have to do it that way).

5.1.5 The ARTWORK and the FABRICATION Files

After all files have been created, they should be placed in the same directory on the disk, and MP2D should be run from that same directory. A few output files will also be present in that directory after this program completes its function. Two of these are important: the ARTWORK file which can be plotted; and the FABRICATION file, which can be sent to the chip manufacturer. The ARTWORK file is actually some kind of a chip photomicrograph, like the one shown in Figure 5-18 (some sources use the term *photomicrograph* only to denote the ARTWORK file for the FC VLSI design methodology).

Figure 5-18 depicts the ARTWORK file for a complicated processor chip (in our case the ARTWORK file would be quite simple). The standard cell channels and the interconnection roadbeds are readily visible. Along the edges run the I/O pads, the metalized contacts for the communication with the outside world. Inside each standard cell two numbers exist. One is defined by the designer of the standard cell family (this is the standard cell code), and the other is defined by the designer of the circuit (this is the ordinal number of the standard cell in the circuit). The interconnection roadbed widths can be reduced by iteratively applying the MP2D. In the case of the 32-bit GaAs microprocessor (RCA), the minimal roadbed widths (that is, the minimal chip area) were obtained after seven iterations.

The contents of the FABRICATION file have not been shown here—these are monotonous columns of numbers describing details of all mask layers. This file can be sent to fabrication either by using magnetic media (tapes, floppy disks) or by e-mail. After the financial agreement has been settled, the chips are delivered by mail, sometimes after only a few days.

5.1.6 Summary

Previous sections described, for educational purposes, the use of the CADDAS package. However, the entire practical work in the VLSI laboratories of many universities today is done using the TANNER package by Tanner Research [25]. The user interface of the TANNER package is very good and avoids unnecessary details that are not important to the users. Anyway, the baseline process is the same as with the CADDAS package—schematic entry is done using the standard ORCAD package or the specific S-Edit program (Schematic Editor), logic and timing testing are done using the GATESIM program (gate-level simulation), and placement and routing are done using the L-EDIT program (layout editor). The TANNER package offers various options regarding fabrication, but by far the most attractive one is the possibility of creating the output file in the CIF format, thus enabling the fabrication to be performed using the MOSIS technology. Details can be found in [26].

5.2 Postfabrication Testing

Testing can be discussed in three different contexts. First, there is the functional testing of different candidate architectures which is done before the circuit design has been created. This can be done using the tools based on the languages ISP' and VHDL. Then, there is the logic and timing testing of the completed circuit after it has been properly formatted for computer processing. The tools for this testing method include programs such as LOGSIM (part of the CADDAS package) or GATESIM (part of the TANNER package). Finally, there is the postfabrication testing which occurs after the circuit has been manufactured. This context will be discussed to some extent in the following paragraphs.

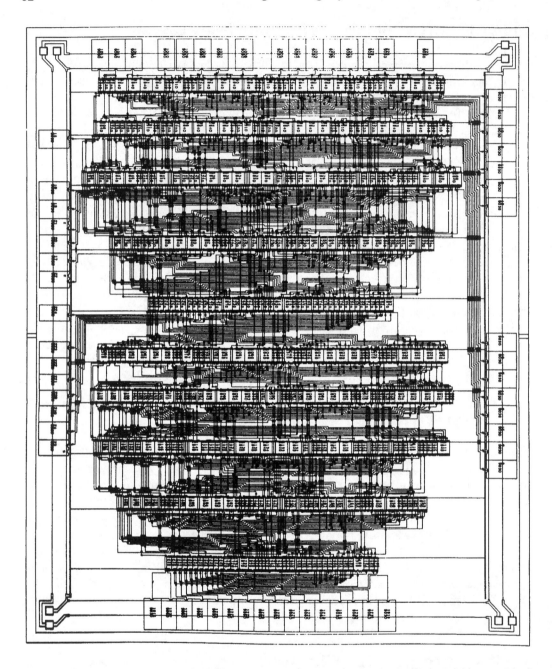

Figure 5-18. An example of practical work using the SC VLSI methodology: a typical layout of the **artwork** file, formed by the MP2D program [24]. The standard cells are laid in columns of the same height, and approximately of the same width. The standard cells are connected through the channels whose height depends on the number of connections to be made. The chip ID is directly ported from the **mmode.dat** file (see Figure 5-14).

The prefabrication testing of the completed circuit and the postfabrication testing of the fabricated chips have a lot in common. The similarities include the test vector creation methodology (it is often the case that the identical test vectors are used in both prefabrication and postfabrication testing). There are, however, some important differences. These differences are mainly because of the impossibility of accessing some important test points in a fabricated chip which are readily accessible in the computer simulation.

The following paragraphs concentrate on the postfabrication testing, but but the discussion also applies to prefabrication testing (especially regarding test vector creation strategies). This discussion is mainly based on [27].

5.2.1 Test Vectors and Fault Coverage

The term *test vector* denotes a sequence of binary symbols which can be used either to test the logic circuit at any given moment or during an interval of time. The *input test vector* is a sequence that is fed to the inputs of the circuit (or to the inputs of the internal elements of the circuit) with the intention of causing the response. The *output test vector* is a sequence which characterizes the response of the tested circuit after it has been subjected to the input test vector. There are two types of output test vectors: the test vector expected to be the output of the circuit, as defined by the designer of the circuit, is called *the expected output test vector;* and the test vector generated either by the software tool (during the prefabrication testing), or the actual output test vector generated by the chip (during the postfabrication testing). The latter is called *the real output test vector*.

A single test vector is totally inadequate for the testing of a nontrivial circuit. This is why a sequence of test vectors is used during the real testing process. The testing is called *exhaustive* if the test vectors cover each and every possible input bit sequence. If the testing is not exhaustive, or if all possible bit sequences are not applied to the circuit inputs, then the testing is *reduced*. Reduced testing does not always have to be suboptimal, since the included test vectors might cover all potentially erroneous states.

Exhaustive testing can often be used with relatively simple circuits. On the other hand, complex circuits require the creation of a relatively small set of input test vectors (reducing the testing time and cost) that covers almost the complete set of potential errors (minimizing the probability of undiscovered errors).

In general, two approaches to testing can be used: functional testing of the chip (or its part) without knowing the internal details; and structural testing of the chip (or its part) with tests performed on each internal element of the chip, without testing the global chip function. These two approaches can be combined. Actually, the best results (regarding time and cost) are obtained by some appropriate combination of these methods.

The input test vectors are most easily generated if there is a suitable algorithm to follow. In that case, test vector generation can be automated, which is relatively easy to do for memory chips; it is almost impossible for processor chips.

Perhaps this is the right moment to point out an important difference between prefabrication testing and postfabrication testing. All test vectors generated during the prefabrication testing are not applicable for the postfabrication testing. Furthermore, some test vectors that are insignificant during the prefabrication testing can be of paramount importance in the postfabrication testing. Generally, these two sets of test vectors partially overlap.

No matter how the test vectors are formed, it is good to have an insight into their quality. Most often, this quality is expressed through fault coverage. *Fault coverage* is defined as the percentage of errors that can be discovered by the test vector set. More to the point, it is defined as the quotient of the error count that can be discovered by the test vector set and the total number of possible errors on the chip. For a given test vector set, fault coverage depends on the utilized fault model.

If the testing is performed on the functional level only, then the fault model includes only the situations present on the input and output pins of the chip (or its part). In this situation, the fault model enables the designer to leave out a number of redundant test vectors.

If the testing is performed on the structural level, then the fault model specifies all erroneous states on the inputs and outputs of each internal element (for example, on each standard cell, if the design methodology is SC VLSI). The errors that can occur but cannot be caught by the fault model are referred to as *Byzantine errors* in the literature.

5.2.1.1 The SSA Fault Model By far the most frequently utilized structural level fault model is the *SSA (single stuck at)* model which is briefly explained below.

This model assumes that the only faults that can occur in an elementary component are the ones where one input or output is stuck at logical one (SA-1) or at logical zero (SA-0). In the case of one gate (see Figure 5-19), the following holds true:

a)   If one input is shorted to the power supply (V_{cc}), this is the SA-1 state;

b)   If one input is disconnected, this can also be the SA-1 state (this depends on the technology—for instance, this holds true for the TTL technology);

c)   If one input is shorted to the ground, this is the SA-0 state;

d)   If one output is fixed at the logic one, this is the SA-1 state;

e)   If one output is fixed at the logic zero, this is the SA-0 state.

As shown in this example, the SSA model does not cover a number of faults that are frequent in the VLSI chips, such as shorted wires or the change in the logic function of a logic element. This model also overlooks the possibility of multiple errors. However, despite these shortcomings, the empirical results show that this model has a fairly high fault coverage. The reason is simple: it is more important to determine whether a part of the chip is inoperative than to discover what exactly has gone wrong. In plain English, the SSA model has a high probability of discovering the presence of errors, but not a high probability of telling us where the fault is and why it is there.

The generation of test vectors consistent with the SSA model is performed according to the *path sensitization (PS)* method. Some bits in the input test vector are chosen in such a way so as to forward the logic zero to one of the test points (to the output pin, or to the point in the chip which can be monitored from some output pin). The rest of the input bits are not significant (X, don't care). This test vector tests for the SA-1 type of fault (if the logic one appears on the selected output). Next, the test vector is created to force the logic one at the same output. If the logic zero appears, then the SA-0 fault exists. The same procedure is applied to all other elements on the chip, leaving out those already tested by the side effects of the previous tests. The total test vector count is therefore less or equal to 2N, where N is the number of chip elements.

In this example, shown in Figure 5-20, the test vector $ABC = 010$ has to be created to see if there is the SA-1 fault at the connection C_4. If the output (C_{14}) shows the logic one, it means that the SA-1 fault exists. The same test vector has the side effect of testing the existence of the SA-0 fault at the connection C_{13}.

The good side of the SSA model is the possibility of automated test vector sequence generation. The bad side of the model is the existence of the nondetectable faults in some circuits. For example, it is not possible to generate the test vector to see whether there is the SA-0 fault at the connection C_4 in the circuit from Figure 5-21. Reference [27] maintains that these cases are mainly present in the poorly designed circuits (that is, in those circuits that contain unnecessary elements). In such cases, the SSA model has a fault coverage of less than one.

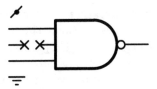

Figure 5-19 Examples of some cases that can be modeled after the SSA (single stuck at) methodology: Input shorted to the voltage supply can be modeled as SA-1; Open input can usually be modeled as SA-1 (TTL logic, for example); Input shorted to the ground can be modeled as SA-0; Output stuck at high logic level can be modeled as SA-1; Output stuck at low logic level can be modeled as SA-0.

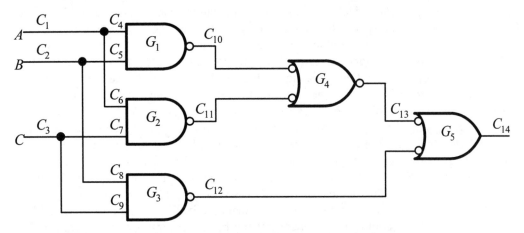

Figure 5-20. An example of test vector generation after the SSA (single stuck at) methodology: input test vector $ABC = 010$ tests for the SA-1 condition at C_4. If the output (C_{14}) shows logic zero, this means that C_4 contains an error of the type SA-1.

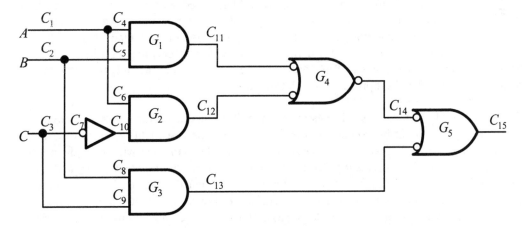

Figure 5-21. An example of the diagram that can not be tested after the SSA methodology: there is no way to generate an input test vector to see if there is an SA-0 type of error at C_4.

5.2.1.2 The Random Test Vector Generation It is interesting to mention that the random test vector generation also gives fairly good results. This is due to the shape of the typical dependence $K = f(N)$, as shown in Figure 5-22. The K axis represents the percentage of the faults discovered, and the N axis represents the number of random test vectors. A very attractive aspect of this method is its simplicity. Less attractive aspects are the impossibility of determining the actual fault coverage and the impracticability of this method for sequential circuits.

5.2.1.3 The SP and BIST Approaches for Sequential and Combinational Circuits The previous discussion focused on combinational circuits. In the case of the sequential circuits, there are two approaches. The first approach assumes the utilization of the PS procedure, which is inappropriate for various reasons; fault coverage is significantly reduced because there are a lot of undetectable faults, and there are some faults which cannot easily fit into the SSA model. The second approach assumes the utilization of the *BIST (built-in self-test)* methodology and the *SP (scan path)* technique, which is a part of BIST.

The basic task of the designer using the BIST method is to create a design for testability. The design has to facilitate efficient testing (with a small number of test vectors giving fault coverage as close to 100 percent as possible) for circuits containing both combinational and sequential elements. The following discussion is based on [28].

If the test vectors are applied to the inputs of circuits containing combinational and sequential elements, then the number of test vectors needed to test the circuit adequately is relatively large. However, if the test vectors can be injected into the circuit interior, their number can be significantly reduced. One of the techniques based on this approach is the *SP technique*. Almost all BIST structures are actually based on one of the SP techniques.

All SP techniques are based on the assumption that all mixed-type circuits (those containing both sequential and combinational elements) can be divided into two parts, one entirely combinational, and the other containing solely sequential elements (for example, D flip-flops, as shown in Figure 5-23). The inputs are labeled X_i ($i = 1, \ldots, n$), and the outputs are labeled Z_i ($i = 1, \ldots, m$). In the original circuit, there are no connections in places labeled with asterisks (*). Therefore, the circuit shown in Figure 5-23 is based on the assumption that the D flip-flops are connected to the rest of the logic by "elastic" connections, and are "taken out" of the circuit without changing its topology. The other assumption made here is that all sequential elements of the circuit are D flip-flops. However, everything said here can easily be generalized for other types of flip-flops or latches, which is important if the SP technique is to be applied to the microprocessors on VLSI chips.

5.2.1.4 The SP Techniques The essence of the SP techniques is the ability to facilitate the test mode of the circuit by connecting the flip-flops and the rest of the circuit in the places labeled with asterisks. In this manner, one shift register has been formed, with the width equal to the number of D flip-flops. This register is called the *SP register (scan path register)* and is used to inject the test vectors into the circuit interior. Next, the inputs to the circuit ($X_1 - X_n$) are set. Then, when the connections labeled with asterisks are broken, the circuit is toggled into the normal mode. After the propagation delay passes through the combinational logic, the circuit enters a new stable state. Now, the clock signal triggers the circuit and writes the new state into the D flip-flops. Then, the circuit is once again toggled into the test mode, and the contents of the flip-flops is read out. The new contents of the *SP* register is actually the output test vector corresponding to the input test vector injected a moment ago. A new input test vector is fed to the flip-flops, in conjunction with the output test vector readout. As stated earlier, the test is performed through comparison between the anticipated and the real output test vectors.

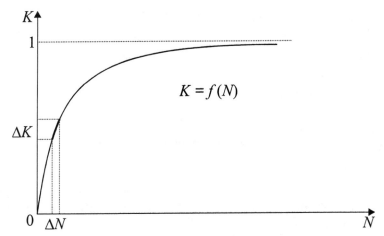

Figure 5-22. Generation of random test-vectors: typical relation of error coverage factor (K) to the number of generated test vectors (N). For small N, insignificant changes ΔN result in significant changes ΔK. This phenomenon enables the designer to achieve relatively good test results from a relatively small number of randomly generated test vectors.

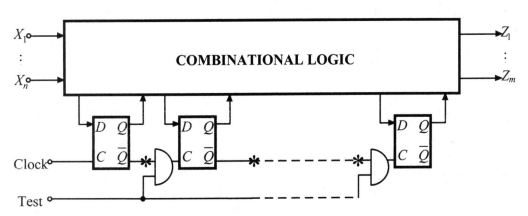

Figure 5-23. General structure of the diagrams inclined toward the SP (scan path) testing methodology. The inputs and outputs are marked X_i ($i = 1, ..., n$) and Z_i ($i = 1, ..., m$), respectively. The nodes marked with $*$ are normally open circuited; they form connections only during the test vector entry and exit.

The most widely used SP technique is the *Stanford SP technique*. It assumes the use of the multiplexed D flip-flops (MDFF), as shown in Figure 5-24. The MDFF is actually a plain D flip-flop with a multiplexer on its D input. The multiplexer has two inputs, D_0 and D_1; the flip-flop has one output, Q, and one control input, T. If $T = 1$, the active input is D_1, and the MDFF is in the test mode with all MDFF elements making up one shift register (the SP register). If $T = 0$, the input D_0 is active, and the MDFF is in the normal mode and connected to the combinational logic.

The test procedure according to the Stanford SP technique (using symbols from Figure 5-24) looks like this:

a)   Setting the test mode:

$T = 1$

b) Entering the input test vector $\vec{y}$ to Q outputs of the flip-flops (Q) using clock CK:

$$\vec{Q} = \vec{y}$$

c) Entering the input test vector $\vec{x}$ to the inputs of the circuit ($\vec{X}$):

$$\vec{X} = \vec{x}$$

d) Setting the normal mode:

$$T = 0$$

e) Circuit stabilizes after the propagation delay; then all flip-flops are triggered to write the output test vector $\vec{Y}$ into the flip-flops Q:

$$\vec{Q} = \vec{Y}$$

f) Setting the test mode ($T = 1$) and taking the output test vector. The output test vectors are taken from the Z outputs and from the SP register (the R output). A new test vector is simultaneously shifted in:

$$T = 1$$

One more thing has to be done before the circuit testing begins, namely the flip-flops also have to be tested. This is usually done by using the *marching zero* and the *marching ones* methods. In the case of marching zero, the test vector contains all ones and a single zero, and that vector is shifted in and out of the SP register. In the case of marching one, the opposite holds true—the test vector contains all zeros and a single one.

As previously mentioned, there are other SP techniques in existence. They all represent modifications of the Stanford SP technique. Two such modifications are shown in Figures 5-25 and 5-26.

The *2PFF-SP technique (two port flip-flop scan path)* is a modified technique that has been used in some RCA products (see Figure 5-25). This technique is essentially the same as the Stanford SP technique, except for the flip-flops which are modified to have two data inputs (D_1 and D_2) and two control inputs (C_1 and C_2) each.

The *LSSD technique (level sensitive scan design)* is a modified technique that has been used in some IBM products (see Figure 5-26). Besides the details shown in Figures 5-24 and 5-25, there are additional latches, labeled $L2\text{-}i$ ($i = 1, 2, \ldots$), which allow the connection of the system latches into one SP register. In the test mode, each system latch $L1\text{-}i$ ($i = 1, 2, \ldots$) has one latch $L2\text{-}i$ ($i = 1, 2, \ldots$) associated with it, and together they make up one D flip-flop. Symbols *SDI (scanned data in)* and *SDO (scanned data out)* refer to the input and output pins for entering and reading out the test vectors (see Figure 5-26). Symbols *TCK* and *CK* refer to the test clock (used in the test mode) and the working clock (used in the normal mode), respectively.

There are two more frequently encountered SP techniques: the *SS method (scan-set)* of UNIVAC, and the *SM method (scan-mux)* of AMDAHL. In the former case, the test data shift registers are used, thus eliminating the need to connect the system latches into one shift register. In the latter case, multiplexers and demultiplexers are used to set and read the system latches, thus eliminating the need for the shift register. As previously mentioned, the system latch based solutions are important in VLSI microprocessors. This is due to the fact that system latches are necessary to realize the arithmetic-logic unit, pipeline, and other microprocessor resources.

Besides the mentioned modifications, which simplify the implementation or widen the field of applicability of the basic SP techniques, there are also improvements oriented towards enhancing the testing efficiency based on the SP techniques. One such improvement is the *ESP technique (external scan path)* elaborated in [28]. This enhancement is based on adding the SP registers associated with input and output pins of the chip being designed. Both the number of test vectors and the testing time can be significantly reduced by using these SP registers.

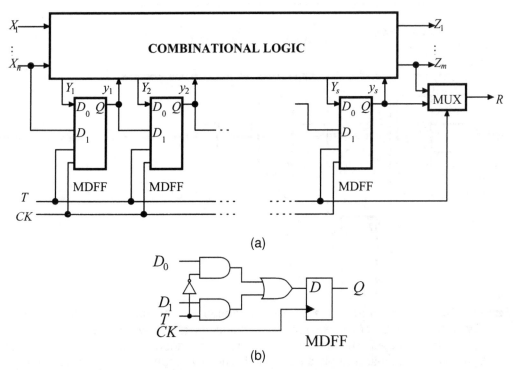

(a)

(b)

Figure 5-24. The structure of the diagrams derived from the Stanford SP (Stanford Scan Path) testing methodology. The inputs and outputs are marked X_i ($i = 1, ..., n$) and Z_i ($i = 1, ..., m$), respectively. The test vectors are entered through the X_n input, and the output test vectors depart through the R output. The symbol MDFF refers to the multiplexed data flip-flop; the input D_0 is active when the control input is $T = 0$ (normal mode), and the input D_1 is active when the control input is $T = 1$ (test mode). Symbol CK refers to the clock signal. The signals y_i and Y_i ($i = 1, ..., s$) refer to the input and output test vectors, respectively.

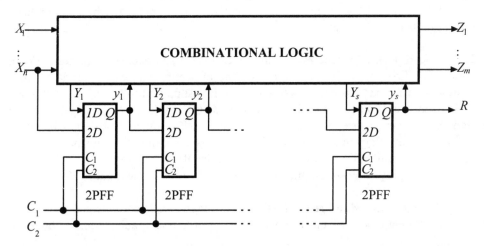

Figure 5-25. The structure of the diagrams corresponding to the 2PFF-SP (two-port flip-flop scan path) testing methodology. The 2PFF flip-flops have two control inputs each (C_1 and C_2) for the two different data inputs (*1D* and *2D*).

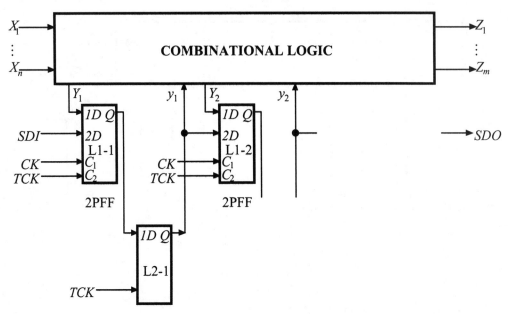

Figure 5-26. The structure of the diagrams corresponding to the LSSD testing methodology. The latches L1-i ($i = 1$, ...) are system latches, and they are a part of the diagram that is being tested. The latches L2-i ($i = 1$, ...) are added to enable the connection of the system latches into a single shift register. The *SDI* (scanned data in) and *SDO* (scanned data out) signals serve the purpose of entering and retrieving the test vectors, respectively. Symbols *CK* and *TCK* refer to the system clock (used in the normal mode), and the test clock (used in the test mode), respectively.

5.2.2   Testing Memory Chips

Memory chips introduce special problems to testing. Testing ROM memories is relatively simple, while testing RAM memories can become quite complicated because of the wide variety of faults that can occur.

5.2.2.1   Testing ROM Memories   There are two basic approaches to the testing of ROM memories. The first approach is based on reading the entire contents of the ROM memory and comparing each address contents to the value it is supposed to have. The fault coverage with this method is 100 percent (if ROM memory sensitivity faults are disregarded, which is allowed, since their occurrence is extremely unlikely). The other approach is based on the control sums. If the algorithm shown in Figure 5-27 is used, then the comparison is not performed for each location, but only once for the entire ROM memory. The number of comparisons is drastically reduced, but the fault coverage drops off to less than 100 percent.

5.2.2.2   Testing RAM Memories   Testing RAM memories is complicated because a variety of very different types of faults can occur. The most frequent faults are listed below:

   a)   Stuck at logic one or logic zero errors, when some bit positions always yield one or zero, no matter what was written in.

   b)   Address decoder errors, when parts of the memory become inaccessible.

1.   *sum* = 0   (* *Skew Checksums* *)
2.   *address* = 0
3.   **rotate_left_1**(*sum*)
4.   *sum* = *sum* + *rom*(*address*)
5.   *address* = *address* + 1
6.   **if** *address* < *rom_length* **then goto** 3
7.   **end**

Figure 5-27.   An algorithm for ROM memory testing.

c)   Multiple write errors, when the "single write" writes to multiple locations.

d)   Slow sense amplifier recovery errors, when reading becomes history sensitive. For instance, after reading 1010101, zero is read correctly, whereas after reading 1111111, it is read incorrectly.

e)   Pattern sensitivity errors, when some patterns are stored correctly and some are not. This is a consequence of the interaction between the physically adjacent memory locations.

f)   Sleeping sickness errors (typical for dynamic RAM memories), when the data are sometimes lost even though the refresh signal is frequent enough.

The order of complexity of the memory testing algorithms is $O(k)$ if the testing time is proportional to N^k for large N, where N is the number of memory locations to be tested. Two simple algorithms of the order $O(1)$ and two more complex algorithms of the order $O(2)$ are described in the following paragraphs.

The most frequently used algorithms of the order $O(1)$ are marching patterns and checkerboards.

The most frequently encountered marching pattern algorithms are marching ones and/or marching zeros. Conditionally speaking, the testing time is $5N$, where N is the number of memory locations that need to be tested, meaning that the algorithm order is $O(1)$. The marching ones algorithm is shown below (the same procedure applies to marching zeros, with zeros and ones switched):

a)   The memory is initialized with all zeros.

b)   Zero is read from the first location, and one is written in instead.

c)   This sequence is repeated for the entire memory.

d)   When the end is reached, one is read from the last location, and zero is written in instead.

e)   This sequence is repeated until the first location is reached.

This algorithm is suitable for discovering the multiple write errors and stuck at errors. It is not, however, efficient for discovering the address decoder errors, slow sense amplifier errors, and pattern sensitivity errors.

The checkerboard algorithm is most frequently realized by working with the alternating zeros and ones in the adjacent locations:

    010101...
    101010...
    010101...

Conditionally speaking, the testing time is $4N$, where N is the number of memory locations that need to be tested, meaning that the algorithm order is $O(1)$. The algorithm is defined in the following manner:

a)   The memory is initialized with alternating zeros and ones in the adjacent bit locations.

b)   The contents of the memory is read.

c)   The same is repeated with zeros and ones switched.

Since it eliminates the chips with easily detectable faults from further testing without wasting too much time, this algorithm [together with other algorithms of the order $O(1)$] is frequently used as an introduction to more complex tests. Furthermore, because it is especially suitable for detecting the pattern sensitivity errors, it is not efficient for other types of errors. The problem with this algorithm is that logically adjacent locations are not always physically adjacent, so the testing equipment often has to be expanded with address scramblers and descramblers.

The most frequently used algorithms of the order $O(2)$ are the *walking patterns (WALKPAT)* and the *galloping patterns (GALPAT)*. The GALPAT algorithm comes in two versions, GALPAT I (galloping ones and zeros) and GALPAT II (galloping write recovery test).

Conditionally speaking, the WALKPAT algorithm is characterized by having the testing time equal to $2N^2 + 6N$, where N is the number of locations to be tested, meaning it has the order $O(2)$. The definition of this algorithm is as follows:

a)   The memory is initialized with all zeros.

b)   One is written into the first location, then all the locations are read, to check if they still contain zeros. Zero is then written into the first location.

c)   The previous step is repeated for all other memory locations.

d)   The entire procedure is repeated with zeros and ones switched.

This algorithm is suitable for detecting multiple write errors, slow sense amplifier errors, and pattern sensitivity errors. It is not suitable for detecting the other types of errors previously mentioned.

Also conditionally speaking, the GALPAT I algorithm is characterized by having the testing time equal to $2N^2 + 8N$, where N is the number of locations to be tested, meaning it is of the order $O(2)$ complexity. This algorithm is equivalent to the WALKPAT algorithm, except that the contents of the location that was written are also read and verified against its supposed value.

The GALPAT II algorithm is (conditionally speaking) characterized with the testing time equal to $8N^2 + 4N$, where N is the number of locations to be tested, meaning it has the order $O(2)$. It starts with arbitrary memory contents, and proceeds like this:

a)   One is written into the first memory location.

b)   Zero is written into the second location, and the first location is read to verify the presence of the one written in a moment ago.

c)   One is written into the second location, and the first location is read again, with the same purpose.

d)   The entire procedure is repeated for all possible pairs of memory locations.

These algorithms are just drops in the ocean of the existing algorithms for testing of RAM memories. Also, there is one more thing to bear in mind. Besides the testing of the logical aspect functionality (the mentioned algorithms fall into that category), there are algorithms for testing the timing aspect functionality (to see if the RAM chip functions satisfy the predetermined timing constraints).

5.3 Summary

This chapter discussed the design and test procedures in general. By now, readers should be able to address the topic of how to design and test. However, since the key question is "what to design and test," the following chapter will focus on the problems related to the VLSI RISC processor design. As indicated, it is generally acknowledged that the process of constructing a new VLSI architecture is a highly creative job, while the process of design and testing is a routine job.

6

RISC: The Architecture

By using adequate architectural solutions, the designer can obtain a much better utilization of the chosen technology for the predetermined application.

6.1 RISC Processor Design Philosophy

The following discussion is based on references [6] and [29]–[36].

The new RISC (Reduced Instruction Set Computer) processors were created as a reaction to the existing CISC (Complex Instruction Set Computer) processors through the attempts to design a processor based on the statistical analysis of the compiled high-level language code. According to one of the existing definitions of the RISC processor design [31], a resource (or an instruction) is incorporated into the chip of the RISC processor architecture if and only if the following occurs:

a) The incorporation of this resource (or instruction) is justified because of its usage probability.

b) The incorporation of this resource (or instruction) will not slow down other resources (or instructions) already incorporated into the chip because of their usage probability, which is higher.

Missing resources are emulated, and missing instructions are synthesized. In fact, the basic problem with both the creation of a new RISC architecture and with the design of a new RISC processor is how to use the available VLSI area wherein the positive effects (for example, the reduced number of machine cycles necessary to execute the entire program) outweigh the negative effects (such as the lengthened machine cycle).

6.1.1 The Technology Domain

Before a new resource or instruction is added to the chip, it is necessary to compare the positive and negative effects of its inclusion, in both the domains of technology and of application.

In the technology domain, it is important to adjust the architecture to conform to the design requirements of the chosen VLSI technology, improving the impedance match between the architecture and the technology. Patterson's principles were defined in accordance with this, and they can be conditionally treated as the basis for the design of the interface between the architecture and the technology base [37].

75

As previously stated, the basic question is how to best use the available VLSI area. Increasing the VLSI area has both positive (although this is not always the case) and negative effects.

The positive effects of enlarging the area of the VLSI chip are the following:

a) The existing resource quantity can be enlarged (for example, we can have 32 instead of 16 registers).

b) New resources can be incorporated (for example, the hardware multiplier can be added, which is very important for some applications).

c) The precision can be enhanced (instead of a 32-bit processor, we can have a 64-bit processor), and so on.

The negative effects of enlarging the VLSI area are the following:

a) The larger the number of gates on the chip, the slower each gate gets, which decreases the microprocessor speed.

b) The larger the chip, the longer the interconnects get, so the only desirable interconnects on the VLSI chip are the nearest neighbor communications.

c) The larger the number of machine instructions, the more complex the decoder logic gets. This slows down all instructions and especially degrades the execution time of the most frequently used instructions which ultimately slows down the entire target application, and so on.

To conclude, the design of a VLSI processor should be done in a way that maximizes the positive effects and minimizes the negative effects.

6.1.2   The Application Domain

In the application domain, it is important to match the architecture to the compilation requirements, with the goal of enabling the optimizing compilers to produce a code that is as efficient as possible. To that end, Wulf's eight principles are defined, and they can be conditionally treated as the base of the RISC architecture to the optimizing compiler interface [38].

In this context, principles exist which must be satisfied during the design of a new architecture. Each deviation results in a special case which must be separately analyzed during the compilation (especially during the code optimization). If the architecture contains many such special cases, the code optimization will be restricted for two reasons: (a) the wish to beat the competition and to launch a new optimizing compiler as soon as possible often means that the special case optimization is not incorporated into the optimizer, and (b) if the compiler has all the special case optimization options built in, the users often deliberately choose to turn off some of the special cases in the optimization analysis in order to speed up the compilation. Wulf's eight principles are summarized below.

a) *Regularity Principle:* if something was done in one way in some instructions, it has to be done the same way in all instructions.

b) *Orthogonality Principle:* for each instruction, the addressing mode, the data type, and the operation type have to be defined independently.

c) *Composability Principle:* combining any addressing mode, any data type, and any operation type must result in a valid instruction.

d) *One Versus All Principle:* the architecture must provide either one solution, or all possible solutions to the problem.

e) *Provide Primitives, Not Solutions Principle:* the architecture must provide primitive operations for solving the existing problem, and not a support for the entire solution.

f) *Addressing Principle:* the architecture must provide efficient solutions for basic addressing modes.

g) *Environment Support Principle:* the architecture must efficiently support the system code, not only the user code.

h) *Deviations Principle:* the architecture must be implementation independent, otherwise each technology change will require the architectural changes as well.

Having this in mind, some differences between the RISC and the CISC architectures can be defined in simple terms: RISC processors provide primitives, and CISC processors provide solutions which are typically not general enough. RISC processors often rely on the reusability of the earlier results, while CISC processors often rely on the recomputation of earlier results. RISC processors provide only one way to solve the given problem, while CISC processors provide many, but not all possible ways.

Each concept is best understood through examples. Therefore, the following section gives details of two basic RISC architectures of interest for this book. For advanced RISC architectures, readers are advised to read the reference [36], and the original manufacturer documentation.

6.2   Basic Examples: The UCB-RISC

This section presents the *UCB-RISC (University of California at Berkeley RISC)* architecture. The architecture of the 32-bit UCB-RISC processor was completely formed in accordance with the described RISC processor design philosophy. This means that the end application was defined at the very beginning; therefore, the statistical analysis of the representable code was performed first. This analysis gave some interesting indications, which had a great influence on further work related to the design of the architecture, and these results will be briefly presented below.

For educational reasons, the following discussion contains some simplifications and/or modifications concerning the original architecture, organization, and design of the UCB-RISC processor.

Figure 6-1 shows the results of the statistical analysis of various high-level language construct frequencies, for C (C) and PASCAL (P). The analysis in question is dynamic, referring to the code in execution, and not the static analysis of the code in memory.

The first two columns (percentage of HLL constructs) refer to the percentage of occurrence of various high-level language constructs in the source code. These two columns show that the **call** and **return** constructs are not too frequent (about 15 percent for PASCAL and about 12 percent for C). On the other hand, the **assign** construct is extremely frequent (about 45 percent for PASCAL and about 38 percent for C).

The third and the fourth columns (percentage of machine instructions) refer to the percentage of machine instructions that are involved in the synthesis of all occurrences of the corresponding high-level language construct.

Approximately one-third of the instructions (about 31 percent for PASCAL and about 33 percent for C) were making up the code that realized the **call** and **return**. The reason for this emphasis of the **call** and **return** instructions, looked from this aspect, is the following:

HLL	Percentage of HLL Constructs		Percentage of Machine Instructions		Percentage of Memory References	
	P	C	P	C	P	C
CALL/RETURN	15±1	12±5	31±3	33±4	44±4	45±9
LOOPS	5±0	3±1	42±3	32±6	33±2	26±5
ASSIGN	45±5	38±15	13±2	13±5	14±2	15±6
IF	29±8	43±17	11±3	21±8	7±2	13±5
WITH	5±5	—	1±0	—	1±0	—
CASE	1±1	<1±1	1±1	1±1	1±1	1±1
GOTO	—	3±1	—	0±0	—	0±0

Figure 6-1. Statistical analysis of benchmark programs that were used as a basis for the UCB-RISC architecture. Symbol *P* refers to the benchmark written in the PASCAL language, and symbol *C* refers to the benchmark written in the C language. These results are derived from a dynamic analysis.

a) The **call** and **return** can be defined on various levels.

b) On the microcode level, these instructions only preserve the value of PC on the stack, and put a new value into it (**call**), or vice versa (**return**).

c) On the machine code level, in addition to the information mentioned above, registers are either saved (**call**) or restored (**return**).

d) On the high-level language level, in addition to the information mentioned above, parameters are passed from the calling program into the procedure (**call**) or results are returned (**return**).

In other words, the realization of all operations regarding the **call** and **return** instructions requires relatively long sequences of machine instructions. Obviously, if those instruction sequences could be shortened through appropriate architectural solutions, the speed of compiled code could be significantly improved (which is usually a goal that new architectures seek to satisfy). This means that, although they do not appear too frequently, the impact of **call** and **return** on the compiled code execution speed is relatively significant.

On the other hand, the number of instructions required to synthesize the **assign** construct is relatively small. The following explains the reasons for deemphasizing the importance of the **assign** construct when looked at from the angle of percentage of machine instructions: it is easy to synthesize the **assign** construct using the machine instructions, because analyses show that about 90 percent of **assign** constructs involve three or less variables, and about 90 percent of operations in the **assign** constructs involve addition or subtraction, enabling the synthesis using minimum of machine instructions (for example, [39]). Therefore, it is not necessary to introduce special hardware for the acceleration of **assign** into the architecture (in fact, it could even slow things down).

The last two columns (percent memory transfers) refer to the percentage of memory transfers involved in the synthesized code for realization of a given construct. That way, about half of the memory transfers (about 44 percent for PASCAL and about 45 percent for C) are involved in the realization of the **call** and **return** constructs. From the perspective of the percentage of memory transfers, the **call** and **return** constructs are emphasized because memory transfers are one of the key bottlenecks in any architecture, and the reduction of these can speed up the code drastically. Obviously, if the number of memory transfers needed in the **call** and **return** constructs could be cut down, the code speedup would result.

Conversely, the number of memory transfers in the **assign** construct is relatively insignificant (about 14 percent for PASCAL and about 15 percent for C). The conclusion is that the **assign** construct has a marginal effect, and does not deserve to be considered in the process of new architecture creation.

In the UCB-RISC processor, the architectural support for the **call** and **return** constructs exists in the form of partially overlapping register windows. The details will be explained later.

This is an appropriate place for a small digression. In the seventies, a lot of effort was put into HLL architectures. However, the attention focused on the static, rather than the dynamic, statistics (probably because of the high cost of memory and the satisfactory code speed when working with underdeveloped applications, which held true in those days). As a consequence, a great deal of attention was devoted to the **assign** construct, and almost none to the **call** and **return** constructs [39].

Figure 6-2 shows the results of the statistical analysis of the appearance of various data types for programs written in PASCAL ($P1$, $P2$, $P3$, and $P4$) and in C ($C1$, $C2$, $C3$, and $C4$). This was a dynamic analysis too. The most important column is the last one, which depicts the average values.

Figure 6-2 makes it clear that scalar variables are by far the most frequent ones, and they represent about 55 percent of the data involved in the ALU operations. Therefore, they should get most of the attention in the new architecture. In the UCB-RISC, this fact influenced the determination of the optimal quantitative values for the most important parameters of the partially overlapping windowed register file. Details follow later on in this chapter.

It is also apparent in Figure 6-2 that variables belonging to complex structures have little importance (they make up only about 25 percent of the variables from this group). In other words, only about 25 percent of the variables involved in the ALU operations come from the complex structures, and they should not be given special treatment in the new architecture. However, if the static analysis were to be used, those variables would receive undue attention; this is precisely what happened with many HLL architectures developed during the seventies.

6.2.1 The UCB-RISC Architecture

Based on this statistical analysis and some other dynamic measurements, and after the candidate architectures were compared, the final UCB-RISC architecture was formed. The basic characteristics of the UCB-RISC are listed below:

a) Pipeline is based on delayed branches.
b) Instructions are all 32 bits wide, with internal fields structured in a manner that minimizes the internal decoder logic complexity.

	P1	P2	P3	P4	C1	C2	C3	C4	Average
Integer Constants	14	18	11	20	25	11	29	28	20±7
Scalar Variables	63	68	46	54	37	45	66	62	55±11
Elements of Complex Data Structures	23	14	43	25	36	43	5	10	25±14

Figure 6-2. Statistical analysis of the frequencies of various data types, in benchmarks that were used as a base for the UCB-RISC architecture. Symbols P_i ($i = 1, 2, 3, 4$) refer to the benchmarks written in the PASCAL language, and symbols C_i ($i = 1, 2, 3, 4$) refer to the benchmarks written in the C language. These are the results of the dynamic analysis.

c) Only the **load** and **store** instructions can communicate with the memory (load/store architecture), and the instruction that uses the data must execute with the delay of at least two clock cycles.

d) Only the most basic addressing modes are supported, and addition is present in each instruction.

e) Data can be one byte wide (eight bits), a half-word wide (16 bits), or a word wide (32 bits).

f) There is no multiplication support in hardware, not even for the Booth algorithm (although the other example, the SU-MIPS, has it).

g) There is no stack in the CPU, neither for arithmetic nor for the context switch.

h) The **call** and **return** support exists in the form of a register file with partially over-lapping windows.

i) The architecture has been realized in the silicon NMOS technology in the first ex-perimental version as RISC I with around 44K transistors, and in the second experi-mental version as RISC II with around 40K transistors on the chip. The differences between RISC I and RISC II architectures are minimal.

j) The architecture has been designed to facilitate code optimization to the extreme limits.

All these characteristics will be detailed in the following text. This architecture has had a strong impact on the architectures of several existing commercial microprocessors.

The concept of a pipeline with delayed branches will be explained with the help of Figure 6-3. It shows one example of the two-stage pipeline. The first stage performs the instruction fetch, and the second stage executes the instruction. If the branch instruction is fetched, then a problem known as the *sequencing hazard* occurs in the pipeline. This problem will be described using Figure 6-3.

Let us assume that the instruction $I1$ is a branch. After the instruction $I1$ has been exe-cuted completely, the address of the next instruction will be known. However, by that time, the instruction $I2$ has been fetched. If the branch does not occur, this is the right instruction. On the other hand, if the branch occurs, that is the wrong instruction, and $I3$ should be fetched. By the time $I3$ has been fetched, $I2$ has completed its execution, which might corrupt the execution environment. Wrong results can be generated as a consequence. This problem is solved by using the mechanism known in the literature as *interlock*. The interlock mecha-nism can be realized in both hardware and software.

6.2.1.1 The Hardware Interlock   The hardware interlock assumes that the architecture includes a hardware resource which recognizes the sequencing hazard and prevents the exe-cution of the wrong instruction.

In the case of the hardware interlock, and in the example from Figure 6-3, one cycle is lost only if the branch occurs. If it does not occur, no cycles are lost. With the hardware interlock, the presence of special hardware decreases the clock speed because of the increased number of transistors. The clock cycle is then equal to the duration of one pipeline stage in the example as shown in Figure 6-3. Therefore, the expected execution time of the N-instruction program is:

$$\overline{T}_H^{DB} = k[N(1+P_B P_J)+1]T.$$

In this equation, k is the base clock cycle extension ($k > 1$), P_B is the probability of the branch instruction, P_J is the probability of branch taken, and T is the duration of the clock cycle. The correction factor 1 (single clock cycle) reflects the fact that one clock cycle is needed to empty out the pipeline. This equation would have a different form for another type of pipeline.

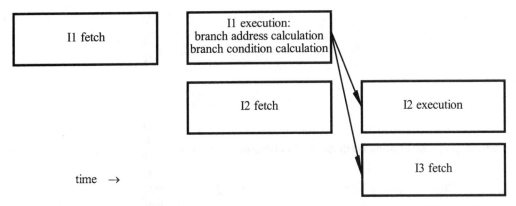

Figure 6-3. An example of the execution of the branch instruction, in the pipeline where the interlock mechanism can be realized in hardware or in software.

6.2.1.2   The Software Interlock   The software interlock assumes the elimination of the hazard during the compilation. When the code is generated, one **nop** instruction is inserted after each branch instruction (as in the example of the pipeline in Figure 6-3), then the code optimizer attempts to fill in some of these slots with useful instructions moved from elsewhere in the code. This is shown in Figure 6-4.

Figure 6-4 shows the code which can be executed properly only in a processor without the pipeline. In order to properly execute the same code in the pipelined machine shown in Figure 6-3, one **nop** instruction has to be inserted after each branch instruction. The execution speed of this code can be increased by moving some useful instructions to places held by the **nop** instructions. In the example shown in Figure 6-4(c) this has been achieved after the instruction **add** 1, *A* was moved from before the **jump** instruction to immediately after it. Since the instruction immediately after the branch executes unconditionally, the instruction **add** 1, *A* will be executed regardless of the branch outcome, because that happens in the pipeline without the hardware interlocks.

The instruction being moved must not be correlated to the branch instruction, that is, the branch address and the branch condition must not depend on it. Details of a widely used algorithm for this optimization will be explained later in this chapter.

	(a) Normal Branch		(b) Delayed Branch		(c) Optimized Delayed Branch	
Address						
100	load	*X, A*	load	*X, A*	load	*X, A*
101	add	1, *A*	add	1, *A*	jump	105
102	jump	105	jump	106	add	1, *A*
103	add	*A, B*	nop		add	*A, B*
104	sub	*C, B*	add	*A, B*	sub	*C, B*
105	store	*A, Z*	sub	*C, B*	store	*A, Z*
106			store	*A, Z*		

Figure 6-4. Realization of the software interlock mechanism for the pipeline from Figure 6-3 (using an example which is definitely not the best one, but helps to clarify the point): (a) Nrmal branch—the program fragment contains a sequencing hazard, as in the case of the pipelined processor,(b) delayed branch—the program fragment does not contain any sequencing hazard if it is executed on a processor with the pipeline as shown in Figure 6-3; this solution is inefficient, because it contains an unnecessary **nop** instruction, and (c) an optimized delayed branch—the previous example has been optimized, and the **nop** instruction has been eliminated (its place is now occupied by the **add** 1, *A* instruction).

In the case of software interlock and the example shown in Figure 6-3, and regardless of the branch outcome, one cycle is lost if the code optimizer does not eliminate the **nop** instruction, and no cycles are lost if it eliminates the **nop**. Therefore, the expected execution time of the N-instruction program is:

$$\overline{T_S}^{DB} = \{N[1 + P_B(1 - P_{COB})] + 1\}T.$$

Here, P_B is the branch instruction probability, and P_{COB} is the probability that the **nop** instruction can be eliminated during the code optimization.

6.2.2 Determining Which Interlock to Use

The question one might now ask is "which interlock is better, and under what conditions?" If, because of the enlarged number of transistors, the prolonged clock cycle is neglected, then the software interlock is better if:

$$1 - P_{COB} < P_J.$$

This is practically always true in the following situations. The existing optimizing compilers easily eliminate about 90 percent of the **nop** instructions, meaning that $P_{COB} \approx 0.9$. On the other hand, if the forward branch probability (forward branches are taken about 50 percent of the time) is approximately equal to the backward branch probability (backward branches are taken about 100 percent of the time), then about 75 percent of the branches are taken, meaning that $P_J \approx 0.75$, that is, the software interlock is better in the example pipeline shown in Figure 6-3.

In the case of deeper pipelines, the number of instructions that are unconditionally executed after the branch instruction increases. The code generator must add n **nop** instructions ($n = 2$, 3, $\ldots$) after the branch instruction. Elimination of several **nop** instructions is extremely difficult. According to some measurements, the situation looks like this:

$$P_{COB}(n = 2) \approx 0.5,$$
$$P_{COB}(n = 3) \approx 0.1,$$
$$P_{COB}(n \geq 4) < 0.01.$$

Therefore, for deeper pipelines, the hardware interlock can become more efficient than the software interlock. Readers should try to write the above mentioned equations for various types of pipelines.

In the case of the **load** instruction, there is a type of hazard that is known in the literature as the *timing hazard*. This problem will be described using the example in Figure 6-5.

Let us assume that the instruction $I1$ is a **load**. The data that is fetched arrives at the CPU at the end of the third pipeline stage, and then it is written into the destination register. If this piece of data is necessary for the execution of the instruction $I2$, then this instruction will produce a wrong result. This is due to the fact that the instruction $I2$ will begin its execution phase before the data has arrived to its destination. This problem is solved through the use of the interlock mechanism. This interlock can be realized in both hardware and software.

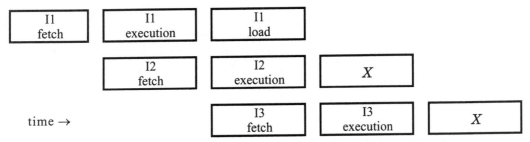

Figure 6-5. An example of the execution of the **load** instruction in a pipeline with either hardware or software interlock. Symbol *X* shows that the third stage is not being used (which is true of all instructions except the **load** instruction).

By definition, the hardware realization of the interlock mechanism assumes that the architecture includes a hardware resource which detects the hazard and prevents the following instruction from executing right away.

In the case of the hardware interlock and the example from Figure 6-5, one cycle is always lost after the **load** instruction. Besides, the increased number of transistors increases the duration of the clock cycle, which is equal to the duration of a single pipeline stage. Therefore, the expected execution time of the *N*-instruction program in the processor with the pipeline from Figure 6-5 will be:

$$\overline{T}_H^{DL} = k[N(1+P_L)+1]T.$$

This equation holds true if the last instruction of the program is not **load**. As before, *k* is the base clock cycle extension ($k > 1$), while P_L is the probability of the **load** instruction, and *T* is the duration of the clock cycle. Of course, in some other type of pipeline the equation would be different.

The software realization of the interlock mechanism relies on the compile-time hazard elimination (see Figure 6-6).

Figure 6-6(a) shows the code fragment which can be correctly executed only in a machine without a pipeline. In the case of a pipelined machine, as in Figure 6-5, the code fragment contains a **load** hazard. This hazard can be eliminated by inserting a **nop** after the **load** instruction during code generation. Like the previous example, the **nop** can be replaced with

Address	(a) Normal Load		(b) Delayed Load		(c) Optimized Delayed Load	
200	**sub**	*R6, R5, R4*	**sub**	*R6, R5, R4*	**load**	*R1*
201	**load**	*R1*	**load**	*R1*	**sub**	*R6, R5, R4*
202	**add**	*R3, R2, R1*	**nop**		**add**	*R3, R2, R1*
203			**add**	*R3, R2, R1*		

Figure 6-6. Realization of the software interlock mechanism for the example of the pipeline shown in Figure 6-5 (again, using an example which is definitely not the best one, but helps to clarify the point): (a) Normal data load—the program fragment contains a timing hazard, in the case of execution on a pipelined processor, (b) delayed data load—the program fragment does not contain a timing hazard, but it is inefficient because it contains an unnecessary **nop** instruction, and (c) optimized delayed load—the previous example has been optimized by eliminating the **nop** instruction (its place is occupied by the instruction **sub** *R3, R2, R1*).

a useful instruction, as shown in Figure 6-6(c). As in the branch hazard example, the moved instruction must not be correlated with the **load** instruction (either with the source address, or with the destination address). The software interlock and the example pipeline from Figure 6-5 cause one cycle to be lost if the optimizer cannot eliminate the **nop**. Therefore, the total expected execution time of the **N**-instruction program would be:

$$\overline{T}_S^{DL} = \{N[1 + P_L(1 - P_{COL})] + 1\}T.$$

This equation holds true if the **load** instruction cannot be the last instruction of the program. Here, P_L is the probability of the **load** instruction, P_{COL} is the probability of the elimination of the **nop**, and T is the duration of the base clock cycle.

Which interlock is better, and under what conditions? If the base clock prolongation is neglected with the hardware interlock, then the software interlock is better if:

$$P_{COL} > 0.$$

This condition is practically always satisfied. To conclude, in the example described, the software interlock is always better.

In the case of a deeper pipeline, the number of **nop** slots increases, and their elimination becomes progressively harder. But, under the described conditions, the software interlock is still better. The readers are advised to try to write the above mentioned equations for different types of pipeline.

6.2.3   Realization of the Pipeline in UCB-RISC I and UCB-RISC II

The actual realization of the pipeline in the UCB-RISC I and the UCB-RISC II is shown in Figure 6-7(a)–(d).

While the UCB-RISC I has a two-stage pipeline [Figure 6-7(a)] similar to the pipeline from Figure 6-3, the UCB-RISC II has a three-stage pipeline [see Figure 6-7(c)], with instruction execution spread across two pipeline stages. During the second stage, two operands from the register file are read and the ALU propagation takes place. During the third stage, both the result write into the register file and the precharging of the microelectronic circuitry take place, which is a characteristic of the chosen technology.

The resource utilization is much better in the UCB-RISC II than in the UCB-RISC I, which is obvious from Figure 6-7(b) and (d).

The RISC I processor has three internal buses, two for register reads and one for register write. The activities of these three buses during one pipeline stage are shown in Figure 6-7(b). The total idle time is significant.

The RISC II processor has two internal buses for register reads. One of them is used for register write. The activities of these two buses during one pipeline stage are shown in Figure 6-7(d). All resources are constantly used.

The assumption made here is that the first pipeline stage of the RISC I is used only for the instruction fetch, and that the second pipeline stage employs the critical datapath (see Figure 6-8). Data are read from the *general-purpose register file (GRF)* through the ports $R1$ and $R2$, and they arrive to the ALU via two internal buses, $B1$ and $B2$. The ALU output can be written into the GRF via the port $W2$, or it can be written into the input/output buffer *I/O_BUF*. The data from the input/output buffer can be written to the GRF via the port $W1$.

Figure 6-7(b) shows that during the first part of the second pipeline stage (lasting about one-third of the clock cycle) the register read is performed, through the ports $R1/R2$, and the results are directed to the ALU via the buses $B1$ and $B2$. At the same time, the bus $B3$ is idle, and the ALU is precharging its circuitry.

During the second part of the second pipeline stage (lasting approximately the same time) all buses are idle, and the ALU operates.

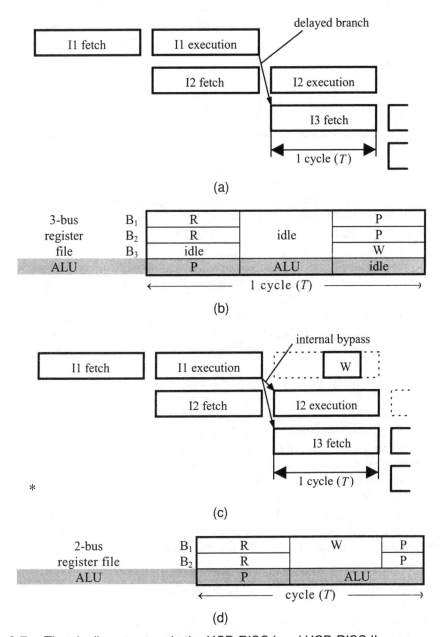

Figure 6-7. The pipeline structure in the UCB-RISC I and UCB-RISC II processors: (a) UCB-RISC I pipeline, (b) UCB-RISC I datapath, (c) UCB-RISC II pipeline; and (d) UCB-RISC II datapath. R—register read; ALU—arithmetic/logic operation; W—register write; P—precharge; IDLE—idle interval.

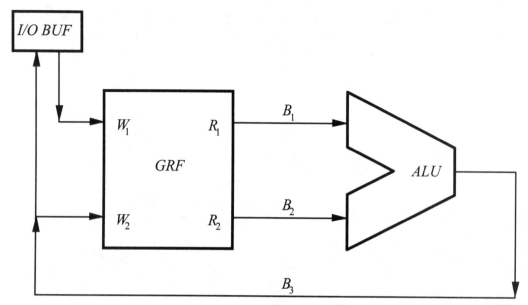

Figure 6-8. An example of the critical data path: *I/O BUF*—input/output buffer; B_1, B_2, B_3—internal busses; *GRF*—general purpose register file; *ALU*—arithmetic and logic unit; R_1, R_2—read port 1, read port 2; W_1, W_2—write port 1, write port 2.

During the third part of the second pipeline stage (lasting approximately the same time), buses B1 and B2 are being precharged, bus B3 is being used to write the result to the GRF (or to the *I/O_BUF*), and the ALU is idle.

To conclude, in the pipeline shown in Figure 6-7(a) and (b), each resource is idle for at least one-third of the clock cycle. Therefore, RISC II has devoted special attention to pipeline optimization and the number of buses was reduced to two. One bus (*B2*) also serves for the result write.

For educational reasons, the following paragraphs discuss the simplified version of the RISC II processor. The quantitative values should be viewed with this restriction in mind. Since the same technology was applied to both RISC I and RISC II, the timing of the second and the third stages of the pipeline in RISC II was approximately the same as the timing of the second pipeline stage in the RISC I. However, faster memory chips (twice as fast) were chosen, with the goal of maximizing the resource utilization. When details of Figure 6-7(a)–(d) are compared, one should remember that the time scales are different.

Figure 6-7(d) shows the second pipeline stage, where the operands are read and transferred to the ALU (via the buses in the first part of the stage), and the ALU operates (in the second part of the stage). During the third pipeline stage, the result write to the GRF and the precharge take place. As shown in Figure 6-7(d), the resources are permanently utilized.

6.2.4   Instruction Format of the UCB-RISC

Figure 6-9 shows the instruction format of the UCB-RISC. The *opcode field* is seven bits wide (bits 25–31) and encodes only 39 instructions with very simple decoder logic. Depending on what is being taken into account, 2–10 percent of the chip area is dedicated to the decoder logic (for example, in the CISC processor Motorola 68000, about 68 percent of the chip area is dedicated to the decoder logic). The *SCC field* (bit 24) defines the purpose of the next field (*DEST*, bits 19–23). It can contain either the destination register address (R_d) or the condition flag specification for the branch instruction (*COND*).

Two basic instruction formats exist: one with a short immediate operand and the other with a long immediate operand.

6.2.4.1   The Short Immediate Operand Format   In the short immediate operand format, the bits 0–18 are organized in the following manner: the R_{S1} field contains the specification of the first operand source register; the *shortSOURCE$_2$* field contains the specification of the second operand source register if bit number 13 is zero (R_{S2}) or the 13-bit immediate operand if bit number 13 is one (*imm*13).

6.2.4.2.   The Long Immediate Operand Format   In the long immediate operand format, bits 0–18 define the 19-bit long immediate operand, as indicated in Figure 6-9.

6.2.4.3   Other Instruction Aspects   The opcode, shown in Figure 6-9, covers only the most elementary operations:

a)   **integer add** (with or without carry)
b)   **integer sub** (with or without borrow)
c)   **integer inverse sub** (with or without borrow)
d)   **boolean and**
e)   **boolean or**
f)   **boolean xor**
g)   **shift ll** (0–31 bits)
h)   **shift lr** (0–31 bits)
i)   **shift ar** (0–31 bits)

All instructions have the three-address format:

$$R_D \leftarrow R_{S1} \text{ op } S_2$$

Here R_D is the destination register, R_{S1} is the first operand source register, and S_2 is the second operand source register. The second operand can be one of the general-purpose registers from the GRF (Figure 6-8), the program counter *PC*, or a part of the instruction register *IR* if the immediate second operand is used.

The fact that the number of supported operations is this restricted can be a surprise. However, the authors of the UCB-RISC architecture claim that the list could have been even shorter had the **integer inverse sub** operation been left out (this operation performs the subtraction of the type $-A + B$, as opposed to the subtraction of the type $A - B$). Originally, this operation was thought to be useful for optimization purposes, but this turned out to be false.

The list lacks the **shift arithmetic left** and **rotate** instructions. They were left out because statistical analyses have shown that they are scarce in compiled code, and they can be easily synthesized from the available instructions.

Further, there are no usual **move, increment, decrement, complement, negate, clear,** and **compare** instructions. All of these instructions can be synthesized using only one instruction and the R_0 register, which is wired to 0 (reading from this register, zero is read; writing to it has no effect):

a)	**move**	**add**	$[R_D \leftarrow R_S + R_0]$
b)	**increment**	**add**	$[R_D \leftarrow R_S + 1]$
c)	**decrement**	**add**	$[R_D \leftarrow R_S + (-1)]$
d)	**complement**	**sub**	$[R_D \leftarrow R_0 - R_s]$
e)	**negate**	**xor**	$[R_D \leftarrow R_S \text{ xor } (-1)]$
f)	**clear**	**add**	$[R_D \leftarrow R_0 + R_0]$
g)	**compare**	**sub**	$[R_D \leftarrow R_{S1} - R_{S2} / \text{set } CC]$

The symbol CC refers to the status indicator and (-1) refers to the immediate operand -1.

6.2.5 The load and store Instructions

As said before, **load** and **store** are the only instructions that can access the memory. The following paragraphs will discuss their actualization in the UCB-RISC. Figure 6-10 shows the **load** instruction and Figure 6-11 shows the **store** instruction.

6.2.5.1 The load Instructions   Figure 6-10(a) depicts the data types that can be stored in the memory, which is byte-addressable. Words (32-bit data) can only be stored on the addresses divisible by four. Half-words (16-bit data) can only be stored on the even addresses. Bytes (8-bit data) can be stored anywhere.

Figure 6-10(b) shows the data transformations that occur during the execution of the five various types of **load**. The **load word** instruction loads a 32-bit value into the corresponding register with no transformations. The instruction **load halfword unsigned** loads a 16-bit value and transforms it into a 32-bit value by zeroing out the high order bits. The instruction **load halfword signed** does the same, except that it extends the sign (bit number 15) of the loaded data into the high order bits. The instructions **load byte unsigned** and **load byte signed** perform the same for the 8-bit values.

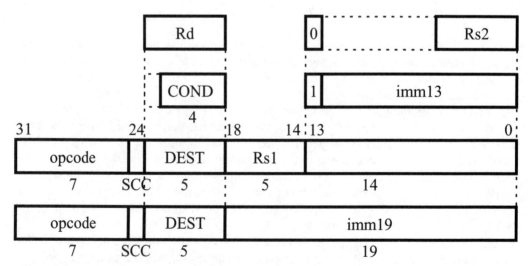

Figure 6-9.   Instruction format of the UCB-RISC: *DEST*—destination; *SCC*—bit that determines whether the *DEST* field is treated as a destination register (R_d) or as a condition code (*COND*); R_{s1}, R_{s2}—source registers; *imm*13, *imm*19—immediate data—13 or 19 bits.

word at address 0				0
word at address 4				4
half-word at address 10		half-word at address 8		8
byte at address 15	byte at address 14	half-word at address 12		12
byte at address 19	byte at address 18	byte at address 17	byte at address 16	16
half-word at address 22		byte at address 21	byte at address 20	20

(a)

word		
0 0 0 0 0 0 0 0 0 0 0 0 0 0 0 0	s	half-word
s s s s s s s s s s s s s s s s	s	half-word
0 0 0 0 0 0 0 0 0 0 0 0 0 0 0 0 0 0 0 0 0 0 0	s	byte
s s s s s s s s s s s s s s s s s s s s s s s	s	byte

(b)

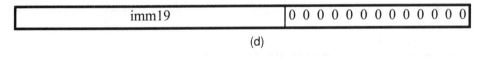

(c)

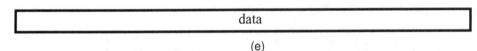

(d)

data

(e)

Figure 6-10. Activities related to the execution of the **load** instruction: (a) Data in memory, (b) register state after **load**, (c) interpretation of immediate data (except **ldhi**), (d) interpretation of immediate data by the **ldhi** instruction, realized in a manner that enables the straightforward formation of the 32-bit immediate operand by using the logical OR (or some other logical function), and (e) data in register after the **load** instruction.

Figure 6-10(c) shows that all instructions (except **ldhi**) work with 13-bit and 19-bit immediate data (*imm*13 and *imm*19). They all load the data into the low order bit positions and extend the sign of the data into the high order bits. This allows the 13-bit immediate operands to be used in many instructions, and the 19-bit immediate operands to be used in a few instructions.

Figure 6-10(d) shows the way in which the **ldhi** instruction treats the 19-bit immediate data. This instruction loads the 19-bit immediate data into 19 high order bit positions, and it zeroes out the 13 low order bit positions. This allows for the synthesis of 32-bit immediate values by using the **ldhi** instruction followed by an **or** instruction with the correct 13-bit immediate value.

Finally, Figure 6-10(e) shows that data in registers can only exist as 32-bit values.

6.2.5.2   The store Instructions   The details of three types of **store** instructions are shown in Figure 6-11(a). The opcode of **store** contains a two-bit field (*WIDTHcode*) which allows the data size to be transferred from the register to the memory. If *WIDTHcode* = 10, then it is the **stw** (**store word**) instruction, and the effective address must have 00 in two low order bits. If *WIDTHcode* = 01, then it is the **sth** (**store halfword**) instruction, and the effective address must have 0 in the lowest order bit position. If *WIDTHcode* = 00, then it is the **stb** (**store byte**) instruction, and the effective address can have any value.

The way in which a low order eight-bit value is written into an eight-bit memory location is depicted in Figure 6-11(b). In this example, in accordance with the table from Figure 6-11(a), two low order bits of the address are 01, and the field *WIDTHcode* contains 00.

	Information Issued by the CPU			Byte Addressed Memory Locations for Write			
Instruction	**WIDTHcodeW**	**WIDTHcodeH**	**eff_addr<1:0>**	**<31:24>**	**<23:16>**	**<15:8>**	**<7:0>**
stw	ON	OFF	00	W	W	W	W
sth	OFF	ON	00			W	W
			10	W	W		
stb	OFF	OFF	00				W
			01			W	
			10		W		
			11	W			

(a)

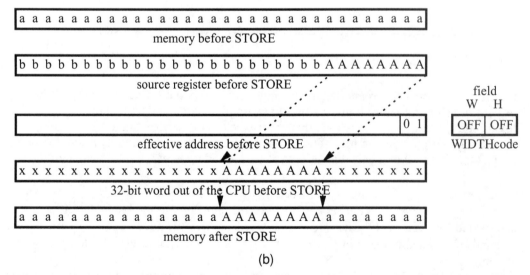

(b)

Figure 6-11.   The **store** instruction related activities: (a) **store** instructions for variable size data which are **stw** (store word), **sth** (store half-word), and **stb** (store byte) and (b) memory write cycle for the **stb** instruction.

6.2.6 The UCB-RISC Addressing Mode

The UCB-RISC has only one addressing mode, and it is used only in the **load** and **store** instructions. In general, the following rule holds true for the **load** instruction:

$$R_D \leftarrow M[R_{S1} + S_2]$$

This means that the effective address is formed by adding the register R_{S1} (one of the general purpose registers) to the register S_2 (one of the general purpose registers, or the program counter, or the immediate data from the instruction register). The register R_D is the destination in the register file.

Through the analogy, the following holds true for the **store** instruction:

$$M[R_{S1} + S_2] \leftarrow R_S$$

Here R_S refers to a source register from the register file. Beginning with this basic addressing mode, three derived addressing modes can be synthesized:

direct (absolute) $M[R_B + imm]$

register indirect $M[R_p + R_0]$

index $M[R_a + R_i]$

In the case of direct addressing, which is used for accessing the global scalar variables, R_B refers to the base register that defines the variable segment starting address of global scalar. In the case of register indirect addressing (used in pointer access), the register R_p contains the address of the pointer. In the case of index addressing (used in accessing the linear data structures), the register R_a contains the starting address of the structure, and R_i contains the displacement of the element inside the structure.

6.2.7 The UCB-RISC Register File Organization

The register file organization in the UCB-RISC has caused some controversy. It was constructed to reduce the number of clock cycles and the number of memory accesses necessary for the **call** and **return** constructs in high-level languages (the statistical analysis pointed out this direction).

By far the greatest number of clock cycles and memory accesses originate from the stack access during the parameter passing and result returning processes in the execution of the **call/return** constructs. Designers of the UCB-RISC architecture came up with an organization, which many claimed was risky rather than RISCy. It covers 138 physical registers inside the CPU, with 32 being visible at any moment. These 32 registers represent a single register bank (this structure is shown in Figure 6-12).

This bank consists of four fields: *HIGH* (six registers), *LOCAL* (10 registers), *LOW* (six registers), and *GLOBAL* (10 registers). The *HIGH* field is used to pass the parameters from the calling procedure to the called procedure. The *LOCAL* field holds the local variables. The *LOW* field is used for passing the results back from the called procedure to the calling procedure. The *GLOBAL* field is used for the global variables.

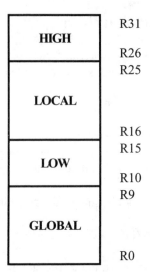

Figure 6-12. Organization of a single register window (bank) in the register file with partially overlapping windows (banks), in the case of the UCB-RISC processor: HIGH—the area through which the data is transferred into the procedure associated to the particular window; LOCAL—the area where the local variables of a procedure are kept; LOW—the area which is used to transfer the parameters from the procedure associated with that window; GLOBAL—the area where the global variables are kept.

Each procedure is dynamically assigned one bank. If the procedure nesting is too deep, the remaining procedures are assigned some space in the memory. Each input/output parameter is assigned a single location in the *HIGH/LOW* fields, and each local/global variable gets its place in the *LOCAL* or *GLOBAL* fields. If the number of parameters exceeds the available space, it gets a place in memory. The number of registers in the *LOCAL, HIGH, LOW,* and *GLOBAL* fields has been chosen in accordance with the results of the statistical analysis. It should be remembered that the R_0 register is wired to zero, leaving nine places in the *GLOBAL* field. Likewise, the program counter is kept in the *LOW* field during calls and actually leaves five registers free.

The banks described are partially overlapping (see Figure 6-13). The bank that will first be assigned to the procedure (A) physically resides in the registers 116–137, plus 0–9; logically, these are the registers $R_0(A)$–$R_{31}(A)$. The bank that will be assigned to the next procedure (B) physically resides in the registers 100–121, plus 0–9; logically, these are the registers $R_0(B)$–$R_{31}(B)$. The total number of these banks is eight. As previously mentioned, a single bank is accessible at a given moment. There is a special pointer guiding it, and it is called *CWP (current window pointer).*

The following conclusions can be drawn from this. First, the *GLOBAL* field physically resides at the same place for all the banks; this is because the global variables must be accessible from everywhere. Second, the *LOW* segment of the bank A (LOW_A), and the *HIGH* field of the bank B ($HIGH_B$) physically reside at the same place, thus allowing efficient parameter passing.

The classical architectures require the parameters from the procedure A (where they are the contents of the LOW_A field) to be transferred first to the memory, and then back to the registers of the processor and into the procedure B (where they become the contents of the $HIGH_B$ field). Since these two fields physically overlap in the UCB-RISC processor (despite their different logical purposes), the complete parameter passing mechanism occurs through the change of a single register contents (*CWP*). Therefore, if the parameter count was N and all parameters were already in the LOW field, the number of memory accesses drops from $2N$ to zero. If some were in the memory (K of them), because there was not enough space in the LOW field, the number of memory accesses drops from $2(N + K)$ to $2K$.

The *CWP* register is updated during the execution of the **call** and **return** instructions. In the case of the call of procedure B from procedure A, one might think that the value of *CWP* changes from 137 to 121; however, since there are eight banks, this need not be so. In fact, *CWP* is a three-bit register, and its contents were changed from seven to six.

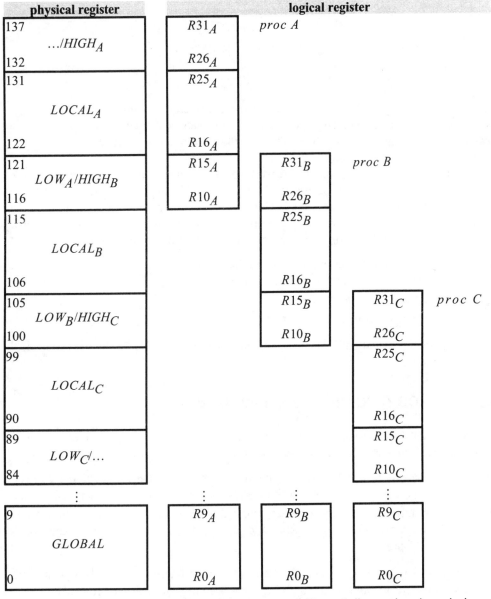

Figure 6-13. Logical organization of the memory with partially overlapping windows: *proc A, B, C*—procedures *A, B, C*.

The entire register file is organized as a circular buffer (see Figure 6-14). This means that the *LOW* field of the last procedure physically overlaps the *HIGH* field of the first procedure. The equation that determines the total number of registers in GRF is:

$$N_{R,TOTAL} = N_P(N_{R,HIGH} + N_{R,LOCAL}) + N_{R,GLOBAL}$$

Here, $N_{R,TOTAL}$ is the total number of registers, N_P is the number of banks, $N_{R,HIGH}$ is the number of registers in the *HIGH* field, $N_{R,LOCAL}$ is the number of registers in the *LOCAL* field, and $N_{R,GLOBAL}$ is the number of registers in the *GLOBAL* field. In the UCB-RISC, the following holds true:

$$N_P = 8,$$

$$N_{R,LOW} = N_{R,HIGH} = 6,$$

$$N_{R,LOCAL} = N_{R,GLOBAL} = 10,$$

$$N_{R,TOTAL} = 138.$$

In the RISC processor SOAR (developed at the University of California at Berkeley, and oriented towards the high-level language Smalltalk), the statistical analysis has shown that it is best to have eight registers in each field. The formula mentioned above gives the total number of registers equal to 136.

Figure 6-14 also shows another three-bit special register, the *SWP (saved window pointer)*. An overflow situation occurs if, during the execution of the **call** instruction, the contents of *SWP* and *CWP* become equal. This means that the procedure nesting is too deep for the architecture and there are no free register banks. In that case, an internal interrupt (trap) is generated wherein the operating system takes over and does the following:

a)   The contents of the bank *A* are stored in the memory,
     making room for the next procedure in line.
b)   The register *SWP* is updated.
c)   The control is returned to the user program.

The reverse situation is called the *underflow*, and it can happen during the execution of the **return** instruction.

6.2.8   The UCB-RISC Processor Test Results

After the UCB-RISC processor was implemented, measurements were performed on real life examples which contained a lot of procedure nesting. The average results were as follows:

a)   The execution speed increased about 10 times over the speed of the Motorola 68000 processor, and about 13 times over the speed of the VAX-11 processor.
b)   The number of memory accesses dropped off about 60 times when compared to the Motorola 68000 processor, and about 100 times when compared to the VAX-11 processor.

These fantastic improvements highlight the fact that wise interventions in the domain of the architecture (for a given application) can bring about a more significant improvement than the careful VLSI design. Therefore, creativity should be directed toward the architecture, and the VLSI design should be considered as the routine task that has to be performed carefully.

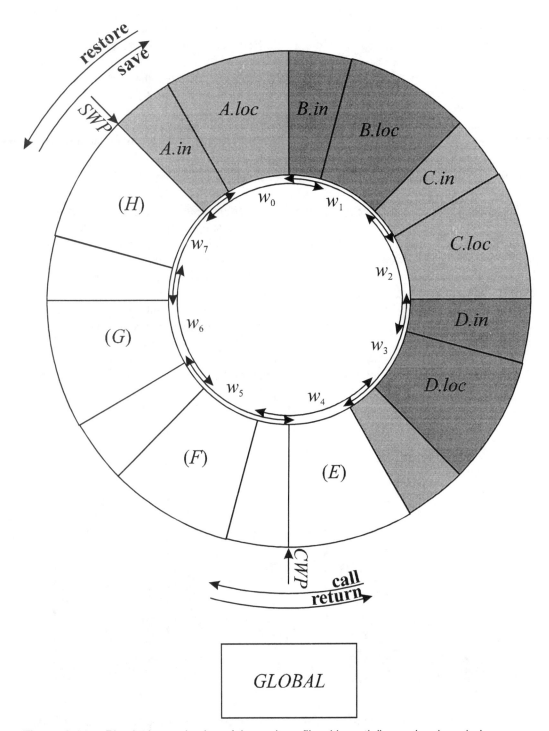

Figure 6-14.   Physical organization of the register file with partially overlapping windows: *CWP*—Current Window Pointer—the contents of this register interacts with the execution of **call** and **return**; *SWP*—Saved Window Pointer—the contents of this register points to the position of the window that has been saved in the main store by the operating system subroutine **save**. Symbols w_i ($i = 0, 1, 2, 3, 4, 5, 6, 7$) refer to the overlapping windows. Symbols *A, B, C, D, E, F, G,* and *H* refer to various procedures. Symbol *GLOBAL* refers to registers R_0–R_9.

Figure 6-15 shows the results of the global speed comparison between the processor UCB-RISC and some other popular machines. Even though the design of the machines used different technologies, results were given in the normalized form. Five benchmarks were chosen, and all without procedure calls (which would be favorable for the UCB-RISC). This way, the influence of the partially overlapping register windows was eliminated; these results should be treated as the minimum performance that can be expected from the UCB-RISC.[*]

Figure 6-15 shows two facts clearly. First, while there is almost no difference between the assembler and high-level language programs for the UCB-RISC, there are vast differences with the other processors—substantial improvements could be achieved if the assembler were used. This is due to the suitability of simple RISC machines for the code optimization. Second, the high-level language code was two to four times faster for the same code optimization technique.

These two facts prove that the RISC architecture can be treated as a HLL architecture. At first, it may seem illogical since RISC instructions are simple, and CISC instructions are complex. However, the prime goal of the HLL architectures is to improve the execution speed of high-level language compiled code. Since RISC processors execute that code faster (two to four times, in the example given in Figure 6-15), they perform better in this role and can therefore be categorized into the HLL architecture class.

All these considerations had a major influence on the modern 32-bit and 64-bit processor design. They should be viewed as the basis for understanding the concepts of modern processors. Because of the evolutionary character of the microprocessor development, the influence of the first 32-bit RISC processors is readily visible in the latest 64-bit microprocessors, too (for example, in the 64-bit microprocessor SuperSparc). For more details on the state-of-the-art 64-bit machines see [36].

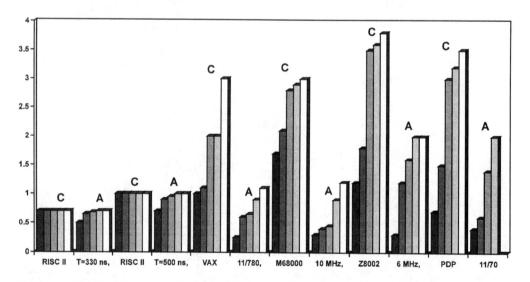

Figure 6-15. An evaluation of the UCB-RISC instruction set: normalized execution times for five procedureless benchmarks, written in C and assembler.

---

[*]Note: According to some researchers, these five benchmarks are rich in integer operations without multiplication, which may create a strong bias in favor of the UCB-RISC.

6.3 Basic Examples: The SU-MIPS

The architecture of the SU-MIPS (Stanford University Microprocessing without Interlocked Pipeline Stages) processor, was also formed in accordance with the general RISC processor design philosophy. This means that like the UCB-RISC, a statistical analysis of the target applications preceded the architecture design.

For educational reasons, this description contains some simplifications or amendments of the basic architecture, organization, and design of the SU-MIPS.

This, again like the UCB-RISC, is also a 32-bit processor. However, the ALU is 34 bits wide, since it supports the Booth algorithm for multiplication (for example, see [34]). The architecture contains 16 general purpose 32-bit registers, and a barrel shifter for shifts of one to 32 bits. There is an instruction that performs the Booth step, with successive two-place shifts. This instruction relies on the 34-bit ALU and the barrel shifter. That way, the multiplication of two 32-bit values takes place in 18 machine cycles.

The pipeline has five stages, and all interlock mechanisms for every type of hazard are realized in software. That means the code is not as easily optimized using the classical methods as with the UCB-RISC. However, significantly greater results can be achieved by using one quite sophisticated code optimization technology. Therefore, the advantages of the SU-MIPS architecture can come to full effect only with good quality code optimization. This is why some researchers view the MIPS design philosophy as the special philosophy of modern microprocessor architecture design.

The architecture of the SU-MIPS processor does not contain condition code, meaning that the computation of the branch condition and the branch itself are performed in the same instruction. In architectures containing condition code, one instruction sets the condition code, and another tests it and executes the branch if the condition is true.

As with the UCB-RISC, the **load** and **store** instructions are also the only ones that can access the memory, and only one addressing mode is supported. Further, because statistical analysis had shown that about 95 percent of the constants can be coded with eight bits, special attention has been devoted to the support of eight-bit constants. Also, the system code support was built in (the majority of previous microprocessor architectures concentrated on providing the user code support only).

6.3.1 Structure of the SU-MIPS Pipeline

Figure 6-16 shows the structure of the pipeline in the SU-MIPS. A new machine instruction is fetched every two clock cycles (one machine cycle).

The *IF stage (instruction fetch)* is used for the new instruction fetch. During the same cycle, the *PC* is incremented by one, and the result is stored into the *PC_NEXT* register:

$$PC\_NEXT = PC + 1$$

The *ID stage (instruction decode)* is used for decoding purposes. Since the time to decode is less than one stage, the rest of the stage time can be used for waiting on a slow memory. The *OD stage (operand decode)* is used differently by various instructions. In each case, the complete datapath cycle is performed, as in Figure 6-8. The memory address is computed during the **load** and **store** instructions. In this stage the ALU operation is performed. For the branch instruction, the branch address is computed and the computed value is placed into the special register *PC_TARGET*. This way, both alternative addresses are defined before the branch condition is known. The condition test is performed during the next pipeline stage.

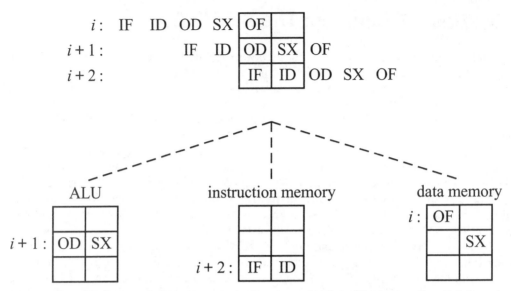

Figure 6-16. The SU-MIPS processor pipeline organization: IF—Instruction Fetch and Program Counter increment; ID—Instruction Decode; OD—Computation of the effective address for **load/store**, computation of the new value of Program Counter in the case of branch instructions, or ALU operation for arithmetic and logical instructions (Operand Decode); SX—Operand read for **store**, compare for branch instructions, or ALU operation for arithmetic and logic instructions (Store/Execute); OF—Operand Fetch (for **load**).

The *SX stage (operand store/execute)* is used differently by various instructions. In each case, the complete datapath cycle is performed, as in Figure 6-8. For the **load** instruction, this stage is used on waiting for the data memory to respond. In the case of the **store** instruction, this stage is used for the transmission of the data to the data bus. This stage can be used to execute a complete ALU operation, meaning that two such operations can take place in one instruction. For the branch instruction, this stage performs the corresponding ALU operation which generates the conditions: these are then tested and the correct value is stored into the *PC*. The value stored is either *PC_NEXT* or *PC_TARGET*. In fact, the outputs of those two registers are connected to the inputs of a multiplexer. Its control input is the corresponding status signal, that is, the condition generated by the ALU.

The *OF stage (operand fetch)* is used only by the **load** instruction.

Figure 6-17 shows all the possible instruction formats of the SU-MIPS. The basic conclusion is that, because the field boundaries are always in the same positions, the instruction decoding is extremely simple. The immediate operands can be 8, 12, 20, or 24 bits wide. However, the eight-bit immediate operand is used in almost all instructions.

6.3.2 Performance Evaluation of the SU-MIPS Processor

Figure 6-18 shows the performance measurement results of the SU-MIPS compared to the Motorola 68000 processor and the superminicomputer DEC 20/60. The results are normalized. The SU-MIPS processor is four to six times faster than Motorola 68000, and marginally slower than DEC 20/60, which is many times more expensive. This high performance is because of the excellent pipeline-aware code optimizer of the SU-MIPS, called the *reorganizer*, which can be treated as a part of the architecture. The reorganizer first moves the

ALU3+ALU2

00$i'i$	dst	alu.3	dst/src	src	alu.2	src2	src1

Jump Based Indirect + ALU2

1110	010i	base	dst/src	src	alu.2	8-bit offset	

Branch Conditionally

1111	000i	cond	src2	src1	12-bit signed offset	

Jump Based

1110	1101	base	20-bit signed offset	

Branch Unconditionally

1110	1110	24-bit signed offset	

Figure 6-17. Instruction formats of the SU-MIPS processor: *alu.2* and *alu.3* refer to the activities in the OD and SX stages of the pipeline. Instruction mnemonics and operand fields are outlined as in the original literature.

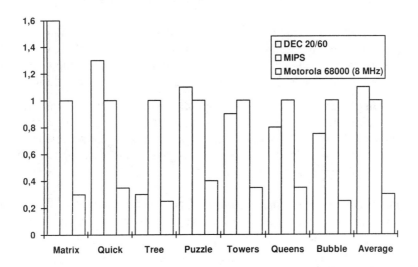

Figure 6-18. Evaluation of the SU-MIPS instruction set: performance data for the eight standard benchmark programs that were formulated at Stanford University, at the request of DARPA, for the evaluation of various RISC processors.

instructions around to avoid the hazards. In places where the hazards cannot be avoided, the reorganizer first inserts the **nop** instructions. Then the instruction packing is performed (if the operation does not use the *OD* or *SX* pipeline stages, one more operation can be inserted next to it, together forming a new instruction with a new operation code). Finally, the assembly process takes place when the machine code is generated.

6.3.3 Definition of Various Hazards

In the following paragraphs, introductory definitions will be given, and then the optimization algorithm for the SU-MIPS processor will be analyzed. The discussion is based on [40]. Generally, there are three hazard types in the pipelined processors: the (nonregister) resource hazards, the (branch-related) sequencing hazards, and the (register-related) timing hazards.

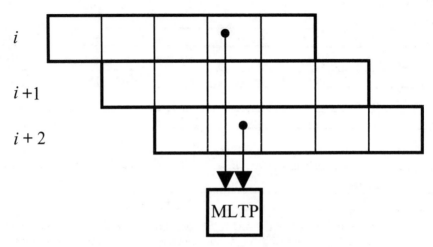

Figure 6-19. An example of resource hazard. Symbol MLTP refers to the hardware multiplier (this is just one possible example).

6.3.3.1 Resource Hazards The *resource hazards* appear when two different instructions in the pipeline require a certain resource simultaneously. One example of the resource hazard is given in Figure 6-19. The instruction i in its fourth pipeline stage, and the instruction $i + 2$ in its second pipeline stage (that is, simultaneously) request the hardware multiplier (MLTP).

6.3.3.2 Sequencing Hazards The *sequencing hazards* appear when n instructions ($n = 1$, 2, ...) which are placed immediately after the branch instruction begin their execution before the branch outcome is known. The actual value of n depends on the processor architecture and organization, and especially on the pipeline organization. This type of hazard was described in some detail earlier in this chapter.

6.3.3.3 Timing Hazards The *timing hazards* appear in a sequence of instructions not containing branches, such as in the cases when inadequate content of a given register is used. There are three subtypes of the timing hazard:

a)   DS (destination-source)
b)   DD (destination-destination)
c)   SD (source-destination)

An example of the *DS hazard* is given in Figure 6-20. In this example, the instruction $i + 1$ reads the contents of the register R_x, before the instruction i writes the new contents into the register R_x. Therefore, the instruction $i + 1$ will read the previous contents of the register R_x. Generally, this will happen if the instruction i is:

$$\textbf{load } R_x$$

and the instruction $i + 1$ is (for example):

$$R_1 = R_2 + R_x,$$

where R_x is the critical register to which the DS hazard is connected.

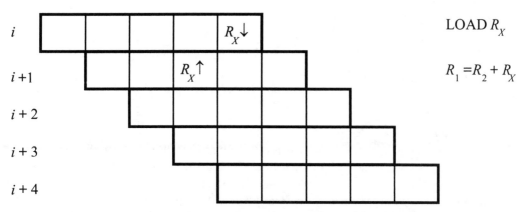

Figure 6-20.   An example of the DS (destination-source) timing hazard: an arrow pointing downwards denotes register write; an arrow pointing upwards denotes register read.

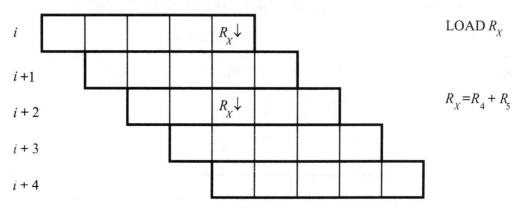

Figure 6-21.   An example of the DD (destination-destination) timing hazard: an arrow pointing downwards denotes register write; an arrow pointing upwards denotes register read.

An example of the *DD hazard* is given in Figure 6-21. In this example, the instructions i and $i + 2$ write to the register R_x simultaneously, the first one in the fifth pipeline stage, and the second one in the third pipeline stage. Therefore, the outcome is uncertain for at least one of the two instructions. Generally, this will happen if the instruction i is:

$$\textbf{load } R_x$$

and the instruction $i + 2$ is (for example):

$$R_x = R_4 + R_5,$$

where R_x is the critical register to which the DD hazard is connected.

An example of the *SD hazard* is shown in Figure 6-22. In this example, the instruction $i + 1$ writes to the register R_x the contents that are supposed to be read by the instruction $i + 2$; however, before it reads the contents of the register R_x, the instruction $i + 3$ writes a new content into the register R_x. Therefore, the instruction $i + 2$ will read the future contents of the register R_x. Generally, this will happen if the instruction $i + 1$ is:

$$R_x = R_1 + R_2,$$

and the instruction $i + 2$ is (for example):

store R_x

while the instruction $i + 3$ is (for example):

$$R_x = R_5 + R_6,$$

where R_x is the critical register to which the SD hazard is connected.

After seeing these examples, it is clear how the mnemonics DS, DD, and SD were coined. The first letter of these mnemonics denotes the usage of the resource by the *earlier* instruction in the sequence, which is either the source (S) or destination (D). The second letter denotes the usage of the resource by the *later* instruction in the sequence, which is either the source (S) or the destination (D).

6.3.4   Examples of Various SU-MIPS Processor Hazards

The examples of various hazards in the SU-MIPS processor will be shown now.

The resource hazard appears only in the case of packing two instructions into one (the first two out of six cases shown in Figure 6-17), and when the resources are accessed which are

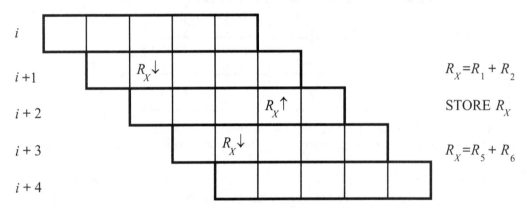

Figure 6-22.   An example of the SD (source-destination) timing hazard: an arrow pointing downwards stands for register write; an arrow pointing upwards stands for register read. In this example, instruction $i + 2$ will read from register R_x the value written there by instruction $i + 3$ (wrong: this is not intended by the programmer who is unaware of the pipeline structure), rather than the value written there by the instruction $i + 1$ (right: this is intended by the programmer, who is unaware of the pipeline structure).

Branch (PC relative) on condition	$n = 1$
Branch (PC relative) unconditionally	$n = 1$
Jump (absolute) via register	$n = 1$
Jump (absolute) direct	$n = 1$
Jump (absolute) indirect	$n = 2$

Figure 6-23.   Sequencing hazards in the SU-MIPS processor: the length of the delayed branch for various instruction types. Symbol n stands for the number of instructions (after the branch instruction) which are executed unconditionally.

physically outside the processor. Therefore, the actual case would depend on the underlying structure of the entire system.

The length of a delayed branch for various instruction types of the SU-MIPS is shown in Figure 6-23. The detailed explanation is given in the figure caption. As previously stated, the delayed branch length n is equal to the number of the **nop** instructions that have to be inserted after the branch instruction during the code generation. These n instructions are always executed unconditionally.

Cases of DS, DD, and SD hazards in the SU-MIPS are depicted in Figure 6-24. A detailed explanation is given in the figure caption. Once again, it is obvious that these hazards can appear only if the instructions are packed.

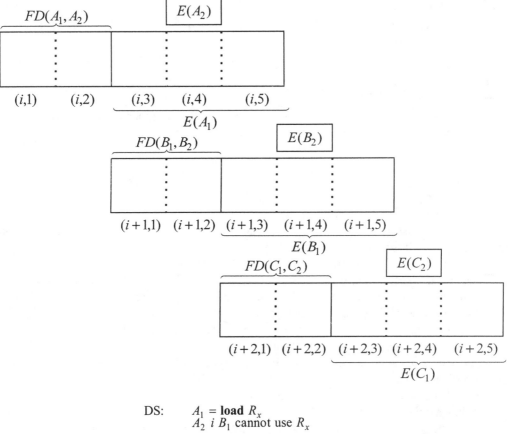

DS: $A_1 = $ **load** R_x
 A_2 i B_1 cannot use R_x

DD: $B_1 = $ **load** R_x
 C_1 cannot use R_x as destination

SD: $C_1 = $ **store** R_x
 C_2 cannot use R_x as destination

Figure 6-24. Timing hazards in the SU-MIPS processor: A_1, B_1, C_1—nominal (primary) instructions; A_2, B_2, C_2—packed (secondary) instructions; i_1, i_2, i_3, i_4, i_5—five stage pipeline for the instruction i; $FD(A_1, A_2)$, $FD(B_1, B_2)$, $FD(C_1, C_2)$—decoding phases for the instructions A, B, C; $E(A_1)$, $E(A_2)$, $E(B_1)$, $E(B_2)$, $E(C_1)$, $E(C_2)$—execution phases for the instructions A, B, C.

6.3.5 Code Optimization

Before the code optimization algorithm is explained, some terms which will be used in the text are to be introduced.

There are two basic approaches to the code optimization (both meant to eliminate hazards) for processors with the software interlock mechanism. They are the *prepass approach*, and the *postpass approach*. In the first case, the optimization is performed before the register allocation, and in the second case it is performed after the allocation. In the first case, better performance is achieved, and in the second case the optimization is simpler. The Gross-Hennessy algorithm [40] uses the postpass approach.

There are two addresses for the branch instruction:

a)   The address t^+ allows the execution to continue if the branch condition is met (branch target).

b)   The address t^- allows the execution to continue if the branch condition is not met (next instruction).

For instance, in the case of the instruction:

    i   **branch on equal** R_1, R_2, L

where *i* is the address of the instruction, and $R_1 = R_2$ is the branch condition, we have the situation where:

$$t^+ = L,$$
$$t^- = i + 1,$$

under the assumption that the above mentioned instruction occupies a single memory location.

The branch instructions can be classified according to the knowledge of t^+ and t^- at compile time. Four classes are obtained this way.

In the first class, t^+ is known at compile time, while t^- has no meaning because this is an unconditional branch. The instructions from this class are: **branch, jump to subroutine**, and **jump direct**. In the second class, both t^+ and t^- are known at compile time. The instruction from this class is **branch on condition**. In the third class, t^+ is not known at compile time, and t^- is known because various system routine calls are in question. The instructions from this class are **trap** and **supervisor call**. In the fourth class, t^+ is not known at compile time, while t^- has no meaning because this class is comprised of the **return from** subroutine and **jump indirect** instructions.

As will be shown later, some optimization schemes are suitable to some branch types, while they are unsuitable for the others.

The order of register reads and writes is also important for the optimization schemes because they move the instructions around. In that sense, a special set $IN(B_j)$ is defined for each basic block B_j ($j = 1, 2, \ldots$); this will be explained later.

6.3.5.1   The Basic Block   The basic block is defined as an instruction sequence beginning and ending in a precisely defined manner. It begins in one of the following ways:

a)   the **org** directive, denoting program beginning,

b)   the labeled instruction, which is a possible branch destination,

c)   the instruction following the branch instruction.

The basic block ends in one of the following ways:

a)   the **end** directive, denoting program end,

b)   the instruction followed by a labeled instruction,

c)   the branch instruction, which is considered to be a part of the basic block.

The basic block is the basis for the Gross-Hennessy algorithm, making it one of the local optimization algorithms. The algorithms that consider the entire code are called global.

The register set $IN(B_j)$ ($j = 1, 2, \ldots$) contains the registers which might be read from before the new contents are written into them by some instructions in the basic block B_j, or by some of the instructions in the basic blocks that follow. This information is routinely being generated during the register allocation process by almost all the optimizing compilers. The importance of the set $IN(B_j)$ will become clear later, when the details of the Gross-Hennessy algorithm are discussed.

6.3.5.2   Three Code Relocation Schemes   Central to the Gross-Hennessy algorithm are three code relocation schemes, which should be combined properly. First, they will be explained, then it will be shown how to combine them in different situations. All three schemes assume that the code generator has already inserted the required **nop** instructions after each branch instruction, regardless of its type (absolute, relative, conditional, or unconditional). The entire analysis holds for each branch type. Here n refers to the number of instructions immediately following the branch instruction, that will be unconditionally executed, regardless of the branch outcome.

Scheme number one, if it can be applied, saves both time (by reducing the number of cycles required for the code execution) and space (by reducing the number of memory locations it occupies) by not executing or storing the **nop** instructions. This scheme relocates the n instructions from the basic block ending with the branch instruction to the place of the n **nop** instructions immediately following the branch instruction. This way, the **nop** instructions are eliminated, saving time (because the **nop** instructions are not executed), and space (because the **nop** instructions are eliminated). This scheme can always be applied if there are no data dependencies between the relocated instructions and both the branch instruction and the instructions that compute the branch condition. The details are shown in Figure 6-25.

Scheme number two (Figure 6-26), if it can be applied, saves time only if the branch occurs; it does not save space. This scheme duplicates the code by copying the n instructions (it starts from the address t^+) over the n **nop** instructions following the branch instruction. The branch address has to be modified so that it will point to address $t^+ + n$. The described code duplication eliminates the **nop** instructions, but it also copies the n useful instructions leaving the code size intact. This scheme can be used to optimize only those branches where t^+ is known at compile time, and the instructions can be copied only if they do not change the contents of the registers in the set $IN(t^-)$. This is necessary to avoid the fatal modification of some register's contents in the case that the branch does not occur, which would result in an incorrect program. If the branch occurs, everything is okay, and n cycles are saved because the branch destination is moved n instructions forward, and the skipped n instructions execute regardless of the branch outcome. If the branch instruction occurs k times, and does not occur l times, this scheme saves $n \cdot k$ cycles and zero memory locations.

In high-level language constructs **do-loop** and **repeat-until,** the loop body usually executes several times, and the loop condition is usually tested at the loop end; the branch occurs more often than not, making scheme number two suitable for these types of loops. The details are shown in Figure 6-26.

Scheme number three (Figure 6-27), if it can be applied, saves time if the branch does not occur; it always saves space. It relocates n instructions from the block immediately following the n **nop** instructions over the **nop**s; these are located immediately after the branch instruction. Since the **nop**s are eliminated, space is saved. This scheme can be used for optimization of the branches where t^- is known at compile time, and the only instructions that can be moved are those which do not change the contents of the registers in the set $IN(t^+)$. This way, if the branch occurs, the instructions following the branch instruction (which are unconditionally executed) will not have fatal consequences on the program execution. If the branch does not occur, everything is okay, and n cycles are saved because the **nop** instructions are not executed. If the branch occurs k times, and it does not occur l times, this scheme saves $n \cdot k$ cycles and n memory locations.

In the high-level language construct **do-while,** the loop body is usually executed several times and the condition is tested at the loop entrance, with high probability that the branch will not occur. Therefore, the scheme number three is suitable for these loops. The details are shown in Figure 6-27.

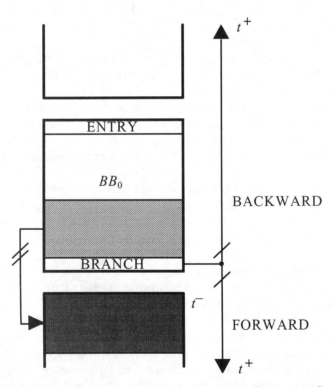

Figure 6-25. Code optimization scheme number one, according to the *Gross-Hennessy* algorithm. The lines with arrowheads and single dash show the possible branch directions, forward or backward. The line with arrowhead and double dash shows the method of the code relocation. The hatched block stands for the initial position of the code that is to be relocated. The crosshatched block stands for the space initially filled (using the **nop** instructions) by the code generator. Symbol BB_0 refers to the basic block that is being optimized.

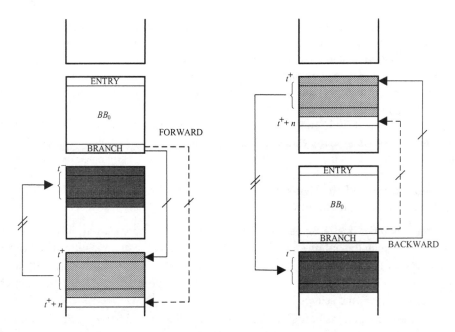

Figure 6-26. Code optimization scheme number two, according to the *Gross-Hennessy* algorithm. The lines with arrowheads and single dash show the possible branch direction, before the code optimization (solid line), and after the code optimization (dotted line). The line with arrowhead and double dash shows the method of code duplication. The hatched blocks stand for the initial code positions before the duplication. The crosshatched blocks stand for the space initially filled (using the **nop** instructions) by the code generator. Symbol BB_0 refers to the basic block that is being optimized.

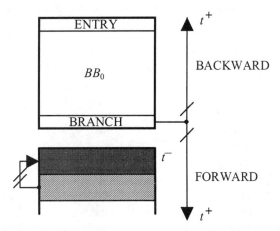

Figure 6-27. Code optimization scheme number three, according to the *Gross-Hennessy* algorithm. The lines with arrowheads and single dash show the possible branch direction. The lines with arrowheads and double dashes show the code relocation. The hatched block stands for the initial position of the block that will be relocated. The crosshatched block stands for the space which is initially left blank by the code generator (that is, it contains the **nop** instructions). Symbol BB_0 refers to the basic block that is being optimized.

In conclusion, scheme number one is always suitable, because it saves both time and space. Scheme number two saves time only when the branch occurs, making it suitable for optimization of backward branches where the probability that the branch will occur is high. Scheme number three saves time only when the branch does not occur; it is suitable for optimization of the forward branches, which have approximately equal probabilities of happening and not happening. This scheme always saves space.

The space saving property is important because in systems with cache memories, saved space also means saved time. In systems with cache memory, the probability that the code will entirely fit into the cache increases as the code length decreases: this influences the code execution speed.

6.3.5.3 Combinations of the Relocation Schemes   The Gross-Hennessy algorithm combines the three schemes in the following way:

a)   Scheme number one is applied first. If the number of eliminated **nop** instructions (k) is equal to n, then the optimization is complete. If $k < n$, the optimization is continued.

b)   The optimization priority is determined (space or time). If time is critical, scheme number two is applied (if possible), and then scheme number three (if possible). If space is critical, the sequence of these two optimizations is reversed.

c)   If all **nop** instructions could not be eliminated, the optimization is finished, and the remaining **nop** instructions stay in the code.

Figure 6-28 shows a segment of the SU-MIPS code before [6-28(a)], and after [(6-28(b)] the optimization where schemes number two and number three were applied.

A segment of the SU-MIPS code where the inadequate register allocation restricted the optimization is depicted in figure 6-29. In the case shown in Figure 6-29(a), the **nop** instruction could not be eliminated as they were in the case shown in Figure 6-29(b). This illustrates the fact that, on average, the prepass optimization gives better results than the postpass optimization.

Figure 6-30 shows two alternative ways of forming the high-level language constructs. The choice of an adequate way can influence the extent of the possible code optimization.

	ld	*A, R6*		ld	*A, R6*
	mov	*#0, R13*		mov	*#0, R13*
	ble	*R6, R13, L3*		ble	*R6, R13, L3*
	nop			sub	*#1, R12*
L1:	sub	*#1, R12*	*L2:*	st	*R12, 3(SP)*
	st	*R12, 3(SP)*		st	*R13, 2(SP)*
	st	*R13, 2(SP)*		jsr	*DUSAN*
	jsr	*DUSAN*		storepc	*1(SP)*
	storepc	*1(SP)*		st	*R0, n(R13)*
	st	*R0, n(R13)*		add	*#1, R13*
	add	*#1, R13*		bgt	*R6, R13, L2*
	bgt	*R6, R13, L1*		sub	*#1, R12*
	nop		*L3:*	...	
L3:	...				
	(a)			(b)	

Figure 6-28.   An example of the code optimization based on the *Gross-Hennessy* algorithm for the SU-MIPS processor: (a) The situation after the code generation and (b) the situation after the code optimization. The details of the SU-MIPS assembly language can be found in [41].

ld	*X, R2*		**ld**	*X, R1*
add	*R2, R0*		**add**	*R1, R0*
ld	*Y, R2*		**ld**	*Y, R2*
bz	*R2, L*		**bz**	*R2, L*
nop			**nop**	

(a)   (b)

Figure 6-29   An example which shows the effects of register allocation on the code optimization: (a) An inadequate register allocation can decrease the probability of efficient code optimization and (b) an adequate register allocation can increase the probability of efficient code optimization. The details of the SU-MIPS assembly language can be found in [41].

6.4   Summary

The architecture and code optimization of the SU-MIPS processor have left a trace in the RISC machine domain. At Stanford University, research continued on the X-MIPS processor which was oriented toward multiprocessing. The MIPS Systems company developed the MIPS architecture into the R2000/R3000/R4000 families, and the more modern families lately such as R10000), which have proven to be very successful in modern workstations. Finally, the SU-MIPS architecture served as the basis of the silicon and GaAs versions of the processors for the MIPS for Star Wars project.

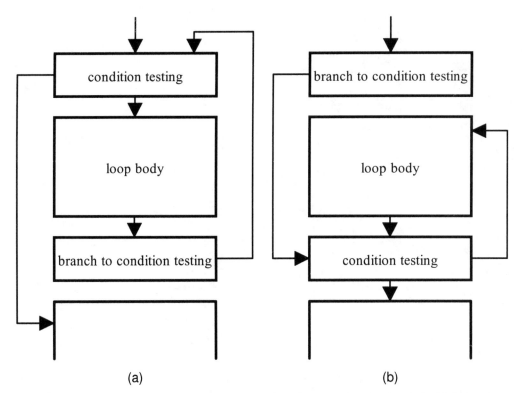

(a)   (b)

Figure 6-30.   Two alternative methods of code generation for the loops in high-level languages: (a) The condition testing is performed at the top and (b) the condition testing is performed at the bottom.

The previously discussed early work on code optimization for pipelined machines has paved the way for the on-going work in branch prediction, speculative execution, and predicated execution in superpipelined and superscalar machines. For more details on these subjects, see [30] and [34], or one of the tutorials presented periodically by Professor Patt at major conferences in the field.

7

RISC: Some Technology-Related Aspects of the Problem

This chapter first discusses the impact of new technologies, and then analyzes a special case: the 32-bit gallium-arsenide microprocessor, a product of RCA (now GE).

7.1 Impacts of New Technologies

Apart from the introductory notes on the achievements of the submicron silicon technology, the rest of this discussion centers on the 1 μm GaAs technology. General aspects of this technology are analyzed, both in the area of direct impact of the technology on the computer architecture (the influence of the reduced chip area and the change in the relative delay between the VLSI chips), and in the area of indirect impact (changes in the way of thinking).

The reason for choosing the GaAs technology for the basis of this chapter is not the belief that some readers will participate in the development of GaAs chips. On the contrary, this is highly unlikely. The real reason is that the technological impact is more dramatic and easier to notice with GaAs than with silicon: the examples are clearer and more convincing.

7.1.1 Submicron Silicon Technology and Microprocessors

Submicron silicon technology enabled the realization of the first 64-bit RISC microprocessors on a VLSI chip. A brief mention of some is in order [36].

The first 64-bit microprocessor was the Intel 860. It existed in two variants, the simpler i860XR (around 1 million transistors) and the more complex i860XP (around 2.5 million transistors). Intel has launched other general-purpose 64-bit microprocessors: the Pentium (around 3.1 million transistors in the 0.8 μm BiCMOS technology), and the PentiumPro.

In 1992, technical details of a few 64-bit microprocessors on the VLSI chip were revealed. Some basic facts on these microprocessors are given below.

The ALPHA microprocessor of DEC (Maynard, MA) was clocked at 200 MHz in 1992. It has a superscalar architecture which can execute two instructions in one clock cycle, and its potential peak speed is 400 MIPS. There are 1.68 million transistors on the chip, which is based on the 0.75 μm CMOS technology. Two 8K cache memories are included into the architecture; one for instructions and the other for data. Also, a 96K secondary data cache.

The SuperSparc microprocessor of Sun Microsystems (Mountain View, CA) and Texas Instruments (Dallas, TX) was clocked at 40 MHz in 1992. It has a superscalar architecture which can execute three instructions in one clock cycle, and its potential peak speed is about 120 MIPS. There are 3.1 million transistors on the chip, which is based on the 0.8 µm BiCMOS technology. Two cache memories are included into the architecture; one is a 20K instruction cache and the other is a 16K data cache.

The microprocessor of Hitachi Central Research Laboratory (Tokyo, Japan) was clocked at 250 MHz in 1992. It has a superscalar architecture which can execute four instructions in one clock cycle, and its potential peak speed is about 1000 MIPS. There are over three million transistors on the chip, which is based on the 0.3 µm BiCMOS technology. Two superscalar processors comprise its architecture, with the total of four 36K cache memories (the cache memory capacity will grow in the versions to follow).

Motorola introduced a series of 64-bit microprocessors under the name PowerPC (in cooperation with IBM and Apple). The first chip in the series is PowerPC 601. This processor has about the same speed as the Pentium for scalar operations, and is about 40 percent faster for the floating-point operations. It was clocked at 66 MHz in 1992. The PowerPC version 602 is oriented toward battery-powered computers. The PowerPC version 603 is oriented toward high-end personal computers, while the PowerPC version 620 is oriented toward high-end workstations.

Other companies like Hewlett Packard and MIPS Systems have their own 64-bit microprocessors (Precision Architecture and MIPS 10000).

7.1.2   GaAs Technology

On the other hand, 1 µm GaAs technology has made practical the realization of a 15-year-old dream of a complete microprocessor on a single GaAs chip. A few microprocessors from this category will be mentioned.

As previously said, the DARPA's first attempt resulted in three experimental microprocessors based on the SU-MIPS architecture. While this attempt did not produce the commercial effect, it showed that a 32-bit microprocessor can be made in GaAs technology.

The following attempt by DARPA was oriented toward the academic environment. Funds were allocated to the University of Michigan and the development lasted from 1992 to 1995. Their research and development was elaborated in several papers (such as [43] and [44]).

Simultaneously, several companies in the US started indigenous efforts to develop central processing units based on the GaAs technology. The CRAY, CONVEX, and SUN were among them. Investors started with the assumption that the CPU cost had little effect on the overall computer system cost (together with the peripherals), and the CPU speed significantly influenced the total speed of the system (for a given application).

In addition, there are several universities cooperating with industry in the research oriented toward the future generations of GaAs microprocessors. Among them are Berkeley, Stanford, and Purdue. This research is multidimensional in its nature (technology, packaging, cooling, superconductivity, and so on). For details, readers are advised to browse through [45] and the more recent references.

7.1.3   The Impact of GaAs Technology on Microprocessor Architecture

The impact of new technologies on the microprocessor architecture can be examined from various angles. Because its effects are very prominent, the following paragraphs will focus only on the influence of the GaAs technology. In addition, this discussion can be viewed as an introduction into the special case analysis, which will follow shortly.

In general, the advantages of the GaAs technology over silicon are:

a) With equal power consumption, GaAs is about one-half order of magnitude faster. In the beginning of eighties, GaAs was a full order of magnitude faster, but since then some significant improvements have been made to the silicon CMOS technology. However, there are two reasons that GaAs is expected to return to the speed one order of magnitude faster than silicon in the future. First, carrier mobility is six to eight times greater with GaAs (at room temperature). Second, GaAs allows a finer basic geometry (λ). Silicon shows problems with λ smaller than 0.25 μm, while GaAs holds on even below 0.1 μm. Of course, the actual values change with time. When first attempting to develop a 32-bit silicon microprocessor for the Star Wars project, DARPA used silicon technology which was more mature than GaAs technology, but it could not be based on less than 1.25 μm; although it was relatively new, the GaAs technology could be based on 1 μm.

b) In GaAs technology, it is relatively easy to integrate the electronic and optical components on a single chip or wafer. This is especially important for connecting microprocessors either to other microprocessors or to the outside environment.

c) GaAs is more tolerant than silicon to temperature variations. GaAs chips function in the temperature range of $-200°$C to $+200°$C. This is important for projects like Star Wars because of low temperatures in space and the upper atmosphere.

d) GaAs is much more rad-hard than silicon (unless special techniques are used). Its resistance to radiation is approximately four times greater (depending upon the certain types of radiation). This is also very important for projects like Star Wars, because missile and aircraft trajectories cross high-level radiation zones.

The disadvantages of GaAs to silicon are:

a) Wafer dislocation density is relatively high. In order to increase the number of faultless chips from the wafer, the chip size must be decreased (under the assumption that the chip is unacceptable if it contains even a single fault, which is not always the case). This leads to relatively small transistor counts for the GaAs chips. The number of transistors in the project described in this book was limited to 30,000. This does not mean that the transistor count of a single GaAs chip is technologically limited to 30,000. It only means that, considering the technology of the period, the technoeconomical analysis preceding the project indicated that the percentage of chips without faults would be unacceptable if the transistor count was increased.

b) GaAs has a smaller noise margin. This can be compensated by increasing the area of the geometric structures, thus increasing the area of standard cells. This effect adds to the problem of low transistor count. If the areas of the standard cells with the same function are compared in GaAs and silicon, the GaAs standard cell will have a somewhat larger area, even though the basic geometry is smaller (1 μm for GaAs, versus 1.25 μm for silicon).

c) The GaAs technology is up to about two orders of magnitude more expensive than the silicon technology. This occurs for two reasons. One is a permanent reason (Ga and As are relatively rare on earth, the synthesis of GaAs is costly, quality tests of that synthesis are also costly, and so on). The other is attributed to temporary factors which might be eliminated through further developments of the technology (compared to the aluminum used in silicon chips, GaAs chips require gold instead for interconnects; also, the GaAs is brittle and easily damaged during the manufacturing process, decreasing the yield still further, and so on).

d)   Testing the GaAs chips is a bit of a problem, because the existing test equipment often cannot test the chip through its full frequency range.

These general properties of GaAs technology have some influence on the design and architecture of microprocessors:

a)   Small chip area and low transistor count lead to complex systems being realized either on several chips in hardware, or predominantly in software with a minimum hardware support.

b)   The relatively large on-chip/off-chip speed ratio (which is the consequence of fast GaAs technology) together with the usage of practically the same packaging and printed circuit board technology silicon uses. This leads to the highly desirable single-chip systems with comprehensive software support as compared to the multi-chip devices. This point will be illuminated later.

c)   The fan-in and fan-out factors of GaAs are lower than in silicon. Standard cells with large fan-in are slower. This makes the usage of the basic elements with low input count more attractive. As a consequence, optimal solutions in the silicon technology are not at all optimal in GaAs, and vice versa. Some solutions which are pointless in silicon show excellent performance in GaAs. Later in this book, several examples illustrating this point will be mentioned.

d)   In some applications, there is a purpose for increasing the wafer yield through the incor-poration of the architectural solutions that enable one or several dislocations on the chip to be tolerated. These methods also increase the transistor count, for a constant yield.

The design of GaAs integrated circuits can be done using various techniques. For instance, in the project described in this book, one team used the bipolar GaAs technology (TI+CDC), the other team used the JFET GaAs technology (McDonnell Douglas), while the third team used the E/D-MESFET GaAs technology (RCA).

7.1.4   Comparative Values Between GaAs and Silicon Chips

Figure 7-1 shows the typical (conservative) data on speed, power consumption, and transistor count. The data on SRAM with capacity of 102.3KB should not be confusing; it represents a laboratory experiment, with the yield almost equal to zero.

A comparison between GaAs and silicon (based on very conservative data) regarding the complexity and speed is shown in Figure 7-2. The point worth remembering is that memory access time depends on the memory capacity (the number of bits per word) and the physical arrangement of the memory and the processor (same chip, different chips on the same mod-ule, different modules on the same printed circuit board, different printed circuit boards, and so on). This is why significant effort is being put into packaging technologies which will enable a large number of chips to be packed into a single module.

Figure 7-3 shows a comparison between GaAs and silicon for an actual 32-bit microproc-essor developed by RCA for the Star Wars project. The marked differences exist in the areas of fan-in and fan-out, noise margins, and transistor count. The CPUs share almost the same complexity, and the drastic difference in transistor counts comes from the inclusion of the on-chip instruction cache memory in the silicon version (if there is room for only one cache memory, the advantage is given to the instruction cache).

Having all this in mind, the question regarding the basic realization strategy of GaAs processors can be answered.

	Speed (ns)	Dissipation (W)	Complexity (K transistors)
Arithmetic			
32-bit adder (BFL D-MESFET)	2.9 total	1.2	2.5
16 × 16-bit multiplier (DCFL E/D MESFET)	10.5 total	1.0	10.0
Control			
1K gate array (STL HBT)	0.4/gate	1.0	6.0
2K gate array (DCFL E/D MESFET)	0.08/gate	0.4	8.2
Memory			
4Kbit SRAM (DCFL E/D MODFET)	2.0 total	1.6	26.9
16K SRAM (DCFL E/D MESFET)	4.1 total	2.5	102.3

Figure 7-1. Typical (conservative) data for speed, dissipation, and complexity of digital GaAs chips.

	GaAs (1 μm E/D-MESFET)	Silicon (2 μm NMOS)	Silicon (2 μm CMOS)	Silicon (1.25 μm CMOS)	Silicon (2 μm ECL)
Complexity					
On-chip transistor count	40K	200K	200K	400K	40K (T or R)
Speed					
Gate delay (minimal fan-out)	50–150 ps	1–3 ns	800–1000 ps	500–700 ps	150–200 ps
On-chip memory access (32 × 32 bit capacity)	0,5–2,0 ns	20–40 ns	10–20 ns	5–10 ns	2–3 ns
Off-chip, on package memory access (256 × 32 bits)	4–8 ns	40–80 ns	30–40 ns	20–30 ns	6–10 ns
Off-package memory access (1k × 32 bits)	10–50 ns	100–200 ns	60–100 ns	40–80 ns	20–80 ns

Figure 7-2. Comparison (conservative) of GaAs and silicon, in terms of complexity and speed of the chips (assuming equal dissipation). Symbols *T* and *R* refer to the transistors and the resistors, respectively. Data on silicon ECL technology complexity includes the transistor count increased for the resistor count.

7.1.5 Basic Realization Strategy for GaAs Processors

Figure 7-4 shows an example of the bit-slice (BS) strategy, from the times when relatively fast bipolar technology with low packaging density was used in CPU realizations (for instance, the AMD 2900 series). This strategy was worthy in the seventies, when this particular silicon technology (which was considered fast in those days) was not linked to the problem of an extremely large off-chip/on-chip delay ratio; this delay ratio is used when comparing GaAs and today's fastest silicon technologies (it is assumed that both use the same packaging and printed circuit board technologies). When the off-chip delays are significant, the horizontal communication losses lead to serious performance degradations (an example of the horizontal communication is the carry propagation between the ALU blocks in BS structures). Still, some companies offer GaAs BS components with a speed advantage of about 50 percent over their silicon counterparts. These are up to an order of magnitude more costly than their silicon counterparts and this seems to defy economic logic. In some cases, however, this might be justified since there are applications in which even a tiniest speedup is important, regardless of the cost.

Figure 7-5 shows an example of the function-slice strategy (FS), which was brought into existence at the time when it was possible to build 16-bit or 32-bit slices of the BS structure (for instance, the AMD 29300 series). This strategy was used in the eighties, and although it almost eliminated the problem of horizontal communications, off-chip delays were still prominent. This strategy offered a 100 percent better performance, which was better than the BS strategy, but it still was not enough for the uncompromised market battle with silicon. There were attempts to realize the Motorola 68000 with this strategy by using several GaAs chips.

The solution seems to be in creating an architecture wherein the microprocessor is on a single chip. In order to put the entire microprocessor on a single GaAs chip, it must be exceedingly simple; meaning that its architecture is bound to be of the RISC type (and very simple, too). Anything not directly supported in hardware must be realized in software; considering the hardware, the supporting software is going to be relatively complex.

In other words, while there is a dilemma in silicon concerning the use of the RISC or CISC processor, the GaAs is bound to the RISC as the only solution. There remains one more question, concerning the type of RISC architecture for GaAs.

7.1.6 RISC Architecture for GaAs

In order to reduce the need for long off-chip delays during the instruction execution, the following things need to be done:

a)   For the instruction fetching, a prefetch buffer is mandatory, and (if there is still some room left on the chip) the instruction cache is useful. Since the execution is sequential (with jumps occurring 10–20 percent of the time), a pipelined organization can speed up the execution.

	GaAs E/D-DCFL	Silicon SOS-CMOS
Minimal geometry	1 μm	1.25 μm
Levels of metal	2	2
Gate delay	250 ps	1.25 ns
Maximum fan-in	5 NOR, 2 AND	4 NOR, 4 NAND
Maximum fan-out	4	20
Noise immunity level	±220 mV	±1.5 V
Average gate transistor count	4.5	7
On-chip transistor count	25,000	100,000–150,000

Figure 7-3. Comparison of GaAs and silicon in the case of actual 32-bit microprocessor implementations (courtesy of RCA). The impossibility of implementing phantom logic (wired-OR) is a consequence of the low noise immunity of GaAs circuits (±200 mV).

b)   For the data fetching, the register file should be large, and data cache is useful if it is large enough. Memory pipelining cannot help much since instructions would still have to wait for the data to arrive to the CPU.

Having this in mind, and knowing that instruction pipelining can be of far greater use than memory pipelining (in the case of limited resources), the best solution is to form as large a register file as possible.[1]

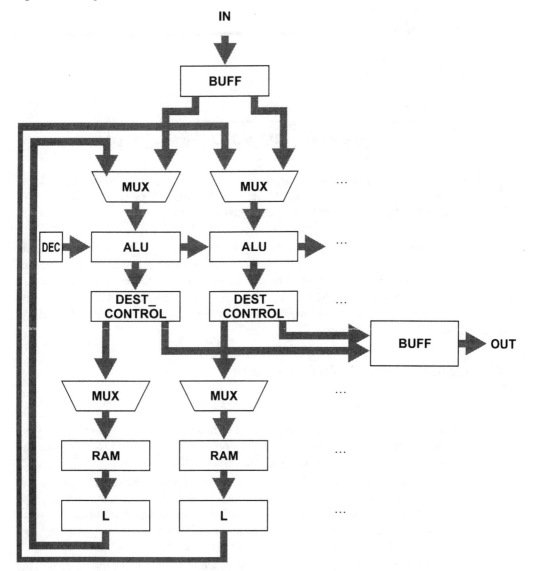

Figure 7-4.   Processor organization based on the BS (bit-slice) components. The meaning of symbols is as follows: IN—input, BUFF—buffer, MUX—multiplexer, DEC—decoder, L—latch, OUT—output. The remaining symbols are standard.

---

[1]In fact, enlarging the register file over some predetermined size (some say it is 32 registers), does not improve things any more; however, because of the restricted transistor count, there is no such danger in GaAs technology today.

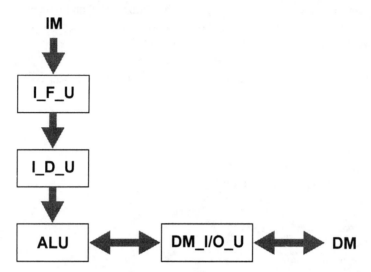

Figure 7-5. Processor organization based on the FS (function slice) components: IM—instruction memory, I_F_U—instruction fetch unit, I_D_U—instruction decode unit, DM_I/O_U—data memory input/output unit, DM—data memory.

Since the large register file absorbs all remaining transistors, there is no chance that any of the other desired storage resources might be incorporated (a small cache might be squeezed in, but there is no use of the small cache; it might even turn out to be degrading to performance). Therefore, instructions must be fetched from the outside environment, and a question arises about the organization of the instruction fetching, as well as about the general arrangement of the processor resources.

7.1.7   Applications of GaAs Processors

GaAs processors have several applications, which are as follows:

a) General purpose processing in aerospace and military environments. This application requires the development of new GaAs microprocessors and their incorporation into workstations [45], or into special expansion cards for the workstations [32].

b) General purpose processing with the goal of replacing the existing CISC processors with faster RISCs. This application assumes not only the development of new GaAs RISC processors, but also the development of new emulators and translators which enable the CISC code written in both the high-level languages and the assembly language to run on the new RISC processors (see [46] and [47]).

c) Special purpose processing in digital signal processing and real-time control. This application assumes the development of relatively simple problem-oriented signal processors [48] and/or microcontrollers [49].

d) Multiprocessing based on the *SIMD (Single Instruction Multiple Data)* and *MIMD (Multiple Instruction Multiple Data)* architectures, both in numerical and nonnumerical applications. This application includes cases such as the systolic processor for antenna signal processing [51], and the multiprocessor system for general purpose data processing [43].

7.1.8   Differences Between GaAs and Silicon Microprocessors

No matter what application will be targeted by the new GaAs microprocessor, the greatest differences exist in the design of the resources of the CPU. These are the register file, the ALU, the pipeline, and the instruction format. The resources traditionally placed outside the CPU are much more alike (the cache memory, the virtual memory, the coprocessors, and the communication mechanisms for multiprocessing).

By far the greatest differences lie in the system software design; this must support the functions not present in the hardware. This includes the functions that must be present in the code optimizer as a part of the compiler. The complexity of the optimizer is mostly because of the deep pipeline, and will be discussed later.

7.1.9   Differences Between GaAs and Silicon Adder Design

There is a wide spectrum of adders, and they vastly differ in complexity and performance. On one end of this spectrum is the *ripple-carry adder (RC),* which has by far the least number of transistors. Generally, this is the slowest adder. On the other end of the spectrum is the *carry lookahead adder (CL)* which, while it is generally the fastest adder, includes the largest number of transistors.

For a model where each gate introduces equal propagation delay (no matter what its fan-in and fan-out are) and where the wires introduce a zero delay, the CL adder is faster than the RC adder for four-bit and wider words (this number can be minimally changed by changing the technology). Since the RC adder requires significantly less transistors, it is used solely for the purpose of making four-bit adders. Often, eight-bit adders are also made as RC adders because they are not much slower and they are still much less complex.

However, the 16-bit and 32-bit processors never use the RC adders. The CL adder is sometimes used, but most often it is an adder which is less complex and somewhat slower than the CL adder.

If all this were taken for granted, one might think that the 32-bit GaAs processor ruled out the use of the RC adder. Surprisingly, it is not so!

If the model is somewhat changed, removing the assumption that the delay does not depend on the fan-in and fan-out, and if the delay through wires is not equal to zero, then the intersection point of the RC and CL delay curves moves from four bits to n bits, where $n > 4$. Now, if $n \geq 32$, the RC adder can be used in 32-bit GaAs processors with better results than for all other adder types.

Reference [52] explains that the point of CL and RC curve intersection lies between 20 and 24 bits for the technology used by RCA. This is because of the large fan-in and fan-out required in CL adders as well as the need for the long wiring. Regardless, the RC adder alone also would not be practical for the 32-bit processor; however, the dropoff in performance is still not unacceptable, and the transistor count is markedly lower. The transistors saved in this way can be used in another resource; this could reduce the number of clock cycles needed for the execution of a given application, making the processor faster than in the case of a slightly reduced clock cycle without any reduction in clock count that would result from the adoption of the CL adder.

However, the 32-bit processor of RCA did not end up with the RC adder, although it was shown that it would be better off with it. The adder incorporated into this processor had

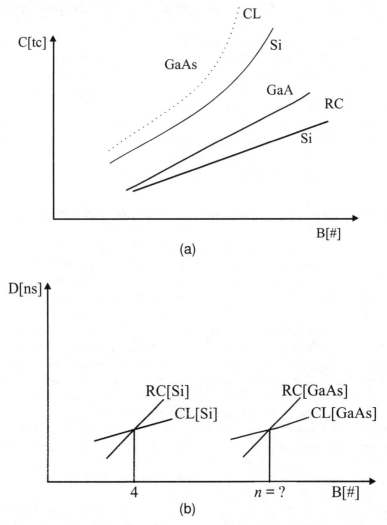

Figure 7-6. Comparison of GaAs and silicon. Symbols CL and RC refer to the basic adder types (*carry lookahead* and *ripple carry*). Symbol B refers to the word size. (a) Complexity comparison: symbol C[tc] refers to complexity, expressed in transistor count and (b) speed comparison: symbol D[ns] refers to propagation delay through the adder, expressed in nanoseconds. In the case of silicon technology, the CL adder is faster when the word size exceeds four bits (or a somewhat lower number, depending on the diagram in question). In the case of GaAs technology, the RC adder is faster for the word sizes up to n bits (actual value of n depends on the actual GaAs technology used).

eight-bit RC blocks, interconnected with the CL logic, to avoid overshooting the required five nanoseconds for the clock cycle [52].

As shown in Figure 7-6, the gate count is slightly larger in GaAs adders than in silicon adders, because the GaAs standard cell family does not contain standard cells with large enough fan-in and fan-out factors. It was necessary to add some standard cells to the design to maintain the needed fan-in and fan-out of certain elements. This phenomenon is more noticeable with CL adders than with RC adders, because the CL adder has a requirement for larger fan-in and fan-out.

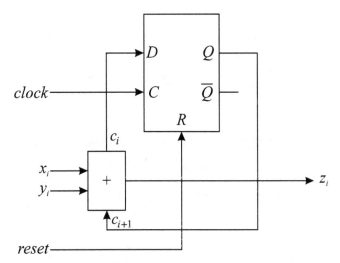

Figure 7-7. Comparison of GaAs and silicon technologies:
an example of the bit-serial adder. All symbols have their standard meanings.

All in all, the conclusion is that the adders present a situation where the most suitable solution for the GaAs is meaningless for silicon. Consequently, the teams that conducted some research before the design began obtained better results than the teams which immediately started designing and based their work right away on silicon technology.

Moreover, the bit-serial arithmetic makes more sense in GaAs than in silicon for arithmetic operations. Bit-serial arithmetic requires less transistors and it is not much slower in GaAs, especially since the internal clock can be faster than the external clock.

Figure 7-7 shows an example of the bit-serial adder, realized using only one D flip-flop and a single one-bit adder. A 32-bit add can be performed in 32 clock cycles, but the clock can be up to 10 times faster than the external clock.

7.1.10   Advanced Issues

It is clear that the principle of bit-serial arithmetic can be applied to the multipliers and other devices. In all these cases, the same conclusions are valid (concerning the relationship between GaAs and silicon).

7.1.10.1   Register File Design   The following paragraphs describe a scenario for a single register cell. Two extreme examples are shown in Figure 7-8. Figure 7-8(a) shows a seven-transistor cell which is used in some silicon microprocessors. Two simultaneous writes and two simultaneous reads are possible. Figure 7-8(b) shows a four-transistor cell which is practically never used in a silicon microprocessor. It enables only one write or read in a single clock cycle. However, the four-bit register cell is very good for GaAs processors. First, it has about one-half the transistor count compared to the seven-transistor cell. The remaining transistors can be used in the struggle against the long off-chip delays. Second, two operands cannot be read simultaneously to be passed to the ALU. Instead, the reading has to be done sequentially; that slows down the datapath, and ultimately the clock, which is not so dangerous in GaAs, as explained next.

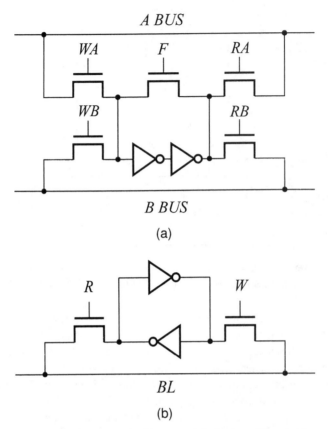

Figure 7-8. Comparison of GaAs and silicon technologies. The design of the register cell: (a) an example of the register cell frequently used in the silicon technology and (b) an example of the register cell frequently used in the GaAs microprocessors. Symbol *BL* refers to the unique bit line in the four-transistor cell. Symbols *A BUS* and *B BUS* refer to the double bit lines in the seven-transistor cell. Symbol *F* refers to the refresh input. All other symbols have their standard meanings.

At first, this solution seems to slow down the application, which is incorrect. Even though it has a slower clock, the pipeline is not so deep; this enables the Gross-Hennessy algorithm to fill in almost all slots after the branch instructions. Therefore, the Gross-Hennessy algorithm almost equalizes the two solutions, and the remaining transistors can be reinvested into the resources which can bring a substantial speedup. One analysis has shown that the speedup ascribed to a larger register file and proper slot filling is much larger than the slowdown ascribed to a decreased clock.[2] All in all, in the case of the GaAs technology, the four-transistor solution is more attractive than the seven-transistor solution.

Once again, it was shown that the solution almost never applied in the silicon technology is a much better one for the GaAs technology.

---

[2]The same reasoning can be applied to the adders, but it was not mentioned when discussing the adder design, because of the presentation sequencing.

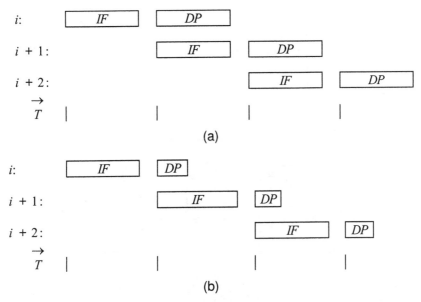

Figure 7-9. Comparison of GaAs and silicon technologies. The pipeline design—a possible design error: (a) two-stage pipeline typical of some silicon microprocessors; (b) the same two-stage pipeline when the off-chip delays are three times longer than on-chip delays (the off-chip delays are assumed to be the same as in the silicon version). Symbols *IF* and *DP* refer to the instruction fetch and the ALU cycle (datapath). Symbol *T* refers to time.

7.1.10.2 Pipelining in GaAs Technology If a well designed silicon processor pipeline [shown in Figure 7-9(a)] was ported to a GaAs processor, the situation shown in Figure 7-9(b) would result, with the datapath unused two-thirds of the time because of the relative slowness of the environment. In this example, the assumptions were made that the packaging and printed circuit board technologies are identical, and that the GaAs technology is exactly five times faster.

7.1.10.3 Approaches to Datapath Utilization The problem of poor datapath utilization can be approached in several ways.

The *interleaved memory approach (IM)*, and the *memory pipelining approach (MP)* are shown in Figure 7-10(a). These are two different organizations with an equivalent timing diagram [see Figure 7-10(a1)]. In the case of short off-chip delays and long memory access times, as in the computers of the sixties (semiconductor CPU and magnetic core memory), the IM method was the only solution [see Figure 7.10(a2)]. In the case of long off-chip delays and short memory access times, as in the GaAs processors of the nineties (CPU and memory in GaAs technology, realized using the classic packaging and wiring technology), both approaches are possible; however, the MP technique is simpler [see Figure 7-10(a3)].

Figure 7-10(b) shows the case of a wide instruction format, where, if data dependencies allow it, multiple ALU instructions are all fetched at once, and are executed in time multiplex.

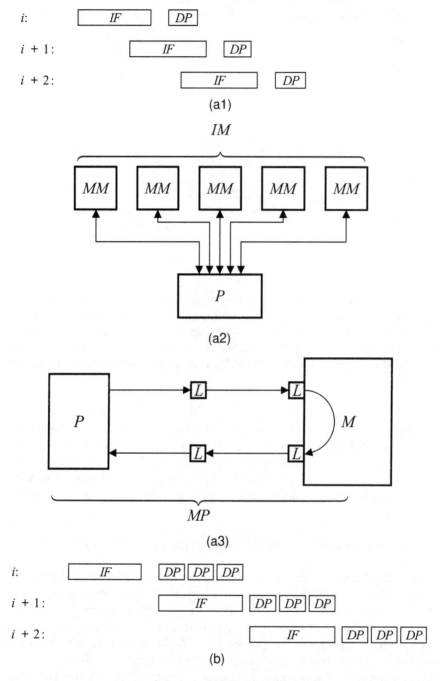

Figure 7-10. Comparison of GaAs and silicon technologies. The pipeline design—possible solutions: (a1) timing diagrams of a pipeline based on the IM (interleaved memory) or the MP (memory pipelining); (a2) a system based on the IM approach; (a3) a system based on the MP approach and (b) timing diagram of the pipeline based on the IP (instruction packing) approach. Symbols *P*, *M*, and *MM* refer to the processor, the memory, and the memory module. The other symbols were defined earlier.

7.1.11 Admonitions

Readers are advised to try to develop a case in which a slow and simple resource (such as bit-serial arithmetic), or a slow and complex resource (for example one pipeline cycle such as Fast Fourier Transform) is used. This enables a shallow pipeline, and the Gross-Hennessy algorithm gives excellent results. However, this approach is justified only for special purpose processors.

The pipeline mechanisms described here and applied in the GaAs processors are not used in the silicon processors; they prove that the traditional way of thinking has to be changed if the technology is changed.

Finally, the instruction format also has to experience some changes. The instruction packing (used in the SU-MIPS processor) has since been abandoned in the silicon processors. However, this approach is fully justified for the GaAs processors because it fully utilizes the pipeline. An example is shown in Figure 7-10(b).

7.2 GaAs RISC Processors: Analysis of a Special Case

A complete review of the architecture of the 32-bit GaAs RISC processor developed through the cooperation between the Purdue University and the RCA is given here. It presents the apex of this book—all the material presented in this book so far can be viewed as the prerequisite necessary for mastering the concepts and tools for the complete realization of the microprocessor under consideration (on a single chip).

At the end, the experiences gained through this project are summarized and the basics of the catalytic migration are also explained. This methodology was reached through the analysis of the experiences, and it is believed that it can be used to solve the basic problems of the GaAs microprocessor design, and generally, of any microprocessor design based on a low on-chip transistor count and a high on-chip/off-chip speed ratio technology.

7.2.1 Technological Restrictions

The basic problems concerning the architecture, organization, and design of our 32-bit GaAs microprocessor were dictated by various technology restrictions.

With the semiconductor technology, the restrictions were mainly in the area of fan-in and fan-out factors, especially with the NAND gates. This can be compensated by creating a fan-out tree, like the one shown in Figure 7-11(a). There were also the restrictions concerning the nonexistence of three-state and wired-or logic. The solutions to these problems were found in the use of multiplexers, as shown in Figure 7-11(b). Of course, all these problems could have been avoided altogether, or at least their severity could have been reduced, by using the FC VLSI design methodology.

Regarding the wiring and packaging technology, restrictions occurred with the printed circuit board technology, as well as with the packaging of a number of chips in a single package. The printed circuit boards were made using the *SL technique (stripline),* instead of the *MS technique (microstrip),* as shown in Figure 7-12. In the case of packaging of several chips into one module, the *MCM technique (multi-chip module)* was used. This had a limitation in the number of chips that could be put in a single module, and stressed the importance of distributing efficiently the processor resources across the modules.

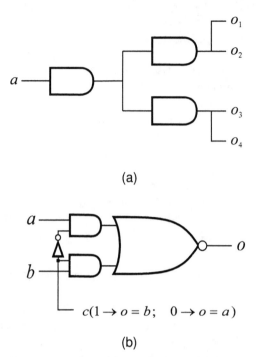

(a)

$c(1 \to o = b; \quad 0 \to o = a)$

(b)

Figure 7-11. The technological problems that arise from using GaAs technology: (a) An example of the fan-out tree, which provides a fan-out of four, using logic elements with the fan-out of two and (b) an example of the logic element that performs a two-to-one one-bit multiplexing. Symbols *a* and *b* refer to data inputs. Symbol *c* refers to the control input. Symbol *o* refers to data output.

Regarding the architecture and organization of the system, the restrictions arose because different parts of the system (containing 10–20 modules with 10–20 chips each) were in different clock phases (because of the slow off-chip signal propagation). This was why some solutions that are never used in silicon chips were used for GaAs chips. Two examples will follow.

In the case of the **load** instruction in silicon processors, the register address is passed from the instruction register directly to the corresponding address port of the register file, where it waits until the data arrive from the main memory (all addresses in main memory are equally distant from the CPU in terms of time). If such an approach were to be used in a GaAs microprocessor, it would create a problem based on the fact that different parts of the main memory are not equally distant from the CPU. The following code would then result in data ending up in the wrong registers (they would switch places):

$$i: \qquad \textbf{load } R1, MEM - 6$$
$$i + 1: \qquad \textbf{load } R2, MEM - 3$$

where $MEM - 6$ is a memory location six clock cycles away from the CPU, and $MEM - 3$ is a memory location three clock cycles away. The destination swap would take place because the $R1$ address would reach the register file address port first, and the data from location $MEM - 3$ would be the first one to arrive to the register file. One way to avoid this would be to send the register address to the memory chip and back (together with the data from memory).

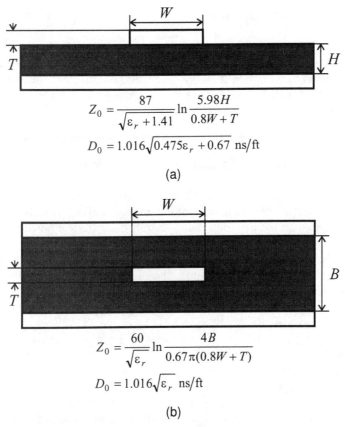

$$Z_0 = \frac{87}{\sqrt{\varepsilon_r + 1.41}} \ln \frac{5.98H}{0.8W + T}$$

$$D_0 = 1.016\sqrt{0.475\varepsilon_r + 0.67} \text{ ns/ft}$$

(a)

$$Z_0 = \frac{60}{\sqrt{\varepsilon_r}} \ln \frac{4B}{0.67\pi(0.8W + T)}$$

$$D_0 = 1.016\sqrt{\varepsilon_r} \text{ ns/ft}$$

(b)

Figure 7-12. Some possible techniques for realization of PCBs (printed circuit boards): (a) The MS technique (microstrip) and (b) the SL technique (stripline). Symbols D_0 and Z_0 refer to the signal delay and the characteristic impedance, respectively. The meaning of other symbols is either defined in former figures or they have standard meanings.

In the case of the **branch** instruction, the problem of filling the delayed branch slots arises if the pipeline is deep. The number of these slots in some GaAs processors is five to eight. If the same solution were applied in the silicon processors, the number of unfilled slots (the **nop** instructions) would make up the major portion of the code (the Gross-Hennessy algorithm, or some other algorithm, would not be able to fill in many slots). One possible solution to this problem is to introduce the **ignore** instruction, which would freeze the clock. It would be introduced after the last filled **nop** slot, eliminating the need for the rest of **nop**s. Thus, all the **nop** instructions that were not eliminated by the Gross-Hennessy algorithm would disappear, reducing the code in size. The **ignore** instruction has one operand, that is, the number of clock cycles to be skipped. The loss is relatively small, and it is only in the form of simple logic used to realize the **ignore** instruction. This is another example of a solution that has no effect in silicon, and can produce good results in GaAs.

7.2.2 Explanation of Appendix A

Appendix A contains a reprint of the article that describes the architecture, organization, and design of the RCA's GaAs microprocessor. This article contains all the details relevant to understanding the design and principle of operation, and it represents the symbiosis of everything said so far in this book. The reprint has been included (rather than the abridged version) which will allow the readers to obtain the information from the original source, as well as get accustomed to the terminology.

7.2.3 Lessons Learned and Catalytic Migration

The fact that the design has been successfully brought to an end, and that the product has been rendered operational, does not mean that the project is over. To fully conclude the project, one should think about the experience and learn lessons from it (such as upgrading from direct migration to catalytic migration).

In this case, it has been noticed that the speed of GaAs microprocessors for the compiled high-level language code is not much higher than the speed of its silicon version, as one might expect by merely looking at the speed ratio of the two technologies (as previously mentioned, RCA has worked on both silicon and GaAs versions of the microprocessor). It is clear that this is because of the small size of GaAs chips, as well as significant interchip delays. The question really is how to enhance the architecture, organization, and design to overcome this problem. One possible solution, which came up after the problem had been given serious consideration, was *catalytic migration*, which will now be briefly explained. For more information, one should refer to [53] and [54].

Catalytic migration can be treated as an upgraded concept of direct migration. Direct migration represents a migration of a hardware resource into software in such a way that it speeds up the application code. An example of direct migration is the migration of the interlock mechanism from hardware to software, such as in the SU-MIPS. It is apparent that while direct migration can be of great use in technologies such as GaAs where the chip size is a bit limited (thus enabling a small number of resources to be accommodated on the chip), and the offchip delays are significant, which means that a high price is paid for each unnecessary departure from the chip.

It is very difficult to come up with the examples of direct migration that result in code speed-up. That is why the idea of catalytic migration came into existence. The essence of this concept is the removal of a relatively large resource on the chip (migrant) by putting in a smaller resource (catalyst) which is potentially useful (see Figure 7-13). The catalyst got its name because it enables the migration effects to come into power.

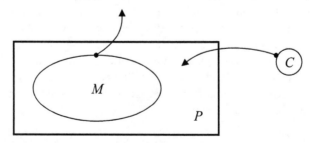

Figure 7-13. The catalytic migration concept. Symbols *M*, *C*, and *P* refer to the migrant, the catalyst, and the processor, respectively. The acceleration, achieved by the extraction of a migrant of a relatively large VLSI area, is achieved after adding a catalyst of a significantly smaller VLSI area.

Actually, the catalyst helps to move the migrant from the hardware to the software, while having a positive effect on the speed of compiled high-level language code. In some cases, this move, or migration (with positive effects), is not possible without adding the catalyst. In other cases, this migration (with positive effects), is possible even before adding a catalyst; however, the effects are much better after a catalyst is added.

Catalytic migration can be either induced (ICM) or accelerated (ACM). In the case of the *induced catalytic migration (ICM),* the code speedup is possible even without the catalyst; in the case of the *accelerated catalytic migration (ACM)* the acceleration might exist without the catalyst, but with reduced effects.

The solutions for the **load** and **ignore** instructions (described globally in this section, and specifically in Appendix A) can be conditionally treated as examples of catalytic migration, and they are now presented in this perspective (see Figures 7-14 and 7-15). There are some

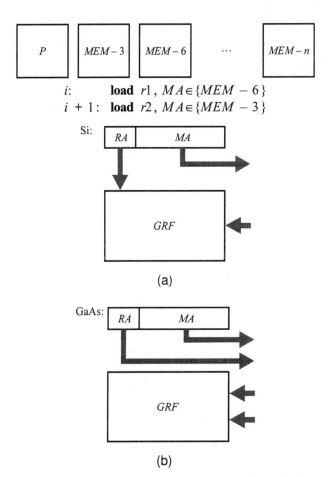

Figure 7-14. An example of the HW (hand walking) type of catalytic migration: (a) before the migration; (b) after the migration. Symbols *P* and *GRF* refer to the processor and the general purpose register file, respectively. Symbols *RA* and *MA* refer to the register address and the memory address in the **load** instruction. Symbol *MEM–n* refers to the main store which is *n* clock periods away from the processor. Addition of another bus for the register address eliminates a relatively large number of **nop** instructions (which have to separate the interfering **load** instructions).

other examples (two of them shown in Figures 7-16 and 7-17) related to **call/return** and **jump/branch**, respectively. The explanations (for all four examples) are given in the figure captions. The explanations are purposefully brief in order to induce and accelerate the readers to think about the details, analyze the problems, and eventually enhance the solutions. Those who wish to obtain complete information about this can review the previously mentioned [53] and [54].

The entire catalytic migration methodology can be generalized. In doing so, this methodology becomes the guide for the type of thinking that leads to new solutions. One possible generalization is shown in Figure 7-18. Applying the catalytic migration has lead to interesting solutions described in [32] and [33], as well as in several of the references of Section 10-2.

7.3 Summary

This concludes the discussion on the impact of the new technologies. This field is extremely fruitful, and represents a limitless source of new research problems and solutions.

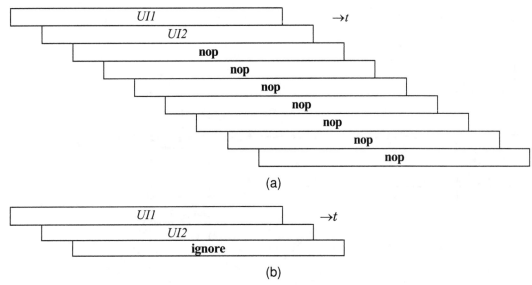

(a)

(b)

Figure 7-15.   An example of the II (ignore instruction) type of catalytic migration: (a) Before the migration and (b) after the migration. Symbol *t* refers to time, and symbol *UI* refers to useful instructions. This figure shows the case in which the code optimizer has successfully eliminated only two **nop** instructions, and has inserted the **ignore** instruction immediately after the last useful instruction. The addition of the **ignore** instruction and the accompanying decoder logic eliminates a relatively large number of **nop** instructions, and speeds up the code, through better utilization of the instruction cache.

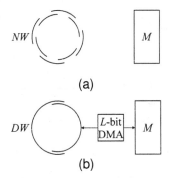

(a)

(b)

Figure 7-16.   An example of the DW (double windows) type of catalytic migration: (a) Before the migration and (b) after the migration. Symbol *M* refers to the main store. The symbol *L*-bit DMA refers to the direct memory access which transfers *L* bits in one clock cycle. Symbol *NW* refers to the register file with *N* partially overlapping windows (as in the UCB-RISC processor), while the symbol *DW* refers to the register file of the same type, this time only with two partially overlapping windows (a working window and a back-up window). The addition of the *L*-bit DMA mechanism, in parallel to the execution using one window (the working window), enables the simultaneous transfer between the main store and the window which is currently not in use (the back-up window). This enables one to keep the contents of the nonexistent $N-2$ windows in the main store, which not only keeps the resulting code from slowing down, but actually speeds it up because the transistors released through the omission of $N-2$ windows can be reinvested more appropriately.

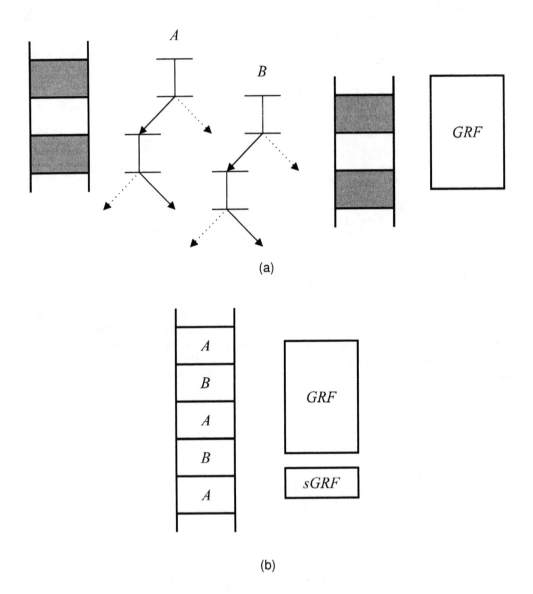

(a)

(b)

Figure 7-17. An example of the CI (code interleaving) type of catalytic migration: (a) Before the migration and (b) after the migration. Symbols *A* and *B* refer to the parts of the code in two different routines that share no data dependencies. Symbols *GRF* and s*GRF* refer to the general purpose register file (GRF), and the subset of the *GRF (sGRF)*. The sequential code of routine *A* is used to fill in the slots in routine *B*, and vice versa. This is enabled by adding new registers (s*GRF*) and some additional control logic which is quite simple. The speed-up is achieved through the elimination of **nop** instructions, and the increased efficiency of the instruction cache (a consequence of the reduced code size). Catalytic migration can be induced (ICM) and accelerated (ACM). In the case of the induced catalytic migration (ICM), the code speed-up is possible even without the catalyst, while in the case of the accelerated catalytic migration (ACM) the acceleration might exist without the catalyst, but with reduced effects.

for $i := 1$ **to** N **do:**

1. *MAE*
2. *CAE*
3. *DFR*
4. *RSD*
5. *CTA*

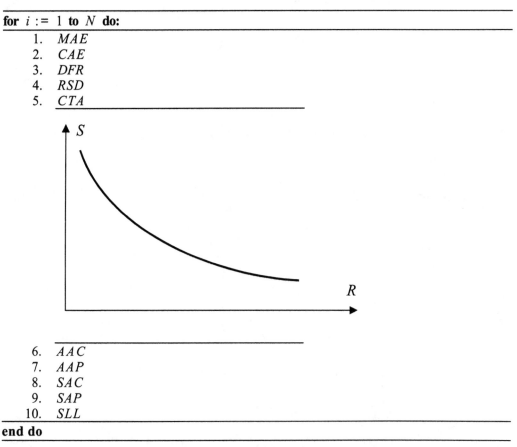

6. *AAC*
7. *AAP*
8. *SAC*
9. *SAP*
10. *SLL*

end do

Figure 7-18. A methodological review of catalytic migration (intended for a detailed study of a new catalytic migration example). Symbols *S* and *R* refer to the speed-up and the initial register count. Symbol *N* refers to the number of generated ideas. The meaning of other symbols is as follows: *MAE*—migrant area estimate, *CAE*—catalyst area estimate, *DFR*—determination of the difference for reinvestment, *RSD*—development of the reinvestment strategy, *CTA*—development of the compile-time algorithm, *AAC*—analytical analysis of the complexity, *AAP*—analytical analysis of the performance, *SAC*—simulation analysis of the complexity, *SAP*—simulation analysis of the performance, *SLL*—summary of lessons learned.

8

RISC: Some Application-Related Aspects of the Problem

So far, we have looked at the general purpose RISC processors. However, the RISC design philosophy can be applied equally well to the design of new specialized processors which are oriented toward specific, precisely defined applications.

The readers of this book are not likely to ever participate in development of a new general purpose RISC processor. The general purpose RISC processor field has entered a stable state, in which the market is dominated by a few established companies such as Intel, Motorola, MIPS Systems, SPARC, and so on, and there is simply no room left for new breakthroughs. On the other hand, at least some of the readers will be put in a situation where he or she will participate in the development of a new special purpose RISC processor. These special purposes include the enhancements of the input/output (in the broadest sense of the word), memory subsystem bandwidth increase, hardware support for various numerical and nonnumerical algorithms, and the like.

In the case of a new application specific RISC processor, there are two approaches that usually give good results. The first assumes the synthesis of a new RISC processor through design of the instruction set which is based on the new understanding of the executable code statistics. This approach is well documented in various sources, such as [56]. The second assumes the synthesis of a new RISC processor (also based on the executable code statistics) with only the basic instruction set and with various, sometimes very powerful, accelerators which could be viewed as on-chip, off-datapath coprocessors. This approach is also well documented in various sources, and it is illustrated in Figure 8-1.

Two examples in the neural network arena will be presented here to illuminate the topic. Conditionally speaking, one solution is based on the first approach, while the other is based on the second approach.

8.1   The N-RISC Processor Architecture

This section will briefly present the architecture of the *N-RISC (Neural RISC)* processor, developed at the UCL (University College, London, England, Great Britain). This topic is discussed extensively and treated in detail in [57].

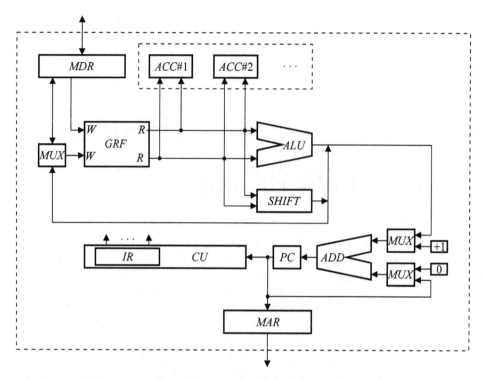

Figure 8-1. A RISC architecture with on-chip accelerators. Accelerators are labeled *ACC*#1, *ACC*#2, ..., and they are placed parallel to the *ALU*. The rest of the diagram is a common RISC core. All symbols have standard meanings.

There were two basic problems associated with the design of the N-RISC processor. The first was the computational efficiency of the following expression:

$$S_j = f\left(\sum_i S_i W_{ij}\right), \qquad j = 1, 2, \ldots$$

which corresponds to the individual neuron structure [see Figure 8-2(a)]. The other one was an efficient data transfer from the neuron's output to the inputs of all neurons which require that piece of data [see Figure 8-2(b)].

In this example, the architecture shown in Figure 8-3 was used. There are many rings in the system. Each ring contains several N-RISC processors called *PEs (processing elements)*. The instruction set of a single N-RISC processor is oriented toward neural network algorithms. Each N-RISC can emulate several neurons in software, which are called *PUs (processing units)*.

The computational efficiency was achieved with the specific architecture for the N-RISC processor (see Figure 8-4). The N-RISC processor has only 16 16-bit instructions (this was an experimental 16-bit realization) and only one internal register.

The communication efficiency was achieved with a *message passing protocol (MPP);* the messages were composed of three 16-bit words:

Word #1: Neuron address
Word #2: Additional dendrite-level specification
Word #3: Data being transferred (signal)

This implementation assumes 64K N-RISC PE elements with 16 PU elements per one PE element. Various applications were also developed (Hopfield, Boltzmann, and the like).

It is appropriate to emphasize the fact that the CPU took up about 8 percent of the chip area, the communication unit took up only about 2 percent, while local memory took up the remaining 90 percent. It is commonly believed that an efficient realization of the N-RISC processor (and neural networks in general) boils down to efficient realization of the memory.

8.2 The Architecture of an Accelerator for Neural Network Algorithms

This section briefly presents an architectural system for the efficient execution of various algorithms in the field of neural networks. This system can be realized as an accelerator in the RISC processor; this will efficiently run the code that emulates certain types of neural networks.

The project was realized at the Milan Polytechnic in Italy [55]. The entire architecture is oriented toward the SC VLSI design methodology. The topology of the architecture is quite regular, and as such it is appropriate for the SC VLSI approach.

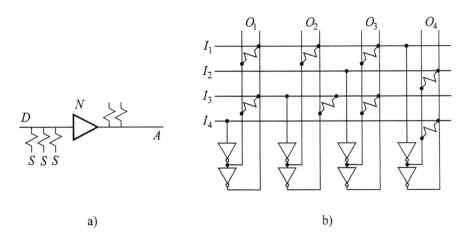

a)   b)

Figure 8-2. Basic problems encountered during the realization of a neural computer: (a) An electronic neuron and (b) an interconnection network for a neural network. Symbol *D* stands for the dendrites (inputs), symbol *S* stands for the synapses (resistors), symbol *N* stands for the neuron body (amplifier), and symbol *A* stands for the axon (output). The symbols I_1, I_2, I_3, and I_4 stand for the input connections, and the symbols O_1, O_2, O_3, and O_4 stand for the output connections.

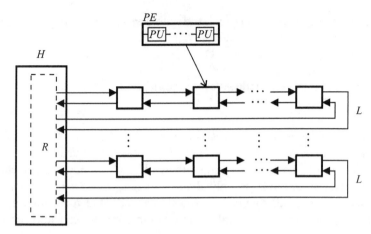

Figure 8-3. A system architecture with N-RISC processors as nodes. Symbol *PE* *(processing element)* represents one N-RISC, and refers to hardware neuron. Symbol *PU* *(processing unit)* represents the software routine for one neuron, and refers to *software neuron*. Symbol *H* refers to the host processor, symbol *L* refers to the 16-bit link, and symbol *R* refers to the routing algorithm based on the *MP (message passing)* method.

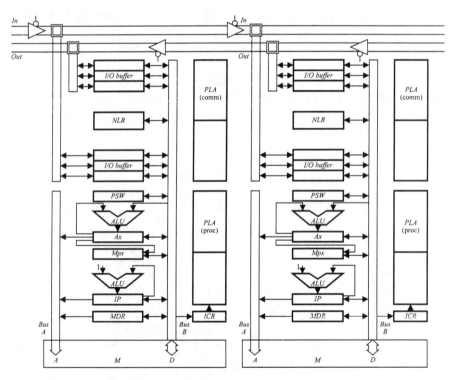

Figure 8-4. The architecture of an N-RISC processor. This figure shows two neighboring N-RISC processors on the same ring. Symbols *A, D,* and *M* refer to the addresses, data, and memory, respectively. Symbols *PLA* (comm) and *PLA* (proc) refer to the PLA logic for the communication and processor subsystems, respectively. Symbol *NLR* refers to the register which defines the address of the neuron (name/layer register). Symbol A_x refers to the only register in the N-RISC processor. Other symbols are standard.

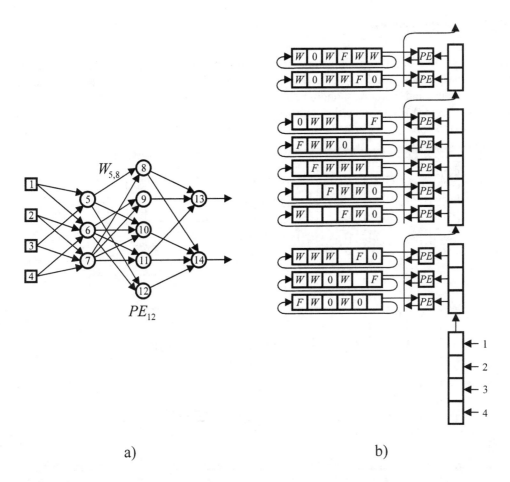

a)   b)

Figure 8-5.   Example of an accelerator for neural RISC: (a) a three-layer neural network and (b) its implementation based on [55]. The squares in Figure 8-5(a) stand for input data sources, and the circles stand for the network nodes. Symbols *W* in Figure 8-5(b) stand for weights, and symbols *F* stand for the firing triggers. Symbols *PE* refer to the processing elements. Symbols *W* have two indices associated with them, to define the connections of the element (for example, $W_{5,8}$ and so on). As an exercise, the exact values of the indices are left for the reader to determine. Likewise, the *PE* symbols have one index associated with them to determine the node they belong to. The exact values of these indices were also left out, so the reader should also determine them.

Figure 8-5 shows both an example of the three layer neural network and the way it was implemented. A simple ALU performs the task of implementing the required arithmetic operations. The communication task falls into the combination of appropriate topology and suitable time multiplexing. Figure 8-6 gives the VLSI layout for the entire architecture. Figure 8-7 shows the timing for the example from Figure 8-5. In short, this is the solution which produces an excellent match of the technology and the application requirements.

8.3 Summary

The general field of RISC architectures for neural network support is extensive and an entire (multivolume) book could be devoted to it. However, this brief discussion pointed out some basic problems and the corresponding solutions, and introduced the readers to this new (and very fast moving) field. Since the field transcends the scope of this book, interested readers are advised to consult [32] and [33].

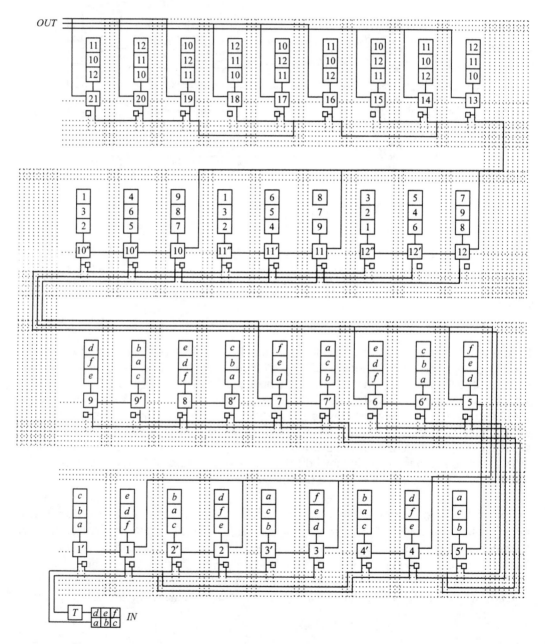

Figure 8-6. A VLSI layout for the complete architecture of Figure 8-5. Symbol *T* refers to the delay unit, and symbols *IN* and *OUT* refer to the inputs and the outputs, respectively.

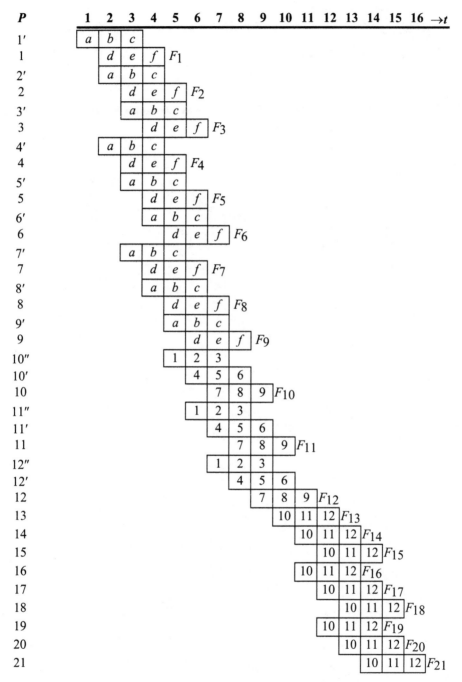

Figure 8-7. Timing for the complete architecture of Figure 8-5. Symbol *t* refers to time, symbol *F* refers to the moments of triggering, and symbol *P* refers to the ordinal number of the processing element.

9
Summary

This chapter contains a short summary of the covered issues, and gives some suggestions for further work.

9.1 What was Done?

After carefully studying this book, the reader (with an appropriate background knowledge) should be able to design (on his/her own) a complete RISC microprocessor on a VLSI chip. Of course, in addition to the theoretical knowledge, other necessary prerequisites are required: access to the right tools, appropriate funding, and a lot of personal enthusiasm.

Special emphasis was given to the lessons learned through the part of the project which is related to the realization of the 32-bit GaAs machine. Note, one can never say that a project is successfully brought to its end if all that is done is that something is implemented and it works. For a project to be truly successful, lessons have to be learned and made available to those that will continue the mission.

Also, with the gained experience one can create new ideas. One idea which was created by the author, after the entire project was over, was to split the data cache subsystem into two distinct parts, one with data that exhibit a predominantly spatial locality (complex data structures), and the other with data that exhibit a predominantly temporal locality (loop control variables, condition control variables, and synchronization variables). The "spatial" part needs no cache hierarchy—only a prefetch buffer. The "temporal" part needs a cache hierarchy, but the capacity of each hierarchy level can be much smaller, since the "temporal" data are just a subset of the overall data. Consequently, approximately the same performance can be obtained with much less VLSI complexity. Details of this idea have been later elaborated in a SCIzzL-5 paper [58], using the basic idea from [59] and the basic methodology from [60].

Another idea which was created by the author, after the entire project was over, was to enable direct injection of data into the cache subsystem, which is of special interest for SMP and DSM systems, and in cases when the impact of the first read/write miss penalty is significant. For details, see [42].

9.2 What is Next?

Further work in the theoretical domain should concentrate on studying new 32-bit and 64-bit RISC architectures. This is a typical subject of many graduate courses at technical universities and preconference tutorials at large conferences.

Further work in the practical domain should concentrate on experimenting with modern commercial packets for functional analysis (VHDL known as the *IEEE 1076* standard), and VLSI design (tools compatible with the MOSIS fabrication). These issues are a typical subject of specialized university courses and conferences which focus on the problem.

Overall theoretical knowledge can be further improved if the references used in this book are read in their original form. A list of all the references used throughout the book is given in the next chapter. Also, one should look at the table of contents of these references for the specialized conferences in the field.

Overall practical knowledge is best improved if the reader takes part in a concrete professional design project, with all the tough deadlines and requirements (no single bug is allowed, no matter how complex the project is). Fabrication is a relatively expensive process, and the chip is always expected to work from the first silicon.

9.3   Doing Your Own Research and Developments

Doing your own research and developments, in order to advance the state of the art, is a special challenge. Once one has a precisely defined statement of work (the problem to solve), while reading about the existing solutions of the same problem, one should constantly think about the ways to solve the problem in a better way (looking from the performance/ complexity point of view). This is easier to achieve if one constantly works on the development of his/her own creativity (simply, one has to believe that he/she is able to create better ideas, in conditions of the full awareness of the existing state-of-the-art). See Appendix D for details on one research and development methodology which is fully applicable in the field of interest for this book.

10

References and Suggested Reading

The knowledge obtained through some kind of formal education can be treated in only one way—as the foundation for further personal development. Since the field treated here is practical in its nature, a lot of hard practical work is necessary in order to gain the required engineering experience. However, the field expands at a fast pace, and a lot of new reading is absolutely necessary in order to keep up with the latest developments. The references listed below represent the ground work that has to be mastered before one decides to try new horizons.

10.1 References

This section contains all the references used in this book. Some of these references contain the facts used to write the book. Other references contain examples created with the knowledge covered in the book.

[1] V. Milutinović, D. Fura, and W. Helbig, "An Introduction to GaAs Microprocessor Architecture for VLSI," *Computer*, Vol. 19, No. 3, Mar. 1986, pp. 30–42.

[2] V. Milutinović et al., "Issues of Importance for GaAs Microcomputer Systems," *Computer*, Vol. 19, No. 10, Oct. 1986, pp. 45–57.

[3] V. Milutinović et al., "Architecture/Compiler Synergism in GaAs Computer Systems," *Computer*, Vol. 20, No. 5, May 1987, pp. 72–93.

[4] W. Helbig and V. Milutinović, "A DCFL E/D-MESFET GaAs 32-bit Experimental RISC Machine," *IEEE Trans. Computers*, Vol. 38, No. 2, Feb. 1989, pp. 263–274.

[5] N. Weste and K. Eshraghian, *Principles of CMOS VLSI Design*, Addison Wesley, Reading, Mass. 1985.

[6] V. Milutinović and Z. Petković, "Ten Lessons Learned from a RISC Design," *Computer*, Vol. 28, No. 3, Mar. 1995, p. 120.

[7] *ENDOT ISP' User's Documentation*, TDT, Cleveland Heights, Ohio, 1992.

[8] *ENDOT ISP' Tutorial/Application Notes*, TDT, Cleveland Heights, Ohio, 1992.

[9] D. Božanić, D. Fura, and V. Milutinović, "Simulation of a Simple RISC Processor," Application Note D#001/VM, TD Technologies, Cleveland Heights, Ohio, Jan. 1993.

[10] M. Tomašević and V. Milutinović, "Using N.2 in a Simulation Study of Snoopy Cache Coherence Protocols for Shared Memory Multiprocessor Systems," Application Note D#002/VM, TD Technologies, Cleveland Heights, Ohio, Jan. 1993.

[11] D. Milićev, Z. Petković, and V. Milutinović, "Using N.2 for Simulation of Cache Memory: Concave Versus Convex Programming in ISP'," Application Note D#003/VM, TD Technologies, Cleveland Heights, Ohio, Jan. 1994.

[12] Z. Petković and V. Milutinović, "An N.2 Simulator of the Intel i860," Application Note D#004/VM, TD Technologies, Cleveland Heights, Ohio, Jan. 1994.

[13] J.R. Armstrong, *Chip Level Modeling With VHDL*, Prentice-Hall, Englewood Cliffs, N.J., 1989.

[14] R. Lipsett, C. Schaefer, and C. Ussery, *VHDL: Hardware Description and Design*, Kluwer Academic Publishers, Boston, Mass., 1990.

[15] *IEEE Standard VHDL Language Reference Manual*, IEEE, Piscataway, N.J., 1987.

[16] C.W. Rose, G.M. Ordy, and P.J. Drongowski, "N.mpc: A Study in University-Industry Technology Transfer," *IEEE Design and Test of Computers*, Vol. 1, No. 1, Feb. 1984, pp. 44–56.

[17] F. Gay, "Functional Simulation Fuels Systems Design," *VLSI Design Technology*, Apr. 1986.

[18] D. Ferrari, *Computer Systems Performance Evaluation*, Prentice- Hall, Englewood Cliffs, N.J., 1978.

[19] J. Archibald and J.K. Baer, "Cache Coherence Protocols: Evaluation Using a Multiprocessor Simulation Model," *ACM Trans. Computer Systems*, Nov. 1986, pp. 273–298.

[20] *Altera User Configurable Logic Data Book*, Altera, San Jose, CA, 1992.

[21] *XC3000 Logic Cell Array Family Technical Data*, Xilinx, Palo Alto, Calif., 1992.

[22] *CADDAS User's Guide*, RCA, Camden, N.J., 1985.

[23] *LOGSIM User's Guide*, RCA, Camden, N.J., 1985.

[24] *MP2D User's Guide*, RCA, Camden, N.J., 1985.

[25] *Tanner Tools User's Documentation*, Tanner Research, Pasadena, Calif., 1992.

[26] *MOSIS Fabrication Facility User's Guide*, MOSIS, Xerox, Palo Alto, Calif., 1993.

[27] R.J. Feugate and S.M. McIntyre, *Introduction to VLSI Testing*, Prentice-Hall, Englewood Cliffs, N.J., 1988.

[28] E.J. McCluskey, "Built-In Self-Test Structures," *IEEE Design and Test of Computers*, Vol. 2, No. 2, Apr. 1985, pp. 29–35.

[29] M.J. Flynn, *Computer Architecture: Pipelined and Parallel Processors*, Jones and Bartlett Publishers, Boston, Mass., 1995.

[30] J.L. Hennessy and D.A. Patterson, *Computer Architecture: A Quantitative Approach*, Morgan Kaufmann Publishers, San Mateo, Calif., 1996.

[31] L. Hoevel and V. Milutinović, "Terminology Risks with the RISC Concept in the Risky RISC Arena," *Computer*, Vol. 24, No. 1, Jan. 1992, p. 136.

[32] V. Milutinović, "RISC architectures for Multimedia and Neural Networks Applications," *Tutorial of the ISCA-92*, Brisbane, Queensland, Australia, May 1992.

[33] V. Milutinović, "RISC Architectures for Multimedia and Neural Networks Applications," *Tutorial of the HICSS-93*, Koloa, Hawaii, Jan. 1993.

[34] D. Patterson and J. Hennessy, "Computer Organization and Design," Morgan Kaufmann Publishers, San Mateo, Calif., 1994.

[35] D. Tabak, *Multiprocessors*, Prentice-Hall, Englewood Cliffs, N.J., 1990.

[36] D. Tabak, Advanced Microprocessors, McGraw-Hill, New York, N.Y., 1995.

[37] D.A. Patterson and D.R. Ditzel, "Case for the Reduced Instruction Set Computer," *Computer Architecture News*, Vol. 8, No. 6, Oct. 15, 1980, pp. 23–33.

[38] W.A. Wulf, "Compilers and Computer Architecture," *Computer*, Vol. 14, No. 7, July 1981, pp. 41–47.

[39] G.J. Myers, *Advances in Computer Architecture*, John Wiley and Sons, New York, N.Y., 1982.

[40] T.R. Gross and J.L. Hennessy, "Optimizing Delayed Branches," *Proc. 15th Ann. Workshop on Microprogramming*, MICRO-15, 1982, pp. 114–120.

[41] J. Gill et al., "Summary of MIPS Instructions," Tech. Report #83-237, Computer System Laboratory, Stanford Univ., Palo Alto, Calif., 1983.

[42] V. Milutinović, "Some Ideas About Future Development of SMP and DSM Systems," Technical Report of the University of Belgrade, Belgrade, Serbia, Yugoslavia, Dec. 1995.

[43] T.N. Mudge et al., "The Design of a Micro-Supercomputer," *Computer*, Vol. 24, No. 1, Jan. 1991, pp. 57–64.

[44] R. Brown et al., "GaAs RISC Processors," *Proc. GaAs IC Symp.*, 1992.

[45] *Microprocessor Design for GaAs Technology*, V. Milutinović, ed., Prentice-Hall, Englewood Cliffs, N.J., 1990.

[46] K. McNeley and V. Milutinović, "Emulating a CISC with a RISC," *IEEE Micro*, Vol. 6, No. 1, Feb. 1987, pp. 60–72.

[47] E. Handgen, B. Robbins, and V. Milutinović, "Emulating a CISC with GaAs Bit-Slice Components," *IEEE Tutorial on Microprogramming*, IEEE CS Press, Los Alamitos, Calif., 1988, pp. 70–101.

[48] H. Vlahos and V. Milutinović, "A Survey of GaAs Microprocessors," *IEEE Micro*, Vol. 7, No. 1, Feb. 1988, pp. 28–56.

[49] V. Milutinović, N. Lopez-Benitez, and K. Hwang, "A GaAs-Based Architecture for RealTime Applications," *IEEE Trans. Computers*, June 1987, pp. 714–727.

[50] V. Milutinović, "A Simulation Study of the Vertical Migration Microprocessor Architecture," *IEEE Trans. Software Eng.*, Dec. 1987, pp. 1265–1277.

[51] J.A.B. Fortes et al., "A High-Level Systolic Architecture for GaAs," *Proc. ACM/IEEE 19th Hawaii Int'l Conf. System Sciences*, IEEE CS Press, Los Alamitos, Calif., 1986, pp. 238–245.

[52] V. Milutinović, M. Bettinger, and W. Helbig, "On the Impact of GaAs Technology on Adder Characteristics," *IEE Proc. Part E*, May 1989, pp. 217–223.

[53] V. Milutinović, "Microprocessor Architecture and Design for GaAs Technology," *Microelectronics J.*, Vol. 19, No. 4, July/Aug. 1988, pp. 51–56.

[54] V. Milutinović, "Catalytic Migration: A Strategy for Creation of Technology-Sensitive Microprocessor Architectures," *Acta Universitatis*, Niš, Serbia, Yugoslavia, 1996.

[55] F. Distante et al., *Silicon Architectures for Neural Nets*, Elsevier Science Publishers, Amsterdam, The Netherlands, 1991.

[56]   W.R. Bush, "The High-Level Synthesis of Microprocessors Using Instruction Frequency Statistics," ERL Memorandum M92/109, Univ. of California at Berkeley, Berkeley, Calif. May 1992.

[57]   P. Treleaven et al., "VLSI Architectures for Neural Networks," *IEEE Micro*, Vol. 9, No. 6, Dec. 1989, pp. 8–27.

[58]   V. Milutinović, M. Tomašević, B. Markovic, and M. Tremblay, "The Split Temporal/Spatial Cache: Initial Performance Analysis," *Proc. of the Fifth International Workshop on SCI-Based High-Performance Low-Cost Computing*, Santa Clara, Calif., March 1996, pp. 63–70.

[59]   V. Milutinoviæ, "Splitting the Spatial and the Temporal Data in the Cache Subsystem," *Technical Report of the University of Belgrade*, Belgrade, Serbia, Yugoslavia, January 1995.

[60]   V. Milutinoviæ, "A Research Methodology in the Field of Computer Engineering for VLSI," *Proceedings of the 20th IEEE International Conference on Microelectronics— MIEL '95*, Nis, Serbia, Yugoslavia, September 1995, pp. 811–814.

10.2   Suggested Reading

Suggestions for further reading include two types of texts. The first type includes the material to help increase the reader's depth of knowledge (that is, the references listed here and their followups). The second type includes the material to help increase the reader's breadth of knowledge (that is, the references from specialized journals and from the proceedings books of the major conferences in the field).

Neural Networks: Concepts, Applications, and Implementations,   P. Antognetti, and V. Milutinović, eds., Prentice-Hall, Englewood Cliffs, N.J., 1992.

B. Furht, and V. Milutinović, "A Survey of Microprocessor Architectures for Memory Management," *Computer*, Vol. 20, No. 3, Mar. 1987, pp. 48–67.

Computer Architecture, D. Gajski, V. Milutinović, H.J. Siegel, and B. Furht, eds., IEEE CS Press, Los Alamitos, Calif., 1987.

C. Gimarc and V. Milutinović, "A Survey of RISC Architectures of the Mid 80's," *Computer*, Vol. 20, No. 9, Sept. 1987, pp. 59–69.

J. Hennessy et al., "Design of a High Performance VLSI Processor," Tech. Report #83/236, Computer Systems Laboratory, Stanford Univ., Palo Alto, Calif., 1983.

E.E. Hollis, *Design of VLSI Gate Array ICs*, Prentice Hall, Englewood Cliffs, N.J., 1987.

M.G.H. Katevenis, RISC Architectures for VLSI, Tech. Report #83/141, Univ. of California at Berkeley, Berkeley, Calif., Oct. 1983.

S. Kong et al., "Design Methodology of a VLSI Multiprocessor Workstation," *VLSI Systems*, Feb. 1987.

S.S. Leung and M.A. Shaublatt, *ASIC System Design with VHDL: A Paradigm*, Kluwer Academic Publishers, Boston, Mass., 1989.

V. Milutinović, M. Bettinger, and W. Helbig, "Multiplier/Shifter Design Trade-offs in GaAs Microprocessors," *IEEE Trans. Computers*, Vol. 38, No. 6, June 1989, pp. 874–880.

V. Milutinović, J. Crnković, and K. Houstis, "A Simulation Study of Two Distributed Task Allocation Procedures," *IEEE Trans. Software Eng.*, Vol. 14, No. 1, Jan. 1988, pp. 54–61.

V. Milutinović, J. Fortes, and L. Jamieson, "A Multicomputer Architecture for Real-Time Computation of a Class of DFT Algorithms," *IEEE Trans. ASSP*, Oct. 1986, pp. 1301–1309.

GaAs Computer Design, V. Milutinović, and D. Fura, eds., IEEE CS Press, Los Alamitos, Calif., 1988.

V. Milutinović, D. Fura, and W. Helbig, "Pipeline Design Tradeoffs in a 32-bit GaAs Microprocessor," *IEEE Trans. on Computers*, Vol. 40, No. 11, Nov. 1991, pp. 1214–1224.

D. Milutinović, V. Milutinović, and B. Souœek, "The Honeycomb Architecture," *Computer*, Vol. 20, No. 4, Apr. 1987, pp. 81–83.

V. Milutinović, "Suboptimum Detection Procedure Based on the Weighting of Partial Decisions," *IEE Electronics Letters*, Mar, 13, 1980, pp. 237–238.

V. Milutinović, "Comparison of Three Suboptimum Detection Procedures," *IEE Electronics Letters*, Aug. 14, 1980, pp. 683–685.

V. Milutinovic, D. Fura, W. Helbig, J. Linn, "Architecture/Compiler Synergism in GaAs Computer Systems," *IEEE Computer*, Vol. 20, No. 5, May 1987, pp. 72–93.

V. Milutinović, "Generalized WPD Procedure for Microprocessor-Based Signal Detection," *IEE Proc. Part F*, Feb. 1985, pp. 27–35.

V. Milutinović, "A Microprocessor-oriented Algorithm for Adaptive Equalization," *IEEE Trans. Comm.*, Vol. Com-33, No. 6, June 1985, pp. 522–526.

V. Milutinović, "GaAs Microprocessor Technology," *Computer*, Vol. 19, No. 10, Oct. 1986, pp. 10–15.

Advanced Microprocessors and High-Level Language Computer Architecture, V. Milutinović, ed., IEEE CS Press, Los Alamitos, Calif., 1986.

V. Milutinović, "A Comparison of Suboptimal Detection Algorithms for VLSI," *IEEE Trans. Comm.*, Vol. 36, No. 5, May 1988, pp. 538–543.

Computer Architecture, V. Milutinović, ed., North-Holland, New York, N.Y., 1988.

High-Level Language Computer Architecture, V. Milutinović, ed., Freeman Computer Science Press, Rockville, Md., 1989.

V. Milutinović, "Mapping of Neural Networks onto the Honeycomb Architecture," *Proc. IEEE*, Vol. 77, No. 12, Dec. 1989, pp. 1875–1878.

D.A. Patterson and C.H. Sequin, "A VLSI RISC," *Computer*, Sept. 1982, pp. 8–21.

S. Przybylski, et al., "Organization and VLSI Implementation of MIPS," Tech. Report No. 84-259, Computer Systems Laboratory, Stanford University, Palo Alto, Calif., 1984.

R.W. Sherburne, Jr., Processor "Design Tradeoffs in VLSI," Tech. Report #84/173, Univ. of California at Berkeley, Berkeley, Calif., Apr. 1984.

A. Silbey, V. Milutinović, and V. Mendoza Grado, V., "A Survey of High-Level Language Architectures, *Computer*, Vol. 19, No. 8, Aug. 1986, pp. 72–85.

J.D. Ullman, *Computational Aspects of VLSI*, Freeman Computer Science Press, Rockville, Md., 1984.

A. Tanenbaum, *Structural Computer Organization*, Third Edition, Prentice-Hall, Englewood Cliffs, New Jersey, 1990.

J. Hayes, *Computer Architecture and Organization*, Third Edition, McGraw-Hill Book Company, New York, New York, 1994.

W. Stallings, *Computer Organization and Architecture*, Fourth Edition, Prentice-Hall, Englewood Cliffs, New Jersey, 1996.

M. Johnson, *Superscalar Microprocessor Design*, Prentice-Hall, Englewood Cliffs, New Jersey, 1991.

10.3 Some of the Recent References of the Author

[1] V. Milutinović, Tutorial on Microprogramming and Firmware Engineering, IEEE Computer Society Press, Los Alamitos, California, 1990.

[2] B. Peruničić, S. Lakhani, and V. Milutinović, "Stochastic Modeling and Analysis of Propagation Delays in GaAs Adders," *IEEE Trans. Computers*, Vol. 40, No. 1, Jan. 1991, pp. 31–45.

[3] V. Milutinović, D. Fura, and W. Helbig, "Pipeline Design Trade-offs in 32-bit Gallium Arsenide Microprocessor," *IEEE Trans. Computers*, Vol. 40, No. 11, Nov. 1991, pp. 1214–1224.

[4] V. Milutinović and L. Hoevel, "Terminology Risks with the RISC Concept in the Risky RISC Arena," *Computer*, Vol. 25, No. 1, Jan. 1992 (Open Channel), p. 136.

[5] M. Tomašević and V. Milutinović, *Cache Coherency Problem in Shared-Memory Multiprocessors: Hardware Solutions*, IEEE Computer Society Press, Los Alamitos, California, 1993.

[6] M. Tomašević and V. Milutinović, "Hardware Approaches to Cache Coherence in Shared-Memory Multiprocessors Part #1," *IEEE MICRO*, Vol. 14, No. 5, Oct. 1994, pp. 52–59.

[7] M. Tomašević and V. Milutinović, "Hardware Approaches to Cache Coherence in Shared-Memory Multiprocessors Part #2," *IEEE MICRO*, Vol. 14, No. 6, Dec. 1994, pp. 61–66.

[8] V. Milutinović and Z. Petković, "Processor Design Using Silicon Compilation: Ten Lessons Learned from a RISC Design," *Computer*, Vol. 28, No. 3, Mar. 1995 (Open Channel), p. 120.

[9] S. Savić, M. Tomašević, and V. Milutinović, "RMS for PC," *Microprocessor Systems*, October 1995.

[10] I. Ekmeoeić, I. Tartalja, and V. Milutinović, "A Taxonomy of Heterogeneous Computing," *IEEE Computer*, Vol. 28, No. 12, Dec. 1995 (Topics), pp. 68–70.

[11] I. Tartalja and V. Milutinović, *The Cache Coherency Problem in Shared-Memory Multiprocessors: Software Solutions*, IEEE Computer Society Press, Los Alamitos, California, 1996.

[12] M. Tomašević, and V. Milutinović, "The World Invalidate Protocol," *Microprocessor Systems*, January 1996.

[13] A. Grujić, M. Tomašević, and V. Milutinović, "A Simulation Study of Hardware DSM Approaches," *IEEE Parallel and Distributed Technology*, Spring 1996, pp. 74–83.

[14] D. Milutinović and V. Milutinović, "New Solutions for New Technologies," *IEEE Computer*, Vol. 29, No. 6, April 1996 (Open Channel).

[15] J. Protić, M. Tomašević, and V. Milutinović, "A Survey of Distributed Shared Memory: Concepts and Systems," *IEEE Parallel and Distributed Technology*, Summer 1996.

[16] I. Tartalja and V. Milutinović, "A Survey of Software Solutions for Cache Consistency Maintenance in Shared Memory Multiprocessors," *IEEE Software*, Fall 1996.

[17] J. Protić, M. Tomašević, and V. Milutinović, *Tutorial on DSM: Concepts and Systems*, IEEE Computer Society Press, Los Alamitos, Calif., 1996.

[18] I. Ekmecić, I. Tartalja, and V. Milutinović, "A Survey of Heterogeneous Computing: Concepts and Systems," *Proc. IEEE*, August 1996.

[19] D. Milićev et al., "Modeling of Modern 32-bit and 64-bit Microprocessors," *IEEE Trans. Education*, 1996.

[20] V. Milutinović, "A Research Methodology in the Field of Computer Engineering for VLSI," *ISSS Scientific Review*, Vol. SE, No. 15, 1996, pp. 125–137.

[21] V. Milutinović et al., "The Split Temporal/Spatial Cache Memory for Next Generation Microprocessors," 1997 (submitted).

[22] V. Milutinović, "Issues of Importance for the Next Generation Multiprocessor DSM Systems in General, and RMS Systems in Particular," 1997 (submitted).

Appendix A

A Model of a Simple RISC Microprocessor

This appendix contains a reprint of the paper:

> D. Božanić, D. Fura, and V. Milutinović, "An ISP' Model of the FURA-RISC Microprocessor," Technical Report of the University of Belgrade, Belgrade, Serbia, Yugoslavia, 1989.

This paper gives an idiot-proof guideline on how to use the ENDOT package in order to develop a simulator of a processor.

Simulation of a Simple RISC Processor

Dragan Božanić, David Fura, and Veljko Milutinović

Introduction

This document is intended for those not familiar with N.2 and for those who already made their first steps into the N.2, and now want to use N.2 for the first time in the design of a real processor. Understanding this attitude very well, we present here the design process for a simple RISC processor simulator. The processor is modeled at the instruction set level.

Simulation of a Simple RISC Processor

The RISC processor discussed here is a slightly modified version of the educational RISC machine developed at Purdue University by David Fura [1], and later used in [2]. It is very similar to the RISC machine in [3], a 200 MHz 32-bit GaAs RISC machine developed within the DARPA's "On-Board Computer for Star Wars" program. Actually, all RISC machines developed under this DARPA's program were functionally simulated using N.2, before they were implemented in VLSI.

The RISC machine under consideration here has a 32-bit word length. It uses a register-to-register execution model; that is, most instruction executions consist of a register file read (of two operands), followed by an ALU operation, and a register file write. The register file holds sixteen 32-bit data words. Data memory is accessed only through the use of *load* or *store* operations. Most instructions require two processor cycles to complete: instruction fetch (IF) and instruction decode & execute (ID&E), both of equal-duration. Instruction pipelining overlaps the ID&E stage of instruction *i* with the IF stage of instruction *i+1*, yielding an effective one-instruction-per-cycle rate of execution. The structure of instruction pipelining is shown in Figure A-1.

The instructions can be divided into four classes. The first of these—the "**ALU class**"—contains all the instructions which conform to the "register read - ALU operation - register write" sequence mentioned above. These instructions are *add*, *subtract*, *move*, *negate*, *and*, *or*, *not*, *shift left*, *shift right*, *set if equal*, and *set if greater than*. All instructions in this class take two cycles to complete: instruction fetch (IF) and instruction decode & execute (ID&E).

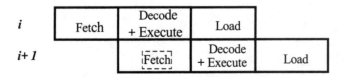

Figure A-1. Structure of Instruction Pipelining

The second instruction class—the "**Branch class**"—contains the instructions *branch on true* and *branch always*. The sequence of microoperations here is: register file read, ALU operation, and (conditional) program counter (PC) write. These two instructions take two cycles to complete (instruction fetch and instruction decode & execute). Because of pipelining, if the condition for branching is satisfied, the effect of the *branch always* instruction or the *branch on true* instruction lasts for an additional third cycle. Because the PC update occurs near the end of the decode & execution cycle, the fetching of the sequential instruction will have been initiated before the PC is updated by the branch instruction being currently executed. Therefore, the effect of the branch instruction is not felt until after the instruction immediately after that branch instruction is executed. This branch handling strategy, where the instruction(s) after the branch instruction are always executed, is known as delayed branching [4]. Generally, only a subset of the instructions in a program can be executed in the slot following a given branch instruction (in most cases of *N*-stage pipelining, this slot is *N-1* processor cycles wide). In systems with delayed branching at compile time, during the code generation phase, an innocious instruction (such as a *no operation, nop*) is placed in the slots behind branches. Then, also at compile time, during the code optimization phase, an attempt is made to eliminate the innocious instruction (typically a *no operation, nop*), by replacing it with a useful instruction from elsewhere in the code. Candidates for replacement are only those instructions which are not correlated with the branch instruction to be optimized (neither the branch target address, nor the branch condition can depend on the instruction to be moved into the delayed branch slot). An example of software optimization for delayed branching is shown in Table A-1.

The third instruction class—the "**Data memory**"—contains the *load* and *store* instructions. From the processor point of view, the *store* instruction needs only two cycles to complete: instruction fetch and instruction decode & execute. The decode & execute cycle includes a register file read, possibly an ALU operation, followed by a write of data and address to output latches. The memory system finishes the *store* instruction independently of the processor. However, the *load* instruction requires three cycles. The first cycle is for the instruction fetch; the second one includes a register file read, possibly an ALU operation, followed by a write of a memory address to an output latch. Near the end of the third cycle, the data operand is transferred from memory into the register file. Obviously the instruction right after a data load instruction cannot use the operand being loaded—it does not arrive in time. In this case, a *no operation* instruction must be placed into the slot behind the *load* instruction. The instruction cycle after the load, the load fill in slot, must be filled, either by the optimizing compiler or by the assembly language programmer, with a useful instruction, just as was required for branch instructions described earlier. Software optimization for delayed load is shown in Table A-2.

The fourth instruction class contains only the *noophalt* instruction. This instruction causes the machine to idle and it does not modify the state of the machine. Also, this instruction may be used for filling the slots behind branches, or behind load instructions. Table A-3. shows the instruction set of the RISC processor under consideration. Figure A-2. shows the instruction formats of the RISC processor under consideration.

We deal here with a processor system, so we need to handle both hardware and software. We can specify hardware at any level: logic gate, register transfer, instruction, or algorithm. This document is orientated towards the instruction level simulation, but it would not be difficult to extend this work to other levels, as well. For software, we can specify the algorithms in some high-level language like C, or in the assembler language. In the case of high-level languages, one must write its own compiler, since N.2 wants to see assembler language code.

Table A-1.   Software Optimization for Delayed Branching

Original code:

instruction	i-1	**ADD** R0, imm32
	i	**JUMP** R1, R2>R3
	i+1	**MOVE** R3, R4
	i+2	**SUB** R5, R6, R7

Code after inserting the *nop* instruction:

instruction	i-1	**ADD** R0, imm32
	i	**JUMP** R1, R2>R3
	i+1	**NOP**
	i+2	**MOVE** R3, R4
	i+3	**SUB** R5, R6, R7

Code after optimization:

instruction	i-1	**JUMP** R1+1, imm32
	i	**ADD** R0, imm32
	i+1	**MOVE** R3, R4
	i+2	**SUB** R5, R6, R7

Table A-2.   Software Optimization for Delayed Load

Original code:

instruction	i-1	**MOVE** R3, R4
	i	**LOAD** R0, MEMORY
	i+1	**ADD** R2, R1, R0

Code after inserting *nop* instruction:

instruction	i-1	**MOVE** R3, R4
	i	**LOAD** R0, MEMORY
	i+1	**NOP**
	i+2	**ADD** R2, R1, R0

Code after optimization:

instruction	i-1	**LOAD** R0, MEMORY
	i	**MOVE** R3, R4
	i+1	**ADD** R2, R1, R0

N.2 requires some files for an instruction-level simulation. They are listed here:

a)   We need to describe our processors. We do this by using a higher-level programming language for hardware description called **ISP'**. With the ISP' you can describe one processor type per input file—these files end with the suffix ".isp," so we see files like "risc.isp," etc. Because of this, we can specify multiple instantiations of one ".isp" file and then connect these instantiations using a topology language.

Table A-3. Instruction Set of the RISC Processor Under Consideration

1. "Add"
   a) **ADD** Rd , Rs1 , Rs2   Rd := Rs1 + Rs2
   b) **ADD** Rd , Rs1 , imm16   Rd := Rs1+ sign_extend(imm16)
   c) **ADD** Rd , PC, imm16   Rd := PC + sign_extend(imm16)

2. "Subtract"
   a) **SUB** Rd , Rs1 , Rs2   Rd := Rs1 - Rs2
   b) **SUB** Rd , Rs1 , imm16   Rd := Rs1 - sign_extend(imm16)
   c) **SUB** Rd , PC, imm16   Rd := PC - sign_extend(imm16)

3. "Move"
   a) **MOV** Rd , Rs1   Rd := Rs1
   b) **MOV** Rd , imm16   Rd := sign_extend(imm16)
   c) **MOV** Rd , PC   Rd := PC

4. "Negate"
   a) **NEG** Rd , Rs1   Rd := - Rs1

5. "Logical AND"
   a) **LAND** Rd , Rs1 , Rs2   Rd := Rs1 .AND. Rs2
   b) **LAND** Rd , Rs1 , imm16   Rd := Rs1 .AND. sign_extend(imm16)

6. "Logical OR"
   a) **LOR** Rd , Rs1 , Rs2   Rd := Rs1 .OR. Rs2
   b) **LOR** Rd , Rs1 , imm16   Rd := Rs1 .OR. sign_extend(imm16)

7. "Logical NOT"
   a) **LNOT** Rd , Rs1   Rd := .NOT. Rs1

8. "Arithmetic Shift Left"
   a) **SLA** Rd , Rs1 , imm5

9. "Arithmetic Shift Right"
   a) **SRA** Rd , Rs1 , imm5

10. "Set If Equal"
    a) **SEQ** Rd , Rs1 , Rs2   if Rs1 = Rs2 then Rd := -1
                                     else Rd := 0

11. "Set If Greater Than"
    a) **SGT** Rd , Rs1 , Rs2   if Rs1 > Rs2 then Rd := -1
                                     else Rd := 0

12. "Branch on True"
    a) **BT** Rd , Rs1   if Rs1 = -1 then PC := Rd

13. "Branch Always"
    a) **BA** Rd   PC := Rd

14. "Load"
    a) **LD** Rd , Rs2   Rd := Mem[Rs2]

15. "Store"
    a) **ST** Rd , Rs2   Mem[Rs2] := Rd

16. "No Operation"
    a) **NOOPHALT**

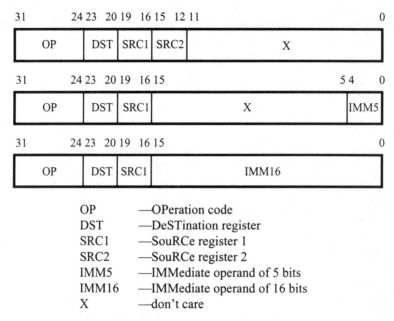

OP	—OPeration code
DST	—DeSTination register
SRC1	—SouRCe register 1
SRC2	—SouRCe register 2
IMM5	—IMMediate operand of 5 bits
IMM16	—IMMediate operand of 16 bits
X	—don't care

Figure A-2. Instruction Formats of the RISC Processor Under Consideration

b)   We also need to descibe our memories, and we use the ISP' language for this, too. These file names tend to look like "mem.isp," for instance. Naturally, processor and main memory have to be connected (because they are usually placed in separate files), using the topology language. In our case here, a main memory description is placed in the same file with the processor description.

c)   We need to convert assembler programs into machine language code. For this purpose, we have to define three things in a file with suffix ".m" (such as "risc.m"):

1)   our machine architecture—really only the bit fields of the machine instructions are needed,

2)   the assembler-to-machine language translator, and

3)   our assembly program.

d)   We need to resolve labels within our assembly program and to load our program into the memory. Label resolution (for instance, the conversion of a label into a number which is really the *address* of that label) is done in a file with suffix ".i," for example "risc.i." Loading the program into memory is done as specified in the topology file. Every ISP' description that contains memory may have a program loaded into it.

e)   In this step we define the topology of the system. We must define the instantiations of the previously created ISP' objects, and then we have to connect these instantiations in the appropriate way, to form a given system. We define the topology of the system in the file with suffix ".t" (that is, "risc.t").

f)   Assembler program for simulation of a processor has to be:

1)   placed in a separated file ("risc.tst") and then "included" into the file with suffix ".m," or

2)   placed directly into the *begin-end* section of the ".m" file. We used this document, the first way, because of the flexibility.

The ".isp" File

In the ".isp" file we describe how our processor works. Memory is passive and can be thought of as just an array of information. The processor does three things:

a)   instruction fetch,

b)   instruction decode, and

c)   instruction execution.

We assume that "instructions" here are the assembled instructions of any assembler program, that is, we can think of each instruction as a sequence of 1's and 0's, with the length of a memory word. In addition, we assume that the instructions have been loaded into program memory, beginning at address zero (PC = 0). In general, instruction *fetching* can be done with an *assignment* statement, instruction *decoding* is done with a *case* statement, and instruction *execution* is done with *assignment* statements including *add*, *subtract*, and so on.

A typical instruction execution cycle consists of register read, followed by an ALU operation, followed by register write. Delayed branching is used; there is no hardware interlock used for sequencing hazards associated with branches; the instruction following a branch is always executed. An exception to this is when the processor execution encounters a sequence of more than one consecutive branch instruction—this phenomenon is too complicated to explain here, and we refer the user to other sources [4]. We assume that the memory system is slow in comparsion with the processor, and that the *load* instruction requires three cycles to complete; a data operand is written into the register file at the end of the third cycle (that is, at the end of the decode & execute cycle of the instruction following the *load* instruction).

1.1 The "Declaration" Part of the ".isp" File

This part contains only declaration data which are placed into **macro**, **state**, **memory**, and/or **format** sections:

The **macro** section contains macro-definitions. Macro-definitions are used to give convenient easily remembered names to ISP' objects. The user is free to use a convenient name, while the ISP' compiler uses the associated value. The names to the left of the "=" are selected by the user, and he can use them throughout the rest of the ".isp" file. The values to the right of the "=" are then associated with the names at the left. Whenever the name is encountered later in this file, the value at the right will be substituted by the ISP' compiler. The "&" separates individual macro-definitions and the ";" ends this section:

> **macro**
> **WORD = 32&,**
> **BYTE = 8&,**
> **NIBBLE = 4&**
>
> ;

The **state** section contains all global variables for an ISP' module. Here we have the processor register (PC, IR, general register file, ...) and simulation variables (histogram array— used to count the number of times an instruction opcode is executed in an assembler program, etc.). All global variables are zero at the time of simulation initiation. Individual global variables are separated by commas, and the section is terminated by the ";". The "number" inside the "<"-">" pair indicates the wordlength (for instance, the number of bits) of a global variable. Arrays can also be used—the dimensionality is specified within the "["-"]" pair:

```
state
    reg[0:15]<WORD>,          ! register file
    pc<WORD>,                 ! program counter
    pastpc<WORD>,             ! previous program counter
    ir<WORD>,                 ! instruction register
    pastop<WORD>,             ! previous opcode
    pastdst<NIBBLE>,          ! previous destination register
    pastval<WORD>,            ! previous value
    hist[0:23]<WORD>          ! histogram array
;
```

The **memory** section contains memory. Memory is like state variables, except that it may be initialized in a specific way, with things like code or data, before simulation, using the topology language (the ".t" file). All locations not explicitly initialized are set to zero at simulation initiation. As in the **state** section, commas separate the memory variables and the section is terminated by the ";". The "<"-">" pair indicates the wordlength and the "["-"]" pair is used for array variables. Symbol "0xfff" represents the hexadecimal value fff, or 4095 in base 10. The prefix "0" can be used to designate an octal number; a prefix of any number except 0 designates a decimal number:

```
memory
    memry[0:0xfff]<WORD>
;
```

The **format** section allow the users to define convenient names for subranges of the previously defined state variables. The use of these names can result in both a more easily read simulation code and in a reduction of errors within the code. In our example, we define instruction fields as subfields of the IR (instruction register). In this way, we obtained variables which represent subranges of the machine-level intructions. The names to the left of the "=" are the user names, while those to the right are the instruction word subranges. Again, commas separate individual format variables, and the ";" terminates the section:

```
format
    op = ir<31:24>,
    dst = ir<23:20>,
    src1 = ir<19:16>,
    src2 = ir<15:12>,
    imm16 = ir<15:0>,
    imm5 = ir<4:0>
;
```

1.2 The "Behavior" Part of the ".isp" File

The **Behavior** part of the ".isp" file describes what our hardware really does. This section contains a set of concurrent tasks. In our case, there is just one task, with the type *main* (works in a continuous loop). The *main* task performs the instruction fetch, instruction decoding, and instruction executing. Instruction feching is performed by the assignment "ir=memry[pastpc]." Instruction decoding is performed by a *case* statement of the following structure:

case op
  0: ...
    .
    .
    .
  23: ...
esac;

Instruction execution is performed by statements that are imbedded within the above mentioned *case* statement. The execution for the opcode of zero (*op=0*, a register-to-register add) is performed by the single statement "*reg[dst]=reg[src1]+reg[src2]*," etc. One very important difference between the ISP' and traditional high-level programming languages is that all ISP' instructions, between two separators of the sequentality, execute concurrently. These separators may be explicit or implicit. One explicit separator of sequentality is the ISP' statement *next*. Implicit separators of sequentality are the ISP' function *delay()* and the end mark for the *main* task—").""

```
main := (                          ! main is an infinitely looping process;
    pastop = op;                   ! keep a copy of the previous opcode;
    hist[pastop] = hist[pastop] + 1;  ! a statistics collecting operation;
    ir = memry[pastpc];            ! this is the instruction fetch;
    pastpc = pc;                   ! pastpc points to the current instruction;
    pc = pc + 1;                   ! pc points to the next instruction;
    delay(1);                      ! all above mentioned statements execute
                                   ! in parallel—they represent the instruction
                                   ! fetch cycle; delay statement stops the
                                   ! program execution for one time unit;
                                   ! besides, delay statement is an implicit
                                   ! separator of sequentality—all statements
                                   ! between these statement and the end mark of
                                   ! the main task work in parallel, too.
    if pastop eql 21               ! if the previous instruction was a load,
        reg[pastdst] = pastval;    ! it is necessary to update the destination register;
                                   ! this statement simulates
                                   ! the "delayed load" strategy;
                                   ! destination load is done in parallel
                                   ! with the decode & execute cycle
                                   ! of the next instruction.
    case op                        ! this statement performs the decode;
                                   ! for each legal opcode,
                                   ! a unique action is specified -
                                   ! this is the execute step.
        0: reg[dst] = reg[src1] + reg[src2]       ! add (reg-reg)
        1: reg[dst] = reg[src1] + imm16 sxt 32    ! add (reg-imm)
        2: reg[dst] = pc + imm16 sxt 32           ! add (pc-imm)
        3: reg[dst] = reg[src1] - reg[src2]       ! sub (reg-reg)
        4: reg[dst] = reg[src1] - imm16 sxt 32    ! sub (reg-imm)
        5: reg[dst] = pc - imm16 sxt 32           ! sub (pc-imm)
        6: reg[dst] = reg[src1]                   ! mov (reg-reg)
        7: reg[dst] = imm16 sxt 32                ! mov (reg-imm)
```

```
    8: reg[dst] = pc                                    ! mov (reg-pc)
    9: reg[dst] = - reg[src1]                           ! negate
   10: reg[dst] = reg[src1] and reg[src2]               ! and (reg-reg)
   11: reg[dst] = reg[src1] and imm16 sxt 32            ! and (reg-imm)
   12: reg[dst] = reg[src1] or reg[src2]                ! or (reg-reg)
   13: reg[dst] = reg[src1] or imm16 sxt 32             ! or (reg-imm)
   14: reg[dst] = not reg[src1]                         ! not
   15: reg[dst] = reg[src1]*/arith (imm5 ext 32)        ! shift left
   16: reg[dst] = reg[src1] /:arith (imm5 ext 32)       ! shift right
   17: if reg[src1] eql reg[src2]                       ! set if equal
           reg[dst] = -1
       else
           reg[dst] = 0
   18: if reg[src1] gtr reg[src2]                       ! set if greater
           reg[dst] = -1
       else
           reg[dst] = 0
   19: if reg[src1} eql -1                              ! branch on true
           pc = reg[dst]
   20: pc = reg[dst]                                    ! branch always
   21: (pastdst = dst;                                  ! load
       pastval = memry[reg[src2]])
   22: memry[reg[src2]] = reg[dst]                      ! store
   23: ;                                                ! noophalt
 esac;
 )                                                      ! end of the "main" process
```

Main characteristics of the *behavior* part of the ".isp" file are shown in Figures A-3. and A-4.

The ".m" File

The translation of assembly instructions into machine language code is the responsibility of this file. We have two major sections: in one of them, we have the translation definition, and in the other one, we have the assembly instructions themselves. The translation definition is given in the *instr*, *format*, and *macro* sections. The assembly language program is placed inside the *begin-end* declaration. The assembly language program is not contained in the ".m" file (it could be), but is instead in another file ("risc.tst") which is "included" into this file. Translation is done by the rules placed in the *macro* section. Each assembly instruction has a macro-definition for assembler-to-machine language translation associated to it.

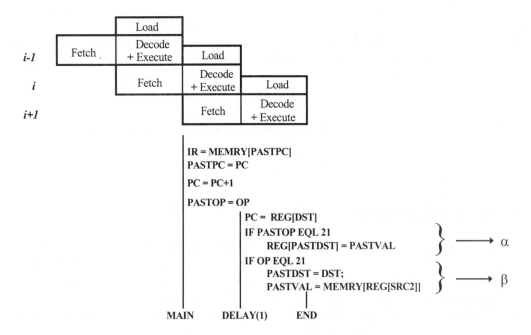

Figure A3. The *main* Process
(See Figure A-4. for the definition of activities α and β.)

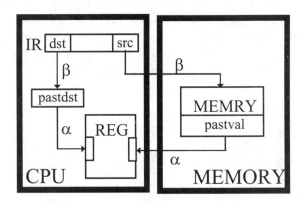

Figure A-4. Delayed Load Strategy
(See Figure A-3 for ISP' statements that correspond to activities α and β.)

2.1 The Instr Section

In this section we define the variable I, a single word containing 32 bits. This variable serves as the place where an assembled instruction is to be stored:

instr

I<32>$

2.2 The Format Section

This section is identical to the format section of the ".isp" file. Here we define local variables which represent subranges of the variable I, needed in the process of translation:

$$
\begin{aligned}
&\textbf{format}\\
&\quad \text{op} = \text{I}<31:24>,\\
&\quad \text{dst} = \text{I}<23:20>,\\
&\quad \text{src1} = \text{I}<19:16>,\\
&\quad \text{src2} = \text{I}<15:12>,\\
&\quad \text{imm16} = \text{I}<15:0>,\\
&\quad \text{imm5} = \text{I}<4:0>\$
\end{aligned}
$$

2.3 The Macro Section

The *macro* section has the same meaning as the *macro* section in the ".isp" file—they both allow one to associate the easily remembered names with certain things. Therefore, they allow the assembly language programmer to use his own instruction mnemonics for each instruction to be assembled, and to associate them with a macro-definition for translation into machine code. The macros are applied to the assembly instructions contained within the *begin-end* pair, at the end of the ".m" file.

In our example, we have two classes of macro-defitions. In the first one, we associate symbolic names for registers (r1, r2, etc.). Now, assembly language programmers can use "*ri*" for register *i*, instead "*i*." The second class of macro-definitions performs the translation. At the left side of the "=," we have the instruction mnemonic with a set of parameters surrounded by parentheses. The parameters are things like register numbers, immediate values, and so on. The need for parentheses is a weakness of the current version of *metamicro*. At the right side of the "=," we see the definition of the translation using the parameters and the variables (which are subrange of I) defined in the *format* section:

```
macro
    r0 = 0&,
    r1 = 1&,
    r2 = 2&,
    r3 = 3&,
    r4 = 4&,
    r5 = 5&,
    r6 = 6&,
    r7 = 7&,
    r8 = 8&,
    r9 = 9&,
    r10 = 10&,
    r11 = 11&,
    r12 = 12&,
    r13 = 13&,
    r14 = 14&,
    r15 = 15&,
    addrr(d,s1,s2)   = op=0; dst=d; src1=s1; src2=s2$&,
    addri(d,s1,i16)  = op=1; dst=d; src1=s1; imm16=i16$&,
    addpi(d,i16)     = op=2; dst=d; imm16=i16$&,
```

```
subrr(d,s1,s2)    = op=3; dst=d; src1=s1; src2=s2$&,
subri(d,s1,i16)   = op=4; dst=d; src1=s1; imm16=i16$&,
subpi(d,i16)      = op=5; dst=d; imm16=i16$&,
movr(d,s1)        = op=6; dst=d; src1=s1$&,
movi(d,i16)       = op=7; dst=d; imm16=i16$&,
movp(d)           = op=8; dst=d$&,
neg(d,s1)         = op=9; dst=d; src1=s1$&,
andrr(d,s1,s2)    = op=10; dst=d; src1=s1; src2=s2$&,
andri(d,s1,i16)   = op=11; dst=d; src1=s1; imm16=i16$&,
orrr(d,s1,s2)     = op=12; dst=d; src1=s1; src2=s2$&,
orri(d,s1,i16)    = op=13; dst=d; src1=s1; imm16=i16$&,
lnot(d,s1)        = op=14; dst=d; src1=s1$&,
sla(d,s1,i5)      = op=15; dst=d; src1=s1; imm5=i5$&,
sra(d,s1,i5)      = op=16; dst=d; src1=s1; imm5=i5$&,
seq(d,s1,s2)      = op=17; dst=d; src1=s1; src2=s2$&,
sgt(d,s1,s2)      = op=18; dst=d; src1=s1; src2=s2$&,
bt(d,s1)          = op=19; dst=d; src1=s1$&,
ba(d)             = op=20; dst=d$&,
ld(d,s2)          = op=21; dst=d; src2=s2$&,
st(d,s2)          = op=22; dst=d; src2=s2$&,
noophalt          = op=23$&$
```

2.4 The Begin-End Section

Here we must define the assembly program for translation into machine code. Actually, our assembly program is in another file, and is "included" here. Consequently, other assembly programs may be assembled by merely changing the filename inside the *include* statement, rather than by rewriting the entire program. Here we have:

```
begin
    include risc.tst$
end
```

The ".i" File

This file allows us to do the following: (1) label resolution, (2) assembled code linking, and (3) program loading into memory.

3.1 The Instr Section

The **instr** section is identical to that in the ".m" file:

```
instr
    I<32>$
```

3.2 The Format Section

The **format** section is identical to that in the ".m" file:

format
       op = I<31:24>,
       dst = I<23:20>,
       src1 = I<19:16>,
       src2 = I<15:12>,
       imm16 = I<15:0>,
       imm5 = I<4:0>$

3.3 The Space Section

The **space** section tells the linking/loader what our address space looks like. It indicates the size of the memory space that we need, and also what the lowest and the highest address are. In general, symbol "<x:y>" indicates that memory from address x to address y will be used:

           space
             <0:4095>$

3.4 The Transfer Section

The **transfer** section describes how memory allocation is to be performed. The loader will put our program into physical memory; however, code segments may not always be stored into *physically* contiguous memory locations by the loader. The amount of pain that this causes depends on whether we have a "vertical" architecture or a "horizontal" architecture.

A *vertical* architecture is one in which the address of the next instruction to execute is not explicitly specified within an instruction. The next instruction in this case is typically the one in the next sequential location in the program (except for branch instructions). If code for a vertical machine is stored into two physically distinct areas in memory, a problem arises when execution wants to proceed sequentially from the end of one area to the beginning of the other area. In order to accomodate this, the linking/loader inserts an unconditional jump instruction into the program at the end of each physical area (except the last one), that is, it adds a *new* instruction, in order to continue program from the new physical segment. So, for vertical machines, we must indicate two things: (1) we must use the keyword *new* to indicate a vertical architecture, and (2) we must tell the linking/loader what an unconditional jump instruction of our processor looks like, so it knows what to insert at the appropriate places.

A *horizontal* architecture is one in which the address of the next instruction to be executed is explicitly given within the current instruction. In this case, when we need to proceed from the end of one area in physical memory to the beginning of another area, we must *modify* the next-address specification within the last instruction of the first area. Therefore, we must use the keyword *old* here to indicate that new instructions are not inserted, but that "old" instructions are modified.

In our example, we choose a vertical architecture. The situation is simplified since we only have one code block; hence, it must be stored into physically contiguous memory, and we do not need to include the unconditional jump statement into the *transfer* declaration:

           transfer
             {new}

3.5 The Mode Section

The **mode** section describes how labels are to be resolved. Labels are not resolved by the meta-assembler; in fact, the meta-assembler completely ignores them. The linking/loader translates a label into address (for instance, immediate operand), and puts that address into the appropriate field of an instruction. Only a few instructions use labels. For each instruction from this group, we must define a way for resolving labels. To make this more clear, look at the "move immediate (movi)" instruction which we defined within the ".isp" and ".m" files. What is not evident from these two files is that the immediate operand could be a label (that is, movi(r0,label)). The meta-asembler ignores labels. The immediate field of the instruction will remain the same (probably zero). It is up to the linking/loader to determine the "value" (for instance, address) of the label and to insert it into the immediate field of the instruction. The linking/loader must be told how to do this. The final address can be a function of two addresses: the program counter, indicated by the variable ".", and the label address, indicated by the variable "address". In our example, we simply put the label address into the immediate field. This can be much more complicated than our simple example, in order to handle a large variety of addressing modes (that is, many processors use the addressing mode "PC+displacement" for branch destination address; the assembly language mnemonic may look like "BR label"; however, the value stored in the immediate field is not the address of the "label", but the address of the displacement (label-PC); in this case, you might see in the mode field, statements such as "imm16~address$," where "." represents the program counter). Note that labels can only legally be used within instructions that are set up for label use in the mode section:

```
mode
    case op eql 7:
    imm16 ~ address$
    break$
    esac,

    default:
    imm16 ~ imm16$
    break$
    esac$
```

The ".t" File

The topology file defines the system structure. It defines some characteristics of ISP' modules and shows how they are interconnected.

4.1 The Signal Section

The **signal** section defines signals that are external to the ISP' modules that the user has created. If we had an example with separate ISP' description for a processor and memory, then signals would be things such as the address and data buses, memory read and write control signals, and so on. Since our example has only one ISP' module containing both processor and memory we have no "external" world, and no need for the signal section.

4.2 The Processor Section

The **processor** section defines some characteristic for each instantiation of an ISP' file that is to be part of the system. If, for example, we have four RISC processors and eight memory modules in our system, we would have a total of 12 "processor" sections in the topology file and two ".isp" files. We have to give each instance of an ISP' module a unique name and define which ".sim" file (for instance, object code version of the appropriate ".isp" file) it is associated with:

processor cpu = "risc.sim";

There is a **time delay** declaration associated with each processor declaration just described. Within the ISP' description for the RISC processor (the "risc.isp" file), there is a keyword "delay(1)" used to indicate the passage of one clock cycle. In the topology file we indicate the amount of time associated with a single clock cycle, using the "time" declaration:

time delay = 100 ns;

There is an **initial** declaration associated with each processor declaration just described. This is how code and/or data is loaded into memory, prior to simulation initiation. In our example, "initial memry=l.out" puts our assembled and linked/loaded program, which is in the file "l.out," into the memory variable *memry*, which was defined within the "risc.isp" file. Note that "l.out" is the default output file of the linking/loader. You can use any filename you wish in the initial declaration, as long as you ensure that the contents of the file "l.out" are copied into the desired file. In the *initial* declaration, we initialize the memory variable defined within the ".isp" file:

initial memry = l.out;

The ".tst" File

The following text shows a sample assembler language program used as the benchmark program for our RISC processor. This program is placed in the separate file ("risc.tst" file) and "included" into the ".m" file (within the *begin-end* section):

High-level representation:

```
/* Bubblesort */
int size;        /* memry[30]*/
int vec[1..size]; /* memry[50..50+size-1] */
int temp;
 for(i=1;i<size;i++)
       for(j=1;j<=size-i;j++)
              if (vec[j]>vec[j+1]) then {
                     temp=vec[j];
                     vec[j]=vec[j+1];
                     vec[j+1]=temp;
              }
```

Assembly language program:

```
               movi(r10,l1)
               movi(r11,l2)
               movi(r0,30)
               ld(r2,r0)
               movi(r4,49)
               movi(r5,50)
               movi(r0,1)
               movi(r3,1)
               movr(r6,r4)
     l1:       movr(r7,r5)
               addrr(r6,r6,r3)
               addrr(r7,r7,r3)
               ld(r8,r6)
               ld(r9,r7)
               noophalt
               sgt(r15,r9,r8)
               bt(r11,r15)
               addri(r3,r3,1)
               seq(r14,r9,r8)
               bt(r11,r14)
               noophalt
               st(r9,r6)
               st(r8,r7)
     l2:       sgt(r15,r2,r3)
               bt(r10,r15)
               movr(r6,r4)
               subri(r2,r2,1)
               sgt(r15,r2,r0)
               bt(r10,r15)
               movi(r3,1)
```

Simulation

6.1 The UNIX Environment

Before you can use N.2 commands, the N.2 home directory must be in your path. This is done differently depending upon which shell you use as follows:

If you use "sh" (your prompt is probably $):

PATH =: /*/endot/bin$PATH; export PATH

If you use "csh" (your prompt is probably %):

setenv PATH:/*/endot/bin$PATH

By putting the appropriate command in your login file (or other appropriate file), you do not have to type this command in every time you want to use N.2. The asterisk in the above commands should be replaced with a letter which depends on the machine that you are using.

For example, on machines EC, ED, EE, EF use the letters b, g, m, and e respectively (at Purdue University).

In addition to the above, the file "nmpc.uof" must be within the directory that you wish to execute from. To get this file, execute:

cp /*/endot/nmpc.uof nmpc.uof

6.2 The VMS Environment

Before you can use N.2 commands, the file "nmpc.uof" must be within your root directory. To get this file, execute:

copy vl$a:[n2]nmpc.uof

There is just one more thing you have to do before every launching of the N.2—you must to execute the following command (at Belgrade University):

@vl$a:[n2]login

By putting this command in your "login.com" file, you do not have to type it in every time you want to use N.2.

6.3 N.2 commands

To create and run an instruction-level simulation, you must execute the following N.2 commands:

ic risc.isp

- This creates the file "risc.sim," the hardware simulator.

micro risc.m

- This creates the file "risc.n."

inter risc.i

- This creates the file "risc.a."

cater risc.a risc.n

- This creates the file "l.out," the software simulator.

ec -b risc.t

- This runs the ecologist, which combines "risc.sim" and "l.out" to produce "risc.e00" and "l.p00."

n2 [-s risc.txt] risc.e00

- This invokes the simulator. The results of simulation may be placed in the file "risc.txt," if option "-s" was used. An example excursion into N.2 simulator is shown in the following text. Every line started with ">" represents the user's input; rest is the computer's output:

  Welcome to N.2. This message is coming from the simulator
  'message of the day' file. Please adjust it to reflect
  information required at your site.

simulation: risc (snapshot = 00)
date created: Wed Oct 22 13:49:02 1992
simulation time = 0
> deposit 1 cpu:pc
> deposit 4 cpu:memry[30]
> deposit 4 cpu:memry[50]
> deposit 3 cpu:memry[51]
> deposit 2 cpu:memry[52]
> deposit 5 cpu:memry[53]
> monitor eql 31 stop cpu:pc
tag 1

> monitor write stop cpu:memry[50,53]
tag 2
tag 3
tag 4
tag 5
> run
2200
      2: write cpu:memry[50] = 00000003
> examine cpu:memry[50,53]
cpu:memry[50] = 00000003
cpu:memry[51] = 00000003
cpu:memry[52] = 00000002
cpu:memry[53] = 00000005
> run
2300
      3: write cpu:memry[51] = 00000004
> examine cpu:memry[50,53]
cpu:memry[50] = 00000003
cpu:memry[51] = 00000004
cpu:memry[52] = 00000002
cpu:memry[53] = 00000005
> run
3900
      3: write cpu:memry[51] = 00000002
> examine cpu:memry[50,53]
cpu:memry[50] = 00000003
cpu:memry[51] = 00000002
cpu:memry[52] = 00000002
cpu:memry[53] = 00000005
> run
4000
      4: write cpu:memry[52] = 00000004
> examine cpu:memry[50,53]
cpu:memry[50] = 00000003
cpu:memry[51] = 00000002
cpu:memry[52] = 00000004
cpu:memry[53] = 00000005
> run
7200

       2: write cpu:memry[50] = 00000002
> examine cpu:memry[50,53]
cpu:memry[50] = 00000002
cpu:memry[51] = 00000002
cpu:memry[52] = 00000004
cpu:memry[53] = 00000005
> run
7300
       3: write cpu:memry[51] = 00000003
> examine cpu:memry[50,53]
cpu:memry[50] = 00000002
cpu:memry[51] = 00000003
cpu:memry[52] = 00000004
cpu:memry[53] = 00000005
> run
10700
       1: eql cpu:pc = 0000001F (= 31)

> examine cpu:hist[0,23]
cpu:hist[0] = 0000000E
cpu:hist[1] = 00000006
cpu:hist[2] = 00000000
cpu:hist[3] = 00000000
cpu:hist[4] = 00000003
cpu:hist[5] = 00000000
cpu:hist[6] = 0000000D
cpu:hist[7] = 00000009
cpu:hist[8] = 00000000
cpu:hist[9] = 00000000
cpu:hist[10] = 00000000
cpu:hist[11] = 00000000
cpu:hist[12] = 00000000
cpu:hist[13] = 00000000
cpu:hist[14] = 00000000
cpu:hist[15] = 00000000
cpu:hist[16] = 00000000
cpu:hist[17] = 00000003
cpu:hist[18] = 0000000F
cpu:hist[19] = 00000011
cpu:hist[20] = 00000000
cpu:hist[21] = 0000000D
cpu:hist[22] = 00000006
cpu:hist[23] = 00000009
> quit

Hopefully, the issues are clear now!

References

[1]   D. Fura and V. Milutinović, "ISP' Simulator of a RISC Machine," Internal Report EE670/87, School of Electrical Engineering, Purdue Univ., West Lafayette, Ind., Dec. 1987.

[2]   D. Božanić and V. Milutinović, "ENDOT Classroom Support Package," Technical Report #ETF-TI-RTI-93-001, School of Electrical Engineering, University of Belgrade, Serbia, Yugoslavia, Jan. 1993.

[3]   W.A. Helbig and V. Milutinović, "A DCFL E/D-MESFET GaAs Experimental RISC Machine," *IEEE Trans. Computers,* Vol. 38, No. 2, Feb. 1989, pp. 263–274.

[4]   J.L. Hennessy and D.A. Patterson, *Computer Architecture—A Quantitative Approach*, Morgan Kaufmann Publishers, San Mateo, Calif., 1990.

Appendix B

An Experimental 32-bit RISC Microprocessor with a 200 MHz Clock

This appendix contains a reprint of the paper:

> W. Helbig and V. Milutinović, "A DCFL E/D-MESFET GaAs 32-bit Experimental RISC Machine," *IEEE Transactions on Computers*, Vol. 38, No. 2, February 1989, pp. 263–274.

This paper describes the crown of the entire effort to realize the GaAs version of the 200 MHz RISC microprocessor, within the "MIPS for Star Wars" program. It was decided that the paper should be reprinted (rather than reinterpreted), so the readers obtain the information from the primary source.

with TriQuint, Inc's DCFL E/D-MESFET.[1] In the DCFL family, NOR gates of 2–5 inputs are present, but NAND gates do not exist. Furthermore, on each input to a NOR gate, a two-input AND gate may be included.

This limitation is the result of the circuit construction technique and the inherent properties of GaAs, one of these being that the voltage swing of the signal in a logic gate is relatively small (± 220 mV), and is centered around the intermediate value of the reference voltage ($+320$ mV). The important factor for the logic designer is that this characteristic causes the power dissipation in a given circuit to be high (since it is always drawing current), thus limiting, severely, the number of logic elements that one may put on a chip, before its internal power consumption becomes prohibitive. Of course, one may design all of the circuits' internal impedances so that they are high (by using small-sized devices). This results in the circuit that has a small fan-out (but permits a large fan-in), uses a small area on the chip, and requires only a small amount of power to operate. On the other hand, a circuit with a larger fan-out tends to permit a smaller number of inputs (smaller fan-in), uses a larger area on the chip, and dissipates more power internally.

The penalty that the logic designer pays by not being able to tie the outputs of two circuits together is even more severe [2]. In other words, one cannot design phantom functions into the logic. With no "off state" in the circuit, tying outputs together does not change the amount of power dissipated, but does decrease the operating noise margin of the resulting logic tree. For the logic designer, this translates into a need to design a system bus, with its many inputs and outputs, as a single entity with only one active load circuit. This means including, in the design, allowances for the function of "bus precharge," and time in each operating cycle to accomplish this precharge. The related loss of time could be substantial and, in the case of the DCFL E/D-MESFET GaAs logic family, is not justified. The reason is that the natural, and easily implemented, logic function AND–NOR is just what is needed to create a multiplexer—a perfect replacement for a bus.

With the above in mind, the choice that was used in the design of the RCA's 32-bit microprocessor was as follows. In those areas where the design was to be handcrafted anyway, and where the speed of operation was not penalized to the point of slowing the system, buses were used. (This occurred in two areas, the general register file and the barrel shifter.) In the remainder of the architecture, multiplexers were used, and this frequently resulted in including additional functional capabilities in the machine, simply because it was cheaper to keep them than to exclude them.

Still another technology-dependent choice made for this design was to use circuits of three different power levels. There was one set of logic gates that had a low power consumption, a low fan-out, and a small chip area requirement. There was also one set that had a high power consumption, a high fan-out, and a large (relatively speaking, of course) chip area requirement. In the third set of logic gates, everything was somewhere between the two extremes.

Interchip communications required very special attention. Because of the circuit limitations, buses could not be used. This decision was reaffirmed later, when it became obvious that the state of the "packaging art" would not allow control signals to be passed freely throughout the system. Furthermore, it was determined that passing signals from one IC to another would be done only with signal delays that are equal to a significant fraction of the CPU cycle time. With a required minimum CPU clock frequency of 200 mHz, and stripline construction on alumina substrates being used for controlled impedance and high-power handling capability, the delays are approximately equal to 5–10 percent of the clock period, per inch of conductor path length. Thus, with any significant amount of conductor length (which is almost a foregone conclusion for paths that go from one board to another), the IC at the sending end could

A DCFL E/D-MESFET GaAs Experimental RISC Machine

WALT HELBIG AND VELJKO MILUTINOVIĆ

Abstract—Design of RCA's 32-bit GaAs microprocessor is presented. We first discuss technology limitations and influences of the software environment. Then we describe the details of the ISA (instruction set architecture) and details of the IES (instruction execution sequence). We underline the essense of the original contributions of the research and the design. Finally, we present the simulated performance evaluation data.

Index Terms—ASIC, DCFL E/D-MESFET GaAs, RISC processor architecture, RISC processor design, 32-bit GaAs microprocessor.

I. INTRODUCTION

This paper describes one microprocessor architecture, the design prepared by RCA of a 32-bit machine intended for implementation using GaAs VLSI. The architecture was patterned along the lines of the basic RISC philosophy. It was designed to include the fundamental operations (to support all functions needed for the intended applications), but limited in VLSI area to what can be put onto a practical size GaAs VLSI chip. As will be seen later, design decisions that we had to make are different enough from typical silicon design decisions.

GaAs has definitely reached the VLSI level of complexity [1], and this work is a part of the effort which was to show that implementation of a 32-bit microprocessor on a GaAs chip is feasible. Still, GaAs chip densities are relatively small, and GaAs designs are characterized with a number of problems not present in silicon designs.

When one is using silicon VLSI, even the newest 1.25 μm technology, the on-chip gate delays are measured in the nanoseconds, and the machine clock cycle time is most often 20 or more times longer. Delays on the board are on the order of 1 percent of the machine clock cycle time per inch of conductor path, the result being that board transmission times are insignificant for planning of the design. In a GaAs design, this percentage is an order of magnitude higher, and must be factored into the architecture. This usually necessitates having interchip communications be pipelined. Furthermore, it means that the board layout must be critically controlled, both at the design level and the architecture level.

II. IMPACTS OF THE TECHNOLOGY

There are a number of computer design related problems with GaAs, as an integration medium, is the limitation on the logic functions that can be created with its devices. RCA chose to work

Manuscript received June 17, 1986; revised February 17, 1987 and September 10, 1987. This work was supported by RCA Corporation.

W. Helbig is with the Advanced Technology Laboratories, RCA Corporation, Morrestown, NJ 08057.

V. Milutinovic is with the School of Electrical Engineering, Purdue University, West Layfette, IN 47907.

IEEE Log Number 8718952.

[1] Only DCFL E/D-MESFET GaAs is treated in this paper.

easily become involved in the clock cycle $n + 1$ before the signals sent during the clock cycle n reach the other IC. Furthermore, by the time the second IC reacts to the signals sent by the first IC, to perform the requested operation and to send the results of its operation back to the first IC, several clock cycles can have elapsed.

This problem is severe, and the designer must consider all of the latencies that might occur in order to construct a design that will operate, no matter how the IC's are placed on the board. Delays will occur in instruction fetch, data store and fetch, as well as in control and address signal distribution. Delays will occur in the distribution of the clock so the IC's will not necessarily be operating in phase with each other. The result may be that the latency in an operation may not be an integer number of clock periods. This phenomenon may also appear in fast silicon designs; however, its impacts are much greater in GaAs designs. On the other hand, the entire system may be designed to be pipelined, wherein the clock is distributed with the data, and at every junction point all signals are reclocked, to remove any variations in delay they might have undergone in making their transit. Then, by having signals distributed out from the CPU, through a series of these junction points, to wherever they are destined to go, and then going back through the same junction points to the CPU, the information will always arrive at the CPU in phase with its clock. Such an approach was chosen for the design of the RCA's 32-bit microprocessor system.

III. Impacts of the Support Software

RISC architecture philosophy is one of allowing the support software to, as much as it can, compensate for decisions made in designing the hardware [3].

The most notable examples of the RISC-type solution are the "branch latency fill-in" and the "load delay fill-in" operations, performed by code optimizer, to give the CPU something useful to do while waiting for its pipeline to complete the operations needed to perform a branch or a load. With respect to these issues, an important difference between silicon and GaAs is that GaAs designs are characterized with much deeper pipelines, and the fill-in algorithms have to be modified [4], [5].

Sometimes, however, there are features that can be added to the hardware to eliminate, from the required support software operation, a function that it can only do crudely at best. Two such features were added to the design of the RCA's 32-bit microprocessor, just for this purpose.

The *first* of these is to allow the system to handle immediate values efficiently. Immediate values typically have the same range of values as addresses and data—equal to the word length of the machine. This means that the machine must have the ability to express or create immediate values of length equal to the data word length, or in this case 32 bits. Creating full word length immediate operands can be done by loading partial length operands, and assembling these by instruction execution (requiring the allocation of at least two general registers for this function). They may also be handled by having an instruction format that includes, for some instructions, a field for an immediate value equal to the word length. Several problems arise here that the architect must handle. First, not all immediate values need to be the full 32 bits in width. In fact, most of the time 8 bits are sufficient [2]. Only a few percent of the time does one need the long immediate field.

Here are two possible ways to get around the problem. The Stanford MIPS machine [6] gets around the problem by including some instructions that have 16-bit immediate fields and some with 24-bit immediate fields but none with 32-bit immediate fields. This leaves the programmer/compiler with the problem of building, at run time, the full word length immediates, or storing all needed immediates in memory and fetching them at run time. An alternative approach was used in the RCA ATMAC [7] where the instruction word was longer (24 bits) than the data word length (16 bits). It worked quite efficiently for this 16-bit machine, because the nonimmediate instructions also required 24 bits to control the ATMAC's horizontal architecture. Other approaches include se-

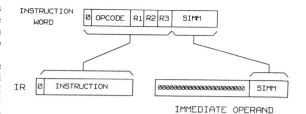

Fig. 1.   One-word format (SIMM: 8-bit short immediate operand).

quences of load and shift instructions, or the special read–shift–OR–replace instruction. RCA's 32-bit GaAs machine handles the problem in a way which is not typical for early RISC machines [8]-[10]. However, we had good reasons for such an approach (see below), and also, we have noticed that some recent (independently generated) designs have employed a similar solution [11].

The instruction format chosen uses one- and two-word instructions. The first part of all instructions is of the same format, specifying the operation code, the three general register file addresses, an unsigned 8-bit immediate value, called SIMM in Figs. 1 and 2 (to take care of 95 percent of the cases where immediate data are needed), and a single bit to designate whether or not there is a second part to the instruction (see Fig. 1). The optional second part of the instruction carries only the 24 most significant (MS) bits of the immediate value, where the 8 bits in the first part of the instruction are the least significant (LS) bits. This arrangement greatly simplifies the instruction decoding logic (see Fig. 2), achieving very efficiently one of the principal goals of RISC machines: improved execution time for compiled HLL code [8]-[10]. As already indicated, a similar approach was used in the AT&T's CRISP microprocessor [11].

While AT&T's motivations behind choosing this solution are as given in [11], our motivations were somewhat different. In designing this microprocessor to fit within the technology limits of a GaAs VLSI circuit, we were looking for simplicity and speed; the two basic demands of a RISC system. We utilized simplicity in the design wherever possible to accomplish as great a gain in performance as possible, while leaving as many as we could of the available devices for other functions. With our approach we were able to inexpensively obtain the full word length immediate operand that we needed for applications that are logic and arithmetic oriented.

The *second* feature added to the architecture of the machine was a way to decrease the time between two executions of two load instructions. Normally, when a load instruction is executed, the data memory address is sent from the CPU, the data are read from the memory, sent back to the CPU, and the value is put into the general register file during the course of execution of the instruction. In a RISC machine, however, especially one made using GaAs IC's, the time available for these operations is too short for any practical memory system. Furthermore, with the interchip communication latency included, several of the machine's clock cycles can have passed between sending the address from the CPU and getting the result back to the CPU (storing the result into the general register file). Each of these clock cycles corresponds to another instruction execution period. In order to keep straight where the data are to go when they get back to the CPU, the normal approach is to hold the general register (GR) file address in the CPU, and have the program not execute another load operation until the first one is completed. The time elapsed is equal to the load latency.

An alternate approach, one that is built into this machine, is to send the destination address (the general register file address) out from the CPU, along with the memory address, to the memory and then have the destination address sent back with the data. When the data finally reach the CPU, the destination register address is with the data, and the data may be properly stored. Therefore, no matter what the interchip communication and the memory system latencies are, and no matter how many load requests are active (initiated but not

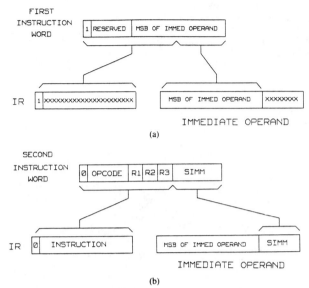

(a)

(b)

Fig. 2. Two-word format. (a) First word. (b) Second word.

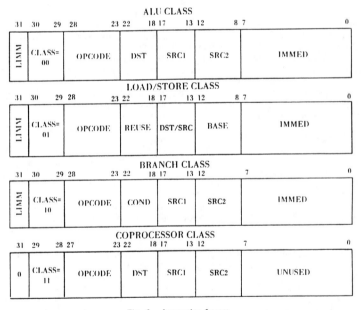

Fig. 3. Instruction format.

completed; we deal here with a relatively deep memory pipeline, as explained in a later section of this paper), at any time everything is kept straight. Consequently, requests for memory load may be issued at every instruction cycle, which would not be possible with standard pipeline organizations.

IV. CPU ARCHITECTURE

Once it is known what the technology and support software guidelines are, the CPU architecture has to be created so as to fit within these guidelines [12], [13]. We created the architecture by including, in the design, those features needed to make the system execute programs efficiently, in the conditions typical of the GaAs technology [12], [13]. Instruction format details are given in Figs. 3–6. A block diagram of the CPU is shown in Figs. 7–10, for various execution phases of a typical instruction.

For this type of pipelined architecture, a stack of registers is required to be connected to the PC, so that the last N values of the instruction memory address can be remembered. These values will be used to restart those instructions that did not finish executing, when an interrupt occurred. Even though these N instructions were fetched, they may not have finished execution when they were stopped, in order for the CPU to execute the called sequence, i.e., the interrupt response program. We have found that the traditional approach to this problem will work well in the GaAs environment,

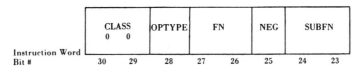

Fig. 4. ALU class op-code field assignments.

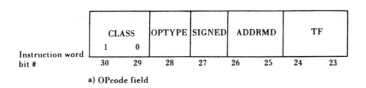

a) OPcode field

b) Cond field (for all except INT & IGN)

Fig. 5. Branch/jump class op-code field assignments.

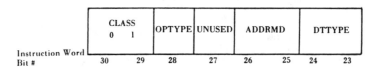

Fig. 6. Load/store class op-code field assignments.

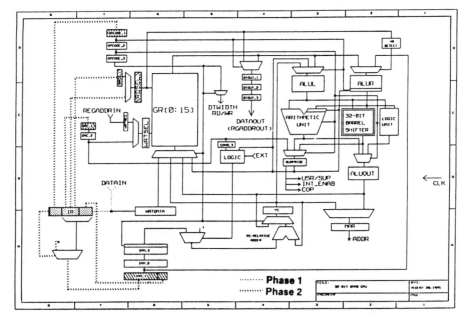

Fig. 7. Instruction read phase.

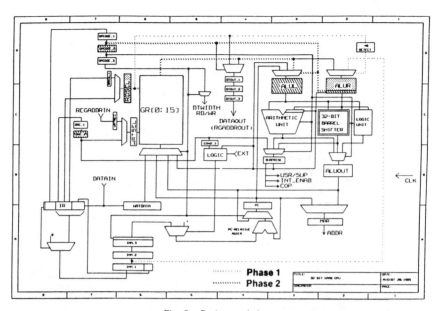

Fig. 8. Register read phase.

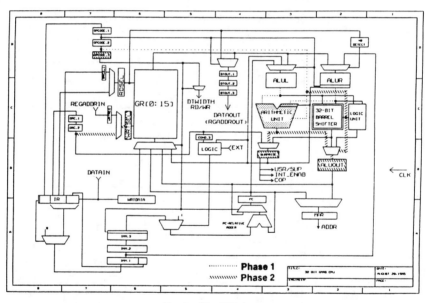

Fig. 9. The ALU phase.

except for differences due to the fact that the value of N is larger [14]–[16].

As each instruction address is generated, it is simultaneously sent to the instruction memory to fetch the instruction, and is pushed onto the register stack containing the last N values. When an interrupt occurs, i.e., when the execution of the interrupt instruction begins, the operation of the stack ceases, while the PC continues to function, first branching to the called routine, and then going through the execution of the called routine. When the interrupt service routine is fully executed, execution of the interrupted routine is restarted, by retrieving the instruction memory addresses from the stack, and refetching the instructions from memory. By the time the execution of the Nth instruction has begun, the CPU will have recovered from the interrupt, and will be back to the point in the interrupted routine where it was interrupted. The PC stack operation is then restarted, and program execution is allowed to proceed normally until another interrupt is received. In this machine, the PC stack is located in the memory controller system rather than in the CPU. This decreased the number of devices to be put on the CPU chip and improved the speed of the recovery process. It allowed the stack to be built with a depth equal to the largest expected N, and still operate efficiently with a small value for N.

One of the major design problems with GaAs microprocessors is the relatively high ratio of off-chip memory access time to on-chip

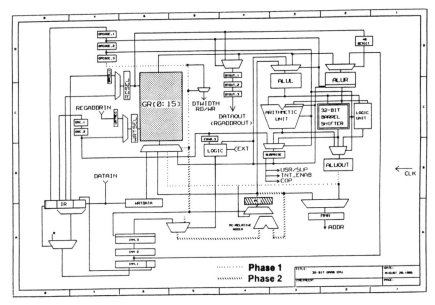

Fig. 10.   The write-back phase.

data path time. With the target execution rate being one instruction per CPU clock cycle, we have defined the system such that more than one instruction is in the process of being fetched.

The first phase of each instruction execution is instruction fetch (MAR loaded with the instruction's address from the PC). In this machine, a series of partial instruction decoders are included between a series of registers that hold the unused portions of the instruction at each stage of the execution cycle. The first of these registers is called the instruction register (IR) and holds the entire instruction. Its output is connected to multiplexers that sequentially use the general register file addresses to access the file, and fetch the two operands that are to be used in the course of the execution of the instruction. Input logic recognizes whether the incoming instruction is the MS bits of an immediate operand OR the following instruction. If that is the case, then the transfer path (to copy the contents of the appropriate bits of the instruction to the immediate operand register for the ALU) is activated (see Fig. 7).

When the next clock cycle of the CPU is completed, the next instruction is ready to be placed into the instruction register, so the present contents must be moved to the "next instruction register." This action occurs at the same time that the operands from the general register file are put into two registers at the input of the ALU, and the immediate operand is put into a third register at the ALU's input (see Fig. 8). At this time, the immediate operand is assembled (using 8 bits from the "second instruction register" and 24 bits from the input to the "first instruction register," if the continuation bit is set) and put into the third ALU input register. If the continuation bit is not set (in the word at the input to the first instruction register), then the 8 bits from the "second instruction register" are put into the third ALU input register, with the 24 most significant bits of this register set to zero. Note the essential difference between this scheme and the "shifted control" scheme used in some other machines.

In order to accomplish all this successfully, with the logic family available, this machine was designed with a two-phase CPU clock system, and two levels of registers for each stage. It also uses a general register file that has one read port and one write port [17], but is fast enough that two pairs of read and write operations may be accomplished during a single CPU clock cycle. In reality, then, the system, on the first clock phase after the instruction is put into the instruction register, reads the first operand out of the general register file, puts it into a temporary holding register, and puts all of the

remaining bits of the instruction into another instruction register. On the second clock phase, the first operand is put into the first ALU input register, the second operand is fetched from the general register file, and put into the second ALU input register. Here, two decisions had to be made.

First, the ALU will only accept two operands, but we have assembled three. So two must be selected from the three. In many machines, the selection is based on the op-code, with some instructions being designed for immediate operands only, and others designed to use two variables only. These machines include an extra bit in the instruction format to specify which operands are to be used: the first and second operands fetched from the register file, or the first operand fetched from the register file, plus the immediate operand. This machine, instead, uses an arrangement to achieve more flexibility (without adding any bits to the instruction format), and to achieve a convenience that is needed later on in the instruction execution cycle. It does this through the implementation of the general register file such that "register zero" does not exist and the file, when register zero is addressed, always puts out a value of zero. Furthermore, the ALU operand selection logic is designed to select the immediate operand, if the second source register address is zero, and select the content read from the general register file, if this address is nonzero. This solution adds a little to the overall complexity of the decoding circuitry, but improves the code density, which is especially important in GaAs machines which have a relatively small instruction cache (located off-CPU-chip/on-CPU-package).

Second, for ALU operations, the first operand is always sent to the ALU unmodified, and the second one may be sent unmodified or complemented, depending on the instruction op-code. However, destinations of operands are determined by the type of operation to be performed. For example, for arithmetic, logic, and shift instructions, the appropriate contents of the ALU input registers are sent to the adder, the logic unit, or the shifter. For coprocessor instructions, CPU operation is meaningless; so any operation is allowed, as long as the result does not disturb a register whose content is to be kept valid from one instruction to the next. For branch instructions, the selected operands are sent to the ALU, but the value in the $R1$ field is used as an extension to the op-code, to specify the test to be performed on the result of the adder operation (to determine if the branch should be taken). In this case, the value in the "immediate operand register" is

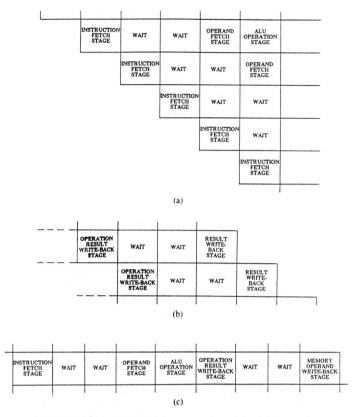

(a)

(b)

(c)

Fig. 11. (a) Instruction execution sequence through the ALU operation phase. (b) The operation result write-back phase of instruction execution. (c) Complete instruction execution cycle.

sent to the PC adder, so that it may be conditionally added to, or subtracted from, the present PC value, for a PC-relative branch. For jump instructions, the values normally selected for the ALU input are sent to the adder, and the adder output is sent later on to the PC, to execute the jump.

The execution of the subtract operation, for the interval when the operands are sent to the ALU, during the next two phases of the CPU clock is illustrated in Fig. 9. Note that, during this cycle, the inputs to the ALU are available at the beginning of the first phase of the clock, and that the selected output of the ALU goes into the ALU "output register" and the "surprise register," at the end of the second phase of the clock. Fig. 11(a) illustrates the phases of the instruction execution sequence through the ALU operation stage. The last stage of the execution of an instruction in the CPU is the stage in which the output of the ALU is sent to its ultimate destination: either to the data memory system as an address, or to the general register file as the result of the computation. In the case of the memory reference, the address goes out, but the result is not sent back immediately, so the information requested by load operation cannot be put into the general register file during the next cycle of the CPU clock. This value will come back later, and will be put into the file then. In the case of the ALU operation, the result is written into the general register file on the first of the two clock phases of this last instruction execution stage (see Fig.10). The alternate phase of operation is used to handle the storage of any data that come from the data memory (from some previously executed load operation). This part of the operation of the machine is illustrated in Fig. 11(b). It shows how the destination address has been delayed during the instruction execution, so that it arrives at the general register file at the same time when the result arrives. The complete instruction execution cycle is shown in Fig. 11(c). Shown also are the two latency periods, the first one related to the instruction fetch, and the second one related to the operand fetch for a load operation.

A number of unique features were added to solve problems caused by the operation of the architecture at a rate of 200 MIPS, a cycle time so short that any interchip communication would use up much of this time (about 0.5 ns per inch of conductor length). This fact mandates the use of memory pipelines, in conjunction with the small number of devices on each related GaAs chip. The first of these added features is the "ignore instruction," to help reclaim some of the instruction memory space lost due to the long branch latency.

In a pipelined machine, following a branch instruction, there are several instructions that will have entered the pipeline, and will be executed, whether the branch is taken or not. For these types of machines it is the job of the code optimizer to find things for the CPU to do, either those that need to be done all the time, or those that are useful sometimes (say when the branch is taken), and harmless the other times (when the branch is not taken). Unfortunately, for the current state of the art compiler technology, code optimizer efficiency is not very high for relatively deep pipelines. Consequently, branch fill-in of one or two instructions being about all that can be accomplished [3]. Therefore, the remainder of the instruction slots in the branch latency area have to be filled in with NoOp instructions. This results in wasting a relatively large part of the memory space.

This space can be reclaimed through the use of the ignore instruction. This is accomplished by having the code optimizer put the ignore instruction following the last useful instruction migrated into the branch latency area. The count in the ignore instruction is

TABLE I
(a) PERCENTAGE OF BRANCH FILLS WITH/WITHOUT THE SQUASH MECHANISM (STATIC NUMBERS). (b) PERCENTAGE OF
NOOP'S (TOTAL NUMBER OF NOOP'S/TOTAL NUMBER OF INSTRUCTIONS). (c) PERCENTAGE OF NOOP'S (TOTAL NUMBER OF
NOOP'S ELIMINATED/TOTAL NUMBER OF NOOP'S BEFORE ORGANIZATION). (d) PERCENTAGE OF CODE REDUCTION
(NUMBER OF INSTRUCTION WORDS REDUCED/TOTAL NUMBER OF INSTRUCTIONS BEFORE REORGANIZATION

benchmarks	total branches	% 3-fills	% 2-fills	% 1-fills	% 0-fills	% fills
REALMM (without)	29	31.0%	20.7%	13.8%	34.5%	49.4%
(with)		42.9%	35.7%	3.6%	17.9%	67.9%
PUZZLE (without)	84	8.3%	9.5%	8.3%	73.8%	17.5%
(with)		33.7%	44.2%	9.3%	12.8%	66.3%
BUBBLE (without)	23	26.1%	17.4%	13.4%	43.5%	42.0%
(with)		29.2%	16.7%	1.3%	41.7%	44.4%
WEIGHT (without)	131	37.4%	17.6%	25.2%	19.1%	57.5%
(with)		40.8%	21.5%	23.1%	14.6%	62.8%

(a)

	without coprocessor			
benchmarks	static		dynamic	
	non-reorg'd	reorganized	non-reorg'd	reorganized
REALMM	66.6%	16.8%	54.2%	17.0%
PUZZLE	39.4%	18.9%	40.0%	10.7%
BUBBLE	48.3%	23.4%	47.4%	20.3%
WEIGHT				
	with coprocessor			
REALMM	48.5%	29.1%	44.2%	26.5%

(b)

	without coprocessor							
	static				dynamic			
	by intrablock reorganztn	by branch optimiztn	by squash	total	by intrablock reorganztn	by branch optimiztn	by squash	total
REALMM	83.3%	5.1%	1.6%	90.0%	68.3%	11.2%	4.5%	84.0%
PUZZLE	68.7%	2.9%	7.4%	79.0%	65.3%	7.9%	11.2%	84.4%
BUBBLE	56.8%	11.1%	1.3%	69.2%	65.2%	5.2%	1.9%	72.3%
WEIGHT								
	with coprocessor							
REALMM	44.4%	9.0%	2.9%	56.3%	43.5%	7.8%	3.1%	54.5%

(c)

	without coprocessor	
	static	dynamic
REALMM	60.2%	49.1%
PUZZLE	45.6%	46.3%
BUBBLE	36.3%	35.3%
WEIGHT		
	with coprocessor	
REALMM	30.5%	24.0%

(d)

then set to cause the CPU to ignore execution of the number of instructions specified, no matter what they are. The memory space following the ignore instruction can be used to hold other instructions.

Most of the decisions made for this processor's design were verified by simulating the execution of compiler-generated code sequences on the alternative architectures, and choosing the best [14]–[16]. In our design, the ignore count was integrated with the branch instruction, putting a count and a control bit in an unused portion of the instruction word. The control bit specified whether the execution of the following N instructions (count field value) should be performed, if the branch is taken or not.

This version of the design, quite similar to the branch squashing technique (e.g., [18]), was simulated for several programs [see Table I]. Two types of statistics were gathered to evaluate the usefulness of this approach. The first statistic showed that, through the use of this technique, the amount of filling of the branch latency area with useful instructions increased on the average about 10 percent (with the best being an improvement from about 17 percent to about 66 percent). It also showed that the number of NoOp instructions in the program memory decreased by an average of about 5 percent (see Table I).

Another place where this technique showed its usefulness was in the area of the elimination of NoOp instructions in the CPU's instruction memory following a coprocessor instruction, and in the execution of NoOp instructions by the CPU while it is waiting for the coprocessor to finish the execution of its instruction. In this case, an average of about 3 percent of the NoOps were eliminated in both the static count of these instructions and about 3 percent in the dynamic execution of the NoOp instructions. These figures could be improved if the count field were larger. Furthermore, the separate instruction is less expensive in terms of device count than the branch squashing approach (see Table I).

A crucial problem in a pipelined machine is that of interrupts. These may be handled totally by hardware on the CPU chip, if there is no external memory pipeline. If a memory pipeline exists in the system, however, no hardware control on the CPU alone can solve the problem conveniently, because of the same reason that necessitated the presence of the memory pipeline in the first place. The problem was solved in this machine by having the interrupt handler logic insert an ''interrupt instruction'' in the instruction stream (when an interrupt request is placed by the external logic) in place of one of the instructions already fetched from memory. The INT was to be used by the hardware with the base register specified as zero. An appropriate ignore field count is also included with this instruction, so that the proper number of instructions already in the memory pipeline (ones that immediately follow the interrupt instruction) are ignored. Note that the PC stack contents mentioned earlier will be used to refetch the instructions which were fetched but not executed, when the interrupt occurred. This will permit their execution upon return from the interrupt.

The two other problem areas found in machines of this type are associated with the implementation of the multiply and divide operations. In the Stanford MIPS computer, these operations were augmented by the inclusion (in the hardware) of special shift registers, called the Hi and Lo registers, and by putting the barrel shifter in series with the adder. This allowed the MIPS to process two multiplier bits and one quotient bit per instruction cycle.

This solution is not applicable in the case of GaAs-oriented design. First, the barrel shifter could not be put in series with the adder. Unlike the MIPS which executed instructions at the rate of one every other machine cycle, this machine was designed to execute instructions at the rate of one every clock cycle, requiring that the critical path be very short. Second, the cost of the Hi and Lo registers was too large for what gain could be achieved in the throughput. Since GaAs chips have to be small, this was felt to be one thing that could be omitted. And finally, the machine was designed to support double precision arithmetic (on a coprocessor), including multiply and divide, and these would make the Hi–Lo register approach even more expensive. As a result, the machine was designed to perform the multiply and divide operations by reading the operands from the general register file, operating on them, and putting them back into the same file. This resulted in a very inexpensive approach that permitted the system to handle single, double, or higher precision operations, without having any ALU or branch latency problems. The result is that multiply is executed at the rate of two multiplier bits for every three machine cycles, for single precision, and every six machine cycles for double precision. Divide is executed at the rate of one quotient bit for every three machine cycles for single precision, and every six machine cycles for double precision.

When it came time to make a decision as to how to do multiply in this machine, we were faced with several ground rules and a difficult choice to make. Without a multiply operation or a barrel shifter, the computer implementation took up all but about 700 of the allowable active devices that could be put on a GaAs VLSI (to assure a "nonzero" fabrication yield). The question that faced us was what to use these remaining devices for. We needed an extendable length multiply and divide operation because the processor had to perform the same operations without the floating point coprocessor, as it did with it. Thus, we had to be able to program both 24 × 24 bit multiplies and 53 × 53 bit multiplies, to provide both the short and the long floating point operations.

We did not want the shifter in series with the adder, because this would double the critical path delay time and, therefore, cut the throughput. We have also performed some preliminary designs and have found out that we could add either the barrel shifter, or the single-length Hi–Lo register combination [10], or a serial multiplier in parallel with the adder, but we could not have more than one of these items without exceeding the device count limit.

Simulations were run on designs of machines that had one of these three items but not the others, to find out which one was the most valuable [16]. The barrel shifter was by far the best choice. Combining it with the designs for the multiplier and divide operation explained before, the average throughput for the machine design was clearly better in almost all benchmark programs tested.

Additionally, it was found that the long divide operations, while simple to program with the chosen approach, would have been costly to implement with the Hi–Lo register approach [10]. Not only did the design permit long divide to be achieved, but multiword multiplies were easy to get as well.

V. Experimenting

Design of the CPU was preceeded by a number of experiments designed to quantify the value of alternate design approaches. Of about one dozen different experiments done at Purdue University

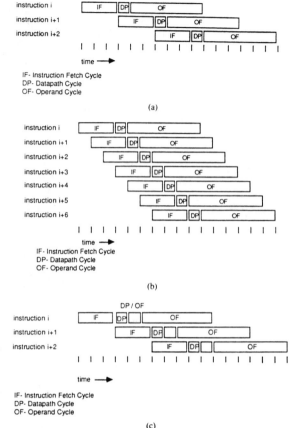

Fig. 12. (a) Silicon-type pipeline, with an on-package instruction cache, and an off-package data cache [14]. (b) Pipelined-memory pipeline, with an on-package instruction cache, and and off-package data cache [14]. (c) Packed pipeline, with an on-package instruction cache, and an off-package data cache [14].

[14]–[16] and RCA Corporation, one which was crucial for many of the decisions was the one related to the design of the pipeline and the evaluation of its efficiency.

The major goal of the pipeline design experiment was to compare the three alternative approaches discussed in [12]. These three approaches are referred to as 1) silicon-type pipeline, 2) pipelined-memory pipeline, and 3) packing-oriented pipeline [14]. The first approach is similar to the Stanford MIPS pipeline implemented in conditions typical of GaAs (large ratio of off/chip to on/chip delays). The second approach is characterized by the branch delay latency equal to the ratio of the off-chip memory access time and the on-chip data-path time (time to read from the general register file, to propagate the signal through the ALU, and to write the result back into the general register file). That is, the approach is characterized by the maximum reasonable depth of the memory pipeline. The third approach is based on the concurrent fetch of more than one operation, and their sequential execution on the single ALU [14]. More details on the three schemes could be found in Fig. 12(a), (b), and (c) and in [14]. The three schemes imply an off-CPU-chip/on-CPU-package instruction cache and an off-CPU-package/on-CPU-board data cache of limited size.

A flexible simulator of all three candidate pipelines was implemented at RCA, and selected benchmarks (described below) were run on each of the candidate pipelines. The results depend on the probability of instruction and data cache hit, as well as on the branch and load fill-in probability.

Note the essential difference between data in Fig. 13 and data in

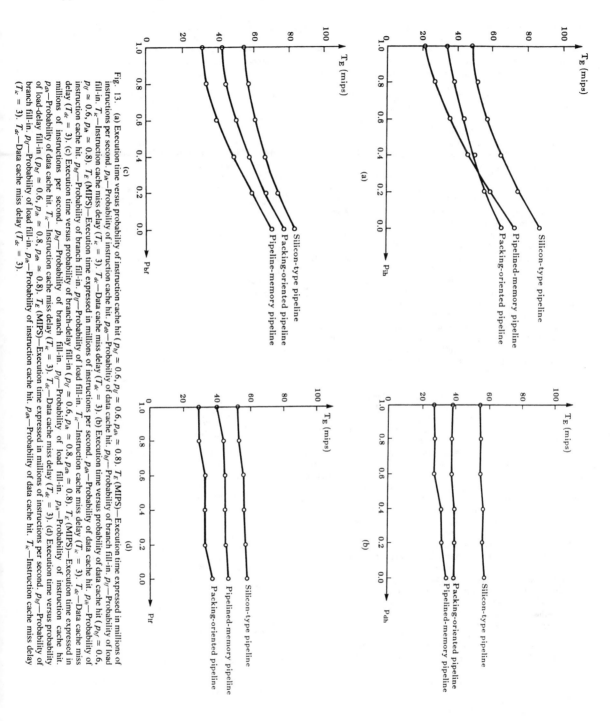

Fig. 13. (a) Execution time versus probability of instruction cache hit ($p_{\mathit{bf}} = 0.6$, $p_{\mathit{lf}} = 0.6$, $p_{\mathit{dh}} = 0.8$). T_E (MIPS)—Execution time expressed in millions of instructions per second. p_{ih}—Probability of instruction cache hit. p_{db}—Probability of data cache hit. p_{bf}—Probability of branch fill-in. p_{lf}—Probability of load fill-in. T_{ic}—Instruction cache miss delay ($T_{\mathit{ic}} = 3$). T_{dc}—Data cache miss delay ($T_{\mathit{dc}} = 3$). (b) Execution time versus probability of data cache hit ($p_{\mathit{bf}} = 0.6$, $p_{\mathit{lf}} = 0.6$, $p_{\mathit{ih}} = 0.8$). T_E (MIPS)—Execution time expressed in millions of instructions per second. p_{dh}—Probability of data cache hit. p_{bf}—Probability of branch fill-in. p_{lf}—Probability of load fill-in. T_{ic}—Instruction cache miss delay ($T_{\mathit{ic}} = 3$). T_{dc}—Data cache miss delay ($T_{\mathit{dc}} = 3$). (c) Execution time versus probability of branch-delay fill-in ($p_{\mathit{lf}} = 0.6$, $p_{\mathit{ih}} = 0.8$, $p_{\mathit{dh}} = 0.8$). T_E (MIPS)—Execution time expressed in millions of instructions per second. p_{bf}—Probability of branch fill-in. T_{ic}—Instruction cache miss delay ($T_{\mathit{ic}} = 3$). T_{dc}—Data cache miss delay ($T_{\mathit{dc}} = 3$). (d) Execution time versus probability of load-delay fill-in ($p_{\mathit{bf}} = 0.6$, $p_{\mathit{ih}} = 0.8$, $p_{\mathit{dh}} = 0.8$). T_E (MIPS)—Execution time expressed in millions of instructions per second. p_{lf}—Probability of load fill-in. T_{ic}—Instruction cache miss delay ($T_{\mathit{ic}} = 3$). T_{dc}—Data cache miss delay ($T_{\mathit{dc}} = 3$).

[14]. The former was obtained through an empirical method from an ENDOT, Inc. simulator [19] and an operational compiler, while the later was obtained via a combined analytical/empirical method, through the SU-MIPS simulator [3], and the precalculation of results to reflect the differences in the pipeline depth of the SU-MIPS machine and the RCA GaAs machine.

Fig. 13(a) gives the performance of three pipelines versus probability of instruction cache hit, for the benchmark mix from Table I, and for the selected values of other relevant parameters. Fig. 13(b) compares the three pipelines from the point of view of their sensitivity to the data cache miss. Fig. 13(c) plots the execution time versus the probability of the branch-delay fill-in. Fig. 13(d) plots the execution time versus the probability of the load-delay fill-in.

Conclusions from the experiments are as follows. In conditions where the probability of fill-in for load and branch delays is relatively high (above 60 percent), the pipelined-memory pipeline performs the best, the packing-oriented pipeline is the next in performance, while the silicon-type pipeline is characterized with a very modest performance. On the other hand, when the probability of the instruction cache hit drops down to below 40 percent, which may happen for extremely small caches, the performance of the pipelined-memory pipeline rapidly decreases. In an extreme case, its performance degrades to being comparable to the performance of the silicon-type pipeline. Also, if one compares results from Fig. 13 and [14], one can conclude that two different methods (one based on the detailed direct-correspondence simulator and an operational optimizer/compiler, the other based on the SU-MIPS simulator/optimizer and precalculation of results to reflect a deeper pipeline) applied to two different but similar benchmark mixes (both oriented to numerical processing with elements of signal processing, data processing, and symbolic processing) have generated very similar results.

With all the above in mind, it was decided to invest maximally into the compiler technology [4], and based on this experiment, a pipelined-memory structure (described previously) was chosen.

Finally, the efficiency of the chosen pipeline was evaluated using the ENDOT, Inc. simulation package, and the related ISP' language [19]. In Table I, some of the benchmarks from [3] are used in their modified form. Realmm(8*8) computes a product of two real matrices of the size eight. Bubblesort(20) performs a bubblesort of twenty integers. Weight (1024) is a computation-heavy program which performs an FFT-based signal transform on a 1024-element signal vector. Puzzle(3) is an iteration-heavy program to solve a three-dimensional cube packing problem. Extrapolated execution speed is given in terms of mega-instructions-per-second (MIPS).

Note that the results from Table I are somewhat different than results from [4], due to the most recent compiler improvements at RCA. Table I(a) presents the percentage of branch fills with and without the squashing mechanism. Table I(b) presents the percentage of NoOp's, for the cases with and without an arithmetic coprocessor [13]. Table I(c) presents the percentage of NoOp's eliminated through the code optimization process, while Table I(d) presents the percentage of code reduction.

One of the main conclusions from Table I is that a major effort is needed to improve the efficiency of delayed branches in deep memory pipelines (which are typical for GaAs microprocessors [20]).

VI. CONCLUSIONS

A project is not undertaken properly if all that is accomplished is that something is built. For any project to be truly successful something should be learned. With this project being one of the first that was to design a computer for construction in GaAs VLSI, a computer that would be patterned after the Stanford MIPS architecture, and like that machine, would have a support software system to make optimum use of the architecture, several lessons were learned in each of the three major areas: technology, architecture, and software.

One was that any significant differences in the lengths of conductors among the lines of parallel paths to carry the bits of a single word would necessitate the use of deskewing buffers at the receiving end. This approach is very inconvenient because of the small amount of logic that can be put on a GaAs VLSI chip today.

Another was that handling one instruction per machine clock cycle increases the problems related to designing the logic for the CPU. All critical paths between registers (such as through the adder and the shifter) must be very short, and typically no more than 20 gate delays long. Furthermore, it was found that the faster the machine operates, the longer the memory pipeline will be. The increasing pipeline length increases the latency that the code optimizer must compensate for: the branch latency, the load latency, and perhaps even the ALU latency. It lengthens the stack that must accompany the program counter to enable the handling of interrupts. It also increases the number of CPU resources that must be "shut down" and then "restarted" properly, during the process of interrupt handling.

Finally, it was proven that in GaAs RISC systems, more than in any silicon RISC systems, the compiler should be considered as an integral part of the architecture. (This is partially due to the deeper memory pipelines of GaAs systems, and partially due to the fact that designers tend to move many traditional hardware functions into the compiler.) However, compiler technology (code optimization technology), not being ready for code optimization in the presence of deep pipelines, caused the execution rate for many benchmarks to be well below the peak execution rate of 200 MIPS.

ACKNOWLEDGMENT

The authors are thankful to B. Heagerty, T. Geigel, and N. Chen for their help.

REFERENCES

[1] S. Karp and S. Roosily, "DARPA, SDI, and GaAs," *IEEE Computer*, pp. 17–19, Oct. 1986.

[2] R. Wedig and T. Lehr, "The GaAs realization of a production system machine," in *Proc. HICSS-19*, Honolulu, Hawaii, Jan. 1986.

[3] T. Gross, "Code optimization of pipeline constraints," Stanford Univ. Tech. Rep. 83-255, Dec. 1983.

[4] V. Milutinović, D. Fura, W. Helbig, and J. Linn, "Architecture/compiler synergism in GaAs computer systems," *IEEE Computer*, May 1987.

[5] J. Linn, "Horizontal microcode compaction," *Microprogramming and Firmware Engineering Methods*. S. Habib, Ed. New York: Van Nostrand Reinhold, 1987.

[6] J. Gill *et. al.*, "Summary of MIPS instructions," Stanford Univ. Tech. Rep. 83-237, Nov. 1983.

[7] W. Helbig and J. Stringer, "A VLSI microprocessor: The RCA ATMAC," *IEEE Computer*, vol. 10, pp. 22–29, Sept. 1977.

[8] R. Colwell *et al.*, "Computers, complexity, and controversy," *IEEE Computer*, pp. 8–20, Sept. 1985.

[9] D. Patterson and C. Sequin, "A VLSI RISC," *IEEE Computer*, pp. 39–47, Sept. 1982.

[10] J. Hennessy *et al.*, "The MIPS machine," in *Dig. Papers, Spring COMPCON 82*, San Francisco, CA, Feb. 1982, pp. 2–7.

[11] D. R. Ditzel, H. R. McLellan, and A. D. Berenbaum, "The hardware architecture of the CRISP microprocessor," in *Proc. ACM/IEEE Int. Symp. Comput. Architecture*, Pittsburgh, PA, June 1987, pp. 309–319.

[12] V. Milutinović *et al.*, "An introduction to GaAs microprocessor architecture for VLSI," *IEEE Computer*, pp. 30–42, Mar. 1986.

[13] V. Milutinović *et al.*, "Issues of importance in designing GaAs computer systems," *IEEE Computer*, pp. 45–57, Oct. 1986.

[14] D. Fura, "Architectural approaches for GaAs exploitation in high-speed computer design," Purdue Univ. Tech. Rep., TR-EE 85-17, Dec. 1985.

[15] M. Bettinger, "Comparison of CMOS silicon and E/D-MESFET GaAs for VLSI processor design," Purdue Univ. Tech. Rep., TR-EE 85-18, Dec. 1985.

[16] V. Milutinović and D. Fura, *Gallium Arsenide Computer Design*. Washington, DC: Computer Society Press, 1988.

[17] W. Helbig, R. Schellack, and R. Zieger, "The design and construction of a GaAs technology demonstration microprocessor," in *Proc. MIDCON 85*, Professional Program Session Rec. 23, Chicago, IL, Sept. 1985, pp. 1–6.

[18] P. Chow and M. Horowitz, ''Architectural tradeoffs in the design of MIPS-X,'' in *Proc. 14th Annu. Int. Symp. Comput. Architecture*, Pittsburgh, PA, June 1987.

[19] C. W. Rose, G. M. Ordy, and P. J. Drongowski, ''M.mPc: A study in university–industry technology transfer,'' *IEEE Design Test*, pp. 44–56, Feb. 1982.

[20] V. Milutinović Ed., Special Issue on GaAs Microprocessor Technology, *IEEE Computer*, Oct. 1986.

Appendix C

An Experimental 64-bit RISC Microprocessor

on over 2 MTR* Complexity

This appendix contains a reprint of the paper:

> V. Milutinović and Z. Petković, "Ten Lessons Learned from a RISC Design," *Computer*, March 1995, p. 120.

This paper describes a followup effort to use ISP' for modeling of a sophisticated 64-bit RISC microprocessor, in a way which is compatible with requirements of a silicon compiler.

---

*MTR = Million Transistors (on a chip)

Ten lessons learned from a RISC design

Lessons can be learned anywhere on earth, and we've accumulated a few from our international project—a 64-bit RISC processor design using silicon compilation (with 2.5 million transistors) that took two years to complete. Project teams were located on three continents: A US company provided the hardware description language; a European group (the two of us) was responsible for generating the HDL-based model that correctly described all signals on all pins for each instruction and every operational mode; and a Japanese company generated over 10 Mbytes of tests. Our team's task was then to successfully pass these tests, after which another US company did the silicon compilation. Finally, another Japanese company did the fabrication. You can imagine the possibilities for complexity! Here are a few of the many lessons we learned.

Lesson #1: It's tough for just one person to understand everything. A silicon compiler's essential value is that it enables one person to fully understand a relatively complex design task; however, it's extremely difficult for one person to manage every detail. In our case, the details were all signals on all pins for every instruction executed in each operational mode. It's important that future HDL extensions contain language constructs to efficiently express such details!

Lesson #2: Coding rules for silicon compilation are underdeveloped. One nice thing about HDLs is that they let you adequately exploit full parallelism at the lowest hardware levels for efficient programming. However, current silicon compilers get "confused" with too much parallelism, so the HDL programmer must serialize the description, which negatively affects programmer productivity. The solution? Develop design rules characterized by maximum parallelism yet without negative effects on synthesis efficiency!

Lesson #3: Don't let silicon compiler warnings get you down. We've noticed that many silicon compilers generate correlated warnings. Consequently, a huge number of warnings results in a mere handful of coding rule violations. Therefore, the generated warnings must be orthogonalized!

Lesson #4: Be careful when naming variables. A silicon compiler shouldn't specify how variable names are created. For example, our register variable names had to start with "r_." This can be confusing, especially if required of the HDL programmers *after* they've mostly completed their task.

Lesson #5: The environment keeps changing. The silicon compiler was fully developed by the time we started our work, but the programming rules that enabled synthesis were not. Consequently, creating rules was a trial-and-error experience. Also, the silicon-compilation design process is still lengthy, so the project requirements are likely to change during the design process. Nothing new!

Lesson #6: Testing is still the bottleneck. The first 90 percent of the project—design—was completed in six months, while the remaining 10 percent—testing—needed another 18 months!

Lesson #7: Beware the NIH problems. People who work in high tech tend to think very highly of themselves, and that characteristic caused some problems of the NIH ("not invented here") variety. When a test failed, entirely too much time was spent trying to determine who made the error rather than getting on with fixing it. The typical reaction was always to blame someone else for the error.

Lesson #8: Working on three continents is both pleasure and pain. If the phone woke you up in the early morning, you *knew* the call was from Japan. If the phone woke you up late at night, you *knew* the call was from the USA. After awhile, you learned the best time of day to send e-mail to get a prompt response. Cultural differences, although a source of fun, can provoke misunderstandings that create hard feelings.

Lesson #9: Time to market is still an issue. A major driver of silicon compiler development is fast time to market. However, the goal has not yet been met to accelerate very sophisticated processor-logic designs adequately. There's *lots* of research room for new methodologies in the over-one-million-transistor arena.

Lesson #10: We're always more clever after the fact! As the saying goes, "hindsight is 20-20." Looking back, it's obvious that better planning up front would have eliminated many problems (although, unfortunately, none of the above!). Better planning would definitely have reduced the 18 months it took to eliminate the last 10 percent of errors. Also, we're all now older and wiser, with two years' more experience!

OUR PROCESSOR DESIGN PROJECT—with all its lessons learned—was one of life's special experiences. During the two long years of work, one of the project team members passed away, and another one received a beautiful new baby. Sometimes, life resembles engineering so much!

Veljko Milutinovic and Zvezdan Petkovic
University of Belgrade
emilutiv@ubbg.etf.bg.ac.yu

Appendix D

A Methodology for

New Research and Developments

This appendix contains a reprint of the paper:

> V. Milutinović, "A Research Methodology in the Field of Computer Engineering for VLSI," *Proceedings of the 20th IEEE International Conference on Microelectronics—MIEL '95,* Niš, Serbia, Yugoslavia, September 1995, pp. 811–816.

This paper describes a research and development methodology which is fully applicable in the field of interest for this book.

A Research Methodology
in the Field of Computer Engineering for VLSI

Veljko Milutinović

Abstract— **This paper presents one research methodology which is applicable both to computer engineering for VLSI and to computer engineering in general. It includes two parts: one related to the methodology of the research work, and the other related to the methodology of presentation of research results. This paper also discusses 15 examples to demonstrate the efficiency of the presented methodology.**

I. INTRODUCTION

This paper aims to highlight a research methodology suited to a wide spectrum of research and development problems. The details of the methodology are elaborated through actual research that was done in the School of Electrical Engineering at the University of Belgrade (the IFACT laboratory) for the leading computer industry worldwide. The research was done by postgraduate students under a tight mentor supervision. All problems elaborated in this paper are related to the next generation of multimedia workstations.

II. ABOUT THE RESEARCH METHODOLOGY

The methodology which is the subject of this paper assumes four phases at the heart of every scientific research. After the customer has defined the problem, the work is carried out through the phases defined next.

A. Survey

The first thing to do is a survey of existing solutions to the problem, and generation of the ideas that might present improvements over the best solutions available in the open literature. Some ideas are rejected through discussions with the customer, and some are retained.

Veljko Milutinović is with the School of Electrical Engineering, University of Belgrade, POB 816, 11000 Belgrade, Serbia, Yugoslavia (emilutiv@ubbg.etf.bg.ac.yu).

Proceedings of the 20th IEEE International Conference on Microelectronics - MIEL'95, Niš, Serbia, Yugoslavia, September 1995.

B. Analytical analysis

The second thing to do is a detailed elaboration of all relevant details for the best K solutions from the open literature (K usually equals one or two), and for the L ideas developed during the previous phase (these ideas are usually the variations of the single base idea). All $K + L$ solutions are treated analytically, with the following purposes:

1) To prove that L generated solutions carry out their function correctly (the proofs for the K solutions from the open literature are typically available in the open literature).

2) To estimate the performance of all $K + L$ solutions. This will aid the early decision whether to perform the laborious simulational analysis or not. The estimate is based upon relatively crude mathematical models.

3) To estimate the complexity of all $K + L$ solutions. This will aid the early decision whether to perform the laborious implementational analysis of the complexity or not. The estimate is, too, based upon relatively crude mathematical models.

4) To compute various initial values for the simulational and/or implemantational analyses to follow later.

C. Simulational analysis

The third thing to do is simulational analysis based on a relatively complex simulational model (often done using HDL languages). The performance is analysed and compared for $k + l$ solutions ($k \leq K$, $l \leq L$), since some of the initial solutions are eliminated after the analytical analysis is over.

D. Implementational analysis

The fourth thing to do is implementational analysis based on a relatively complex implementational model (often done using VLSI design). The complexity is analysed and compared for the same $k + l$ solutions.

After the research is completed, the road is open for the implementation of the market prototype.

III. ABOUT THE PRESENTATION METHODOLOGY

After the work is completed (using the research methodology described in the previous section) the work has to be presented to the public (using the presentation methodology described in this section). The presentation methodology described here is composed of 10 steps. Minor deviations are allowed in the specific conditions of the actual research work:

A. Introduction

Basic facts about the presentation to follow are contained here.

B. Problem statement

A detailed definition of the problem is presented, as well as the explanation of its significance.

C. Existing solutions to the problem and their criticism

A survey of the existing solutions, or references to the sources, is presented here. They are criticized from the standpoint central to the research being done.

D. Proposed solution and its essence

A philosophical and physical essence of the proposed solution is discussed here, and a global argument is given to support the claim that this solution could be better than all solutions available through the open literature, or that the previously spotted defficiencies of these solutions are expected not to appear in the proposed one.

E. Conditions of the analysis to follow

All relevant conditions and assumptions for the following analysis are presented here. Conditions define the actual environment. Assumptions define the simplifications (to the actual environment) with the aim of reducing the amount of work in the analysis to follow, without negative side effects related to the generality and precision of the results.

F. Definition of candidate solutions

Relevant details for the analysis of all $K + L$ solutions should be found in this section.

G. Analytical analysis and comparison

The results of the analytical analysis and comparison are presented here. The appropriate mathematical models are used to accomplish this.

H. Simulational analysis and comparison

The results of the performance comparison are presented here, through the use of appropriate simulational models.

I. Implementational analysis and comparison

The results of the complexity comparison are presented here, through the use of appropriate implementational models.

J. Conclusion

The summary of the work done so far is presented first (from the performance/cost ratio point of view), then the specification of the possible uses of the obtained results is given, followed by a brief summary of the newly open research and development problems that are the consequence of the concluded research. Some elements of this methodology can be found in a references [1] and [2].

Important comments

The report should contain as many figures and references as reasonable. The figures should be language independent, with the mnemonic labels, while the caption accompanying every figure should contain the following five elements: (a) figure title, (b) definition of all mnemonics that appear in the figure, (c) a description of the phenomena shown in the figure, (d) an explanation of the phenomena shown in the figure, and (e) engineering implications of the mentioned phenomena. The figure caption, consequently, contains all local parameters of the figure. On the other hand, global parameters are elaborated in the main text. The references should be formatted and composed after the model presented in the IEEE TRANSACTIONS magazines.

IV. EXAMPLES

Examples of the multimedia workstation related research where the above described methodology gave good results will be shown now.

The first eight examples focused on the internal architecture, organization, and design improvements in multimedia workstations. The research was done for one of the leading multinational corporations in the area of computer technology (X_1), and its world market.

The following four examples are related to the incorporation of multimedia workstations into the DSM (Distributed Shared Memory) systems. The research and the subsequent development were done for one of the leading multinational corporations in the area of real-time applications (X_2), and its world market.

The following two examples are related to the implementation of processors for multimedia workstations. The research and the subsequent development were done for one of the leading Japanese corporations in the area of computer technology (X_3), and its Far East market.

The remaining example is related to the incorporation of multimedia systems into the ATM networks. The research was done for one of the leading multinational corporations in the area of semiconductor technology (X_4), and its Far East market.

All these examples can also be treated as a review of today's basic trends in the area of multimedia workstations. The number of examples per category can also be viewed as the proof of success for the described methodology: the first customer (eight examples) has started five years ago, the second (four examples) four years ago, the third (two examples) three years ago, and the fourth (one example) two years ago.

Along with the presentation of the actual examples, wherever appropriate, the following outline will be adhered to: (a) what was the problem about, (b) what solutions existed at the time, and what were their deficiencies from the research sponsor point of view, (c) what was the essence of the proposed solution, and why it is expected not to have the previously mentioned defficiencies, (d) which references contain the relevant details, and (e) whether the same group made the manufacturing prototype as well, or only did the research.

A. A multiprocessor workstation for multimedia applications

The basic idea of this project assumed the interconnection of N ($N = 4$, 8, or 16) microprocessors (i486, etc...) into a multiprocessor system based on the shared memory, together with the addition of the special accelerators for the critical functions related to the multimedia applications:

1) A hardware solution for the second level cache memory consistency maintenance. The problem here was the realization of the system for maintaining the consistency of the second-level cache memory, in the case when the percentage of branch instructions is relatively low (the first-level cache coherence is best maintained using the solution suggested by the manufacturer of the microprocessor, since the first-level cache is usually present on the same chip along with the microprocessor). The best among the existing solutions to the problem are Berkeley "write-broadcast" and Dragon "write-update" types. Both use the block as the broadcast/invalidation unit. The proposed solution uses the word as the invalidation unit. If the number of invalidated words (of a block) crosses a predetermined boundary N_c, then the entire block is invalidated. It is shown that $N_{c,opt} = 1$. This solution is better when the percentage of branch instructions is relatively small, which was the case in the customer's intended applications. The details of this research are given in references [3], [4], [5], [6], and [7]. Only a research prototype of the solution core was done.

2) A software solution for the cache memory consistency maintenance. The problem here was the optimal software method of the cache consistency maintenance, in the conditions of a relatively high probability that the same process remains in the state of execution on the same processor. The best among the known solutions to the problem are proposed by Smith (static) and Veidenbaum (dynamic). Both use the critical region as the consistency maintenance element, and clean up the cache prior to leaving the critical region. The proposed solution combines the best properties of both static and dynamic approaches; however, it cleans up the cache memory prior to entering the critical region. This solution obviously works better for the applications with a relatively high probability of current process continiung the execution on the same processor upon the reentry. The details of this research are given in references [8], [9], [10], and [11]. Only a research prototype of the solution core was done.

3) *An accelerator for windowing environments.* The problem here was the optimal algorithm for quick refresh of the contents of the temporarily overlapped window, for VGA (or higher resolution) video adapters. Existing solutions generally fall into two extremes: recalculation of the window contents (cheap, but slow), and redrawing of the saved window contents (fast, but expensive). The proposed solution is based on the partial recalculation, using the partially saved contents, and it achieves the performance/complexity ratio far in excess of the existing solutions. Details of this research are given in references [12], [13], and [14]. Both a research prototype of the solution core and an industrial prototype of the entire solutions were made.

4) *An accelerator for database environments.* The problem here was the determination of the optimal structure of the accelerator for the most frequently used operations in database applications, in the case of the accelerator implemented as a separate plug-in card which is incorporated into a PC system via the system bus. The existing solutions generally fall into two categories: utilization of the random logic, and utilization of the separate coprocessor. The proposed solution is oriented toward the acceleration of the bit-manipulation instructions, using an accelerator in the form of a simple RISC/MIPS chip, with the added bit-manipulation hardware. Extreme acceleration is possible when applications contain the abundance of bit-manipulation instructions. The details of this research are given in reference [15]. Only a research prototype of the solution core was done.

5) *An accelerator for disk cache memory.* The problem here was the determination of the optimal structure of the chip for increasing the efficiency of the disk cache memory, in conditions when it is necessary to perform the prediction of the program execution path, and data prefetching. The existing solutions generally fall into two categories: the cache memory cleanup, and a dynamic prediction in addition to the cache memory cleanup. The proposed solution uses both mentioned methods, plus a static prediction. Excellent results are obtained in this way, even if dynamic prediction fails to deliver any improvement at all. The details of this

research are given in references [16], [17], and [18]. Only a research prototype of the solution core was done.

6) *An accelerator for JPEG compression.* The problem here was the optimal structure for the JPEG algorithm chip. The existing solutions were either based on the random logic, or they were using a coprocessor. The proposed solution is based on the on-chip accelerators for the most commonly used operations. The details are given in references [19] and [20].

7) *An accelerator for MPEG compression.* The problem here was the optimal structure for the MPEG algorithm chip. The existing solutions were either based on the random logic, or they were using a coprocessor. The proposed solution is based on the on-chip accelerators for the most commonly used operations. The details are given in references [21] and [22].

8) *An accelerator for ASCII compression.* The problem here was the optimal structure for the LZ algorithm chip. The existing solutions were either based on the random logic, or they were using a coprocessor. The proposed solution is based on the on-chip accelerators for the most commonly used operations. The details are given in references [23] and [24].

B. Incorporation of PC computers into DSM systems

The basic idea of this project assumed the interconnection of N ($N = 16$, 32, or 64) PC computers into a DSM system based on the RMS algorithm. The existing RMS systems included up to nine superscalar computers. The increase in the node count required the improvements of the RMS algorithm.

1) *An improvement of the "single word transfer" RMS algorithm.* The problem here was the modification of the basic RMS algorithm to make it more efficient when the number of RMS bus nodes increases significantly. The proposed solution can be conditionally classified as a UMA (Uniform Memory Access) DSM algorithm. Five improvements to the basic solution have been proposed, and their details are given in reference [25]. After the research was done, the prototype board intended for volume production has been made, along with a dozen FPGA VLSI chips.

2) *An improvement of the "multiple word transfer" RMS algorithm.* The problem here was the modification of the RMS algorithm that transfers data streams across the RMS bus, using some sort of DMA. One improvement has been proposed, and its details are given in reference [26].

3) *A comparison of DSM algorithms.* The problem here was to survey all DSM algorithms [27], [28], and [29], and to compare the RMS with the four rival algorithms (KSR, SCI, DDM, and DASH), aiming to speed up the RMS bus to the same performance level [30], and eventually to improve on the DSM in general. As of now, no improvements were generated in the architecture domain, but only in the organization domain (the design domain was not considered).

4) *Advances in heterogeneous processing.* The problem here was the improvement of an existing algorithm related to the allocation in the heterogeneous systems, in conditions of certain technology shifts. Four orthogonal improvements are proposed (design, organization, architecture, and system software). The lessons learned are given in reference [31].

C. Silicon compilation

The basic idea of this project was exploration of the possibilities in the domain of the HDL based silicon compilation.

1) *The i860XP.* The problem here was the determination of the optimal algorithm for utilization of the special HDL (ISP') in the case of a project involving the design of a new RISC processor with the transistor count over one million. Existing methodologies did not take this important aspect into account. The proposed methodology is based on an iterative approach together with the systematic corrections of the previous iteration, only after the effects of the following iteration are visible. The details are given in references [32], [33], and [34]. After the research was concluded, the model of the chip for the volume production was developed.

2) *A comparison of convex and concave HDL programming.* The problem here was the determination of the effects introduced by the convex programming (with maximal serialization) to the effects of the concave programming (with maximal parallelization). Several solutions were proposed, having the maximal performance/cost ratio. The details are given through four application notes.

D. ATM routing

The basic idea of this project was the efficient incorporation of the PC technology into ATM. The most pronounced obstacle on this road is the search through relatively large routing tables.

A hash based ATM router. The main problem was the search for the optimal structure of the ATM router chip, under the conditions when the routing table contains over 10,000 input-output transformation pairs. The existing solutions are based on the CAM algorithm, but are unable to cover medium to large size tables, due to the implementation problems. The proposed solution contains the standard RAM and uses a hash function, which means that a certain number of ATM cells can be lost. However, if the RAM has enough capacity, the loss probability will be below the limit tolerated by the ATM. On the other hand, the cost is significantly lower. The details are given in reference [35], and they can be compared to the alternative approach which does not waist the ATM cells [36].

V. CONCLUSION

All above mentioned research was done during the period between January 1st 1990 and December 31st 1994. The described methodology was followed in almost all cases. It seems that the postgraduate students have successfully mastered the entire "methodological system" and that they have become fully competent to tangle with the most complex problems in the industry today.

REFERENCES

[1] Milutinović, V., "Projektovanje i arhitektura RISC procesora za VLSI", Nauka, Belgrade, Serbia, Yugoslavia, 1994. (English translation: Milutinović, V., "Surviving the Design of a 200 MHz RISC Microprocessor: Lessons Learned," *IEEE Computer Society Press*, Los Alamitos, California, USA, 1996.)

[2] Milutinović, V., Božanić, D., Polomčić, D., Aleksić, M., "Uvod u projektovanje računarskih VLSI sistema," Nauka, Belgrade, Serbia, Yugoslaia, 1994.

[3] Tomašević, M., Milutinović, V. (editors), "Tutorial on Cache Consistency in Multiprocessor Systems: Hardware Methods," *IEEE Computer Society Press*, Los Alamitos, California, USA, 1993.

[4] Tomasević, M., Milutinović, V., "A Survey of Hardware Solutions for Maintenance of Cache Consistency in Shared Memory Multiprocessor Systems: Part 1 (Basic Issues)," *IEEE MICRO*, October 1994.

[5] Tomasević, M., Milutinović, V., "A Survey of Hardware Solutions for Maintenance of Cache Consistency in Shared Memory Multiprocessor Systems: Part 2 (Advanced Issues)," *IEEE MICRO*, December 1994.

[6] Tomasević, M., Milutinović, V., "A Simulation Study of Snoopy Cache Coherence Protocols," *Proceedings of the HICSS-92*, Koloa, Hawaii, USA, January 1992, pp. 427-436.

[7] Tomašević, M., *Ph.D. Thesis*, School of Electrical Engineering, Belgrade, Serbia, Yugoslavia, 1992.

[8] Tartalja, I., Milutinović, V. (editors), "Tutorial on Cache Consistency in Multiprocessor Systems: Software Methods," *IEEE Computer Society Press*, Los Alamitos, California, USA, 1995.

[9] Tartalja, I., Milutinović, V., "An Approach to Dynamic Software Cache Consistency Maintenance Based on Conditional Invalidations," *Proceedings of the HICSS-92*, Koloa, Hawaii, USA, January 1992, pp. 457–466.

[10] Tartalja, I., Milutinović, V., "A Survey of Software Solutions for Maintenance of Cache Consistency in Shared Memory Multiprocessors," *Proceedings of the HICSS-95*, Maui, Hawaii, USA, January 3–6, 1995 .

[11] Tartalja, I., *Ph.D. Thesis*, School of Electrical Engineering, Belgrade, Serbia, Yugoslavia, 1995.

[12] Aleksić, M., Milutinović, V., "Architecture Support for Window Environment," *Proceedings of the HICSS-92*, Koloa, Hawaii, USA, January 1992, 506–514.

[13] Aleksić, M., Milutinović, V., "RISC Architecture for Window Environments: A Simulation Study," *Proceedings of the APS-93 Symposium—Workstations*, Hagen, Germany, May 24–27, 1993, pp. 17–25 (VDE Publishing Company, Frankfurt, Germany, 1993).

[14] Aleksić. M., *Ph.D. Thesis*, School of Electrical Engineering, Belgrade, Serbia, Yugoslavia, 1992.

[15] Jovanov, E., *Ph.D. Thesis*, School of Electrical Engineering, Belgrade, Serbia, Yugoslavia, 1994.

[16] Deletić, D., Lazarević, P., Milutinović, V., Zlatković, S., "Simulation Analysis of an Improved Disk Cache Controller for Utilization of 'Silence'," *Proceedings of the IEEE ICSI-94*, San Paulo, Brasil, August 1994 pp. 434–440.

[17] Cirić, J., Deletić, D., Lazarević, P., Milutinović, V., Zlatković, S., "A RISC Architecture for Disk Cache Control Using Lattice FPGA VLSI," *Proceedings of the ESONE RTS `95 International Seminar for Real Time Data,* Warszaw, Poland, September 1995.

[18] Lazarević, P., *Ph.D. Thesis*, School of Electrical Engineering, Belgrade, Serbia, Yugoslavia (in progress).

[19] Car, A., Đurić, D., Milutinović, V., "A RISC Architecture for JPEG, " *Proceedings of the ESONE RTS `95 International Seminar for Real Time Data,* Warszaw, Poland, September 1995.

[20] Đurić, D., *Ph.D. Thesis*, School of Electrical Engineering, Belgrade, Serbia, Yugoslavia (in progress).

[21] Škorc, A., Milutinović, V., "A Comparison of Two DCT Preprocessor Architectures for VLSI Image Compression," *Proceedings of the HICSS-94*, Maui, Hawaii, USA, January 1994, pp. 312–320.

[22] Škorc, A., *Ph.D. Thesis*, School of Electrical Engineering, Belgrade, Serbia, Yugoslavia (in progress).

[23] Marković, P., Milutinović, V., " A RISC Architecture for Lossless Data Compression in Multimedia Applications," *Proceedings of the ESONE RTS `95 International Seminar for Real Time Data,* Warszaw, Poland, September 1995.

[24] Marković, P., *Ph.D. Thesis*, School of Electrical Engineering, Belgrade, Serbia, Yugoslavia (in progress).

[25] Savić, S., Tomašević, M., Milutinović, V., "Improved RMS for PC Environments," (to be published).

[26] Jovanović, M., Tomašević, M., Milutinović, V., "A Simulation-Based Comparison of Two Reflective Memory Approaches," *Proceedings of the HICSS-95*, Maui, Hawaii, USA, January 3–6, 1995.

[27] Protić, J., Tomašević, M., Milutinović, V. (editors), "Tutorial on Distributed Shared Memory," *IEEE Computer Society Press*, Los Alamitos, California, USA, 1995.

[28] Protić, J., Tomašević, M., Milutinović, V., "A Survey of Distributed Shared Memory Approaches," *Proceedings of the JINR XVI International Symposium on Nuclear Electronics*, Varna, Bulgaria, September 12–18, 1994.

[29] Protić, J., Tomašević, M., Milutinović, V., "A Survey of Distributed Shared Memory Systems," *Proceedings of the HICSS-95*, Maui, Hawaii, USA, January 3–6, 1995 .

[30] Grujić, A., Tomasević, M., Milutinović, V., "A Simulation Study of Hardware Oriented Distributed Shared Memory Approaches," *Proceedings of the IEEE TENCON-94*, Singapore, August 1994, pp. 386–390.

[31] Ekmečić, I., Tartalja, I., Milutinović, V. ""A contributon to Taxonomy of Heterogeneous Computer System," *IEEE Computer, 1995* (Hot Topics).

[32] Milutinović, V., Petković, Z., "Ten Lessons Learned from/a RISC Design," Vol. 28, No. 3, *IEEE COMPUTER*, March 1995 (Open Channel).

[33] Petković, Z., Milutinović, V., "An Approach to Processor Logic Desing Using HDL for Silicon Compilation," *Proceeding of the IEEE MIEL-95,* Niš, Serbia, Yugoslavia, Septembar 1995.

[34] Petrović, M., Tartalja, I., Milutinović, V., "Branch Delay in Deep Pipelines" (to be published).

[35] Rašković, D., Jovanov, E., Janićijević, A., Milutinović, V., "An Implementation of Hash-Based ATM Router Chip," *Proceedings of the HICSS-95*, Maui, Hawaii, USA, January 3–6, 1995.

[36] Janićijević, A., Jovanov, E., Rašković, D., Milutinović, V., "A Comparison of Two Approaches to ATM Router Chip Design," *Proceedings of the JINR XVI International Symposium on Nuclear Electronics*, Varna, Bulgaria, September 12–18, 1994

Note: Paper [6] was awarded.

Appendix E
Acronyms and Abbreviations

2PFF-SP:	Two-Port Flip-Flop Scan-Path
BiCMOS:	Bipolar Complementary Metal Oxide Semiconductor
BIST:	Built-In Self-Test
BS:	Bit-Slice
CADDAS:	Computer Aided Design & Design Automation System
CCITT:	Commiteé Consultatif International de Telegraph e Telephone
CIF:	Caltech Intermediate Format
CISC:	Complex Instruction Set Computer
CMOS:	Complementary Metal Oxide Semiconductor
DARPA:	Defense Advanced Research Project Agency
E/D-MESFET:	Enhancement/Depletion mode MESFET
ECL:	Emitter Coupled Logic
ENDOT:	A Software Package for Hardware Simulation (TD Technology): N.
ESP:	External Scan Path
FBL:	Functional Behavior Level
FC VLSI:	Full Custom VLSI
FS:	Function Slice
FSK:	Frequency Shift Keying
GA VLSI:	Gate Array VLSI
GaAs:	Gallium Arsenide
GE:	General Electric
GTL:	Gate Transfer Level
HDL:	Hardware Description Language
IM:	Interleaved Memory
ISP':	A Hardware Description Language: Instruction Set Processor'
JFET:	Junction Field Effect Transistor
LOGSIM:	LOGic SIMulation system
LSI:	Large Scale Integration
LSSD:	Level Sensitive Scan Design
MCM:	MultiChip Module

MDFF:	Multiplexed Data Flip Flop
MESFET:	MEtal Semiconductor Field Effect Transistor
MIPS:	Million Instructions Per Second *or* Microprocessor without Interlocked Pipeline Stages
MOS:	Metal Oxide Semiconductor
MOSIS:	MOS Implementation System
MP:	Memory Pipelining
MP2D:	MultiPort 2-Dimensional placement and routing system
MS:	MicroStrip
MSI:	Medium Scale Integration
N-RISC:	Neural RISC
NMOS:	N-type Metal Oxide Semiconductor
OrCAD:	A Software Package for Schematic Entry
PL VLSI:	Programmable Logic VLSI
PS:	Path Sensitization
RAM:	Random Access Memory
RCA:	Radio Corporation of America
RISC:	Reduced Instruction Set Computer
ROM:	Read Only Memory
RTL:	Register Transfer Level
SC VLSI:	Standard Cell VLSI
SDI:	Strategic Defense Initiative
SL:	StripLine
SM:	Scan Mux
SOAR:	Smalltalk Oriented Architecture for a RISC
SP:	Scan Path
SSA:	Single Stuck At
SSI:	Small Scale Integration
SU-MIPS:	Stanford University Microprocessor without Interlocked Pipeline Stages
TANNER:	A Software Package for Standard Cell VLSI Design (Tanner Research)
UCB-RISC:	University of California at Berkeley RISC
VHDL:	Vhsic HDL
VHSIC:	Very High Speed Integrated Circuit
VLSI:	Very Large Scale Integration

Appendix F

Short Biographical Sketch
of the Author

Veljko M. Milutinović (born in 1951) received his BS in 1975, MS in 1978, and PhD in 1982, all from the University of Belgrade, Serbia, Yugoslavia.

Prior to 1982, he was with the Michael Pupin Institute in Belgrade, the nation's leading research organization in computer and communications engineering. At that time he was active in the fields of microprocessor and multimicroprocessor design. Among the projects that he successfully realized completely on his own, the major ones are:

- A data communications codec for the speed of 2400 bps;
- a prototype of a two-processor modem for the speeds up to 4800 bps;
- a DFT machine based on 17 loosely coupled microprocessor systems organized as a MISD architecture;
- a bit-slice machine for signal processing (partially done at the University of Dortmund in Germany);
- a study on the microprocessor based modem design for speeds up to 9600 bps (partially done at the University of Linkoeping in Sweden); and
- a study on the utilization of microprocessors in general data communications (partially done at the University of Warsaw in Poland).

In 1982, he was appointed a tenure track assistant professor at the Florida International University in Miami, Florida. One year later, in 1983, he moved to Purdue University in West Lafayette, Indiana, and worked first as a visiting assistant professor, and then (starting in 1987) as a tenure track assistant professor. He was with Purdue University until late 1989. While at Purdue University he was involved in a number of projects. The major ones were:

- A design of a 32-bit 200 MHz GaAs RISC microprocessor on a VLSI chip (for RCA) which is the subject of this book;
- a study of a systolic array with 2^{14} GaAs processors, each one working at the speed of 200 MHz (for RCA);
- a simulation study of cache memory for a 40 MHz silicon RISC (for RCA);
- a design of a specialized processor based on the new concepts of vertical and catalytic migration (for NCR);
- a study of high-level language machines (for NCR); and
- a simulation of technology influences on advanced microprocessor architectures (for NCR).

During the decade of the eighties, he was consulting for a number of high-tech companies, including, but not limited to: RCA, NCR, IBM, GE, Intel, Fairchild, Encore, Honeywell, Aerospace Corporation, Electrospace Corporation, NASA, AT&T, Mitsubishi, Fujitsu, NEC, and OKI.

Early in 1990, he moved back to Europe, where he teaches the advanced VLSI architecture and multiprocessor/multicomputer design courses in a number of universities. He is a cofounder of IFACT—a research and development laboratory active in high-tech research and development for European, US, and Far East sponsors. A number of successful projects were completed under his leadership. The most recent ones include:

- A design of HDL based simulators for selected 64-bit microprocessors;
- a design of the model of a 2.5-million-transistor processor, for silicon compilation;
- a design of a board which enables a PC to become a node in a distributed shared memory system;
- a simulation study of hardware oriented distributed shared memory concepts;
- a design study of the ATM router table search chip; and
- a development study of new approaches to heterogeneous processing and distributed shared memory in modern multimicroprocessor systems.

Milutinovic has published more than 100 papers (over 50 in IEEE journals and books). Some of his papers have been translated and republished in Japanese, Chinese, Russian, Polish, Slovenian, and Serbian. He has published four original books (two as a single author), and edited 20 books (six as a single editor) for Prentice-Hall, Elsevier-Science, ACM Press, and IEEE Computer Society Press. Some of them have been used as textbooks in universities around the world. For two of his books forewords were written by Nobel Laureates Leon Cooper and Kenneth Wilson.

His work is widely referenced and can be found in over 50 SCI citations, in over 100 citations of IEEE conference proceedings books and textbooks of major US publishers, and in more than 1,000 INSPEC references.

Milutinovic has given more than 100 invited talks on five continents and over a dozen cities. His current interests include multimicroprocessor and multimicrocomputer research, plus specialized VLSI architectures for the acceleration of multimedia and networking applications.

Index